TAKE A WALK ON THE ODD SIDE

This weird collection boasting thousands of the most peculiar, outrageous, and mind-boggling tidbits of trivia is guaranteed to shock even as it entertains. Here is all the unusual information you ever wanted to know but never had the time to find out—or were too embarrassed to ask. Almost 100 lists (nearly 10,000 items in all!) include 4 of the Stupidest Initiation Rites, 19 Things You're Not Supposed to Do to the United States Flag, and 15 Last Suppers of Famous Death-Row Prisoners. This is the ultimate compendium of the craziest kitsch ever. Enjoy!

The
ODD
Index

STEPHEN J. SPIGNESI is the author of many books on popular culture, including *The Official "Gone with the Wind" Companion*. He lives in East Haven, Connecticut.

The ODD index

The Ultimate Compendium of Bizarre and Unusual Facts

Stephen J. Spignesi

A PLUME BOOK

PLUME
Published by the Penguin Group
Penguin Books USA Inc., 375 Hudson Street,
New York, New York 10014, U.S.A.
Penguin Books Ltd, 27 Wrights Lane,
London W8 5TZ, England
Penguin Books Australia Ltd, Ringwood,
Victoria, Australia
Penguin Books Canada Ltd, 10 Alcorn Avenue,
Toronto, Ontario, Canada M4V 3B2
Penguin Books (N.Z.) Ltd, 182–190 Wairau Road,
Auckland 10, New Zealand

Penguin Books Ltd, Registered Offices:
Harmondsworth, Middlesex, England

First published by Plume, an imprint of Dutton Signet,
a division of Penguin Books USA Inc.

First Printing, August, 1994
10 9 8 7 6 5 4 3

℗ REGISTERED TRADEMARK—MARCA REGISTRADA

LIBRARY OF CONGRESS CATALOGING-IN-PUBLICATION DATA:
Spignesi, Stephen J.
The odd index : the ultimate compendium of bizarre and unusual facts / Stephen J.
Spignesi.
p. cm.
ISBN 0-452-27103-7
1. Curiosities and wonders—Encyclopedias and dictionaries.
I. Title.
AG243.S75 1994
031.02—dc20   94-608
                                                                      CIP

Printed in the United States of America
Set in New Baskerville
Designed by Leonard Telesca

Have you tried thinking like a shower?
—CHRIS STEVENS

I'm looking at the Big Sky.
—KATE BUSH

Acknowledgments

My special thanks to the following friends of the odd:

My wife, Pam, for not thinking me *too* odd;

John White, for having an awesome library and allowing me to play in it;

Ed Stackler, my editor on this project, for fielding the strangest questions with an absolutely straight face, and even more important, for always having the perfect answer and/or advice;

Liz Torke and Leah Bassoff, Ed's assistants, for their charming manners and gracious willingness to chat, even when they were too busy for chatting;

Michael Hoy and his amazing company, Loompanics, for their help, for the free books, and especially for the company's admirable big balls philosophy;

Penguin USA, for their continued interest and support;

Dan Fasano, "Mr. Cousin Dan," for his computer advice and for having a readily accessible Hindu friend;

Hugh Klockars and Frank Myjak, two commendable constables and truly fine friends;

Tom Schultheiss and Pat Curtis, for their continued friendship, and for understanding why I couldn't revisit Jessie or the Waste Lands this year;

Erik Leeming, for his wonderfully disgusting jokes, not a single one of which we could print;

Linda Beavis and Tommy K Video, for their truly twisted cult movie department;

Tim Berra, William Poundstone, and Richard Spears, for their wonderful writings;

The East Haven Public Library; and

The University of New Haven Library.

Contents

Introduction
The Alphabet of Odd
A Lexicon of the Loony

Aberrant, abnormal, absurd, amazing, anomalous, atypical.

Bizarre, bohemian.

Curious, crazy.

Deranged, demented, deviant, different, droll.

Eccentric, enigmatic, erratic, exotic, extraordinary.

Fantastic, far-out, fascinating, foolish, freaky, frivolous, funny.

Ghostly, goofy, grotesque.

Humorous.

Impossible, inane, incredible, inexplicable, insane, intriguing, ironic, irrational.

Jolting.

Kinky.

Lunatic.

Mad, maniacal, marvelous, mysterious, mystical.

Novel, nonconformist, nuts.

Oddball, offbeat, outlandish.

Peculiar, preposterous, preternatural, puzzling.

Quaint, queer.

Rare, raunchy, remarkable, ribald, ridiculous, rude.

Silly, special, spooky, startling, strange.

Tantalizing, terrifying.

Uncommon, unconventional, unearthly, unexpected, unfamiliar, unique, unorthodox, unknown, unusual.

Vicious, vile, violent.

Wacky, weird.

Xenophilic.

Yawping.

Zany.

Welcome to Odd.

The Land of Odd is a place where playing cards can tell the future, where there are sixteen crucified saviors other than Jesus Christ, where there are real people with names such as League of Nations and Rudolph Goldshitter (as well as people who can blow smoke out of their eyeballs), where statues bleed real blood and the Virgin Mary appears to thousands, and where there are 228 ways to say "sexual intercourse."

The Odd Index is an attempt to not only chronicle the bizarre and unusual, but to satisfy that most frustrating of emotions, curiosity. The information presented here consists of things most people would absolutely love to know, but wouldn't know how to go about finding (or might even be embarrassed to be caught searching for!).

The Odd Index is the ultimate compilation of humorous, peculiar, outrageous, gross, mind-boggling, raunchy, infuriating, enlightening, disgusting, and just plain useless information ever assembled—almost 10,000 items of bizarre information in all.

Just reading the table of contents will be enough to suck you in.

And then you're mine.

It's a weird world.

Knowledge is power.

Read on.

39 Acts of Select Mayhem in 2 Three Stooges Films, *Brideless Groom* and *Disorder in the Court*

Hey, Moe! Hey, Larry!—Curly

It is a truism that women don't get the Three Stooges, while men, on the other hand, can't get enough of them.

Why do men roll around in paroxysms of hilarity every time Moe pokes Larry in the eyes, or Curly lets out with a "Woo, woo, woo," while a woman will just sit there with a bewildered look on her face, wondering what the hell *else* she doesn't know about this guy she's chosen to spend the rest of her life with?

Whatever the reason, there ain't *nobody* like the Stooges.

This feature looks at 39 favorite, particularly choice, moments of mayhem from two especially memorable Stooges features, both of which include a segment in which a Stooge head is crushed in a letter press.

I found myself laughing as I wrote that line, and I was in hysterics while I took notes on the two Stooge films. My wife, the charming Mrs. Spignesi, just shook her head and left the room.

Go figure.

Brideless Groom
(starring Moe Howard, Larry Fine, and Shemp Howard)

"Gimme Susquehanna 2-2-2-2."—Shemp

1. Shemp whacks Larry on the head with a conductor's cue.
2. Shemp knocks Larry's elbow off a piano causing Larry to fall and bang his head.

3. Moe drags Shemp by his hair to a pay phone.
4. Moe and Shemp tie each other up with a phone cord.
5. Moe dials Shemp's eyes, thinking his face is a phone.
6. Shemp bites himself on the hand, thinking it belongs to Moe.
7. Moe stabs Shemp in the calf with a sewing needle.
8. Moe breaks through the bottom of a dresser drawer with his head when he comes up too quickly with the drawer open.
9. Moe breaks the drawer over Larry's head.
10. Larry burns his hand with an iron.
11. Miss Hopkins slaps Shemp in the face five times, hits him on the chest twice, and then hauls off and punches him in the mouth, knocking him backward through a door and taking the door off its hinges.
12. Moe slams Shemp's face into the piano wires.
13. Shemp pulls a piano wire out of the piano. The wire snaps and hits Moe in the eye.
14. Shemp gets tangled in the piano wires and Moe and Larry attempt to pull him out of the tangle. They set him down to "get a new grip" and the tension of the wires pulls Shemp along the floor and slams him face first into the leg of the piano. Twice.
15. One of Shemp's fiancées grabs Larry by the hair and slams him face first into a door.
16. One of Shemp's fiancées rips out a handful of Shemp's hair.
17. One of Shemp's fiancées smashes a bird cage on the minister's head.
18. One of Shemp's fiancées grabs him in a headlock and drags him over to a letter press. She inserts his head in the press and begins tightening it down. He complains to her that he's getting a headache.
19. Larry slams Moe in the head with the butt of a rifle.
20. One of Shemp's fiancées grabs Moe by the hair and sends him flying backward into a chair in which there just happens to be an open bear trap. Moe sits in the trap.

Disorder in the Court
(starring Moe Howard, Larry Fine, and Curly Howard)

"Soitenly, Judgy."—Curly

MOE: "Hey, Jasper, what comes after 75?"
LARRY: "76."
MOE: "That's the spirit."

1. Moe pokes Curly in the eyes with his index and middle fingers.
2. Moe slaps Larry in the face.
3. Curly falls backward out of the witness stand.
4. Curly shoots a cello bow "arrow" into the court reporter's mouth using the cello strings as his "bow."
5. Curly slams himself in the belly with a cello.
6. Larry removes a guy's toupee with a violin bow.
7. Curly slams Moe's foot with a hammer trying to kill the toupee they all believe is a tarantula.
8. Moe fires five shots into the toupee with a revolver.
9. Moe hits Curly in the head with a conductor's cue.
10. Curly slaps Moe on the back, causing him to swallow a harmonica.
11. Curly and Larry "play" Moe by pumping his arms up and down.
12. Moe hits Curly in the head with a hammer.
13. Moe inserts Curly's head into a letter press and begins tightening it down.
14. The steel tightening wheel on top of the letter press spins rapidly backward, flies up in the air, and comes down on Moe's head.
15. Moe bops Curly on top of his head to pop it back into shape after its being compressed in the letter press.
16. A parrot lands on the heads of five jurors and Curly hits each one on the head with a hammer in an attempt to subdue the bird.
17. Larry smashes a Stradivarius with a hammer.
18. Moe instructs Curly to grab his own ear and he then drags

him around as Curly holds onto his ear, making a convenient "handle" with his arm.

19. Curly soaks just about everyone in the courtroom with a fire hose.

10 Astonishing Abilities Manifested by "Idiot" Savants

I am still learning.—Michelangelo's motto

Savant syndrome, as it has come to be known, points up just how difficult it is to truly understand the functioning of the human brain.

In his groundbreaking 1989 study *Extraordinary People,* Dr. Darold Treffert defined *savant syndrome* as "an exceedingly rare condition in which persons with serious mental handicaps, either from developmental disability (mental retardation) or major mental illness (Early Infantile Autism or schizophrenia), have spectacular islands of ability or brilliance which stand in stark, markedly incongruous contrast to the handicap." He went on to say that it occurs in males six times more frequently than in females.

Savants usually have extremely low IQs, some as low as in the 30s and 40s, and yet possess "islands of ability" that are so extraordinary as to seem almost supernatural. People who cannot see can draw like Old Masters; people who cannot speak can sing entire scores of Broadway musicals; people who appear almost catatonic in their daily lives can sit at a piano and flawlessly play complete classical concertos after hearing the piece only once. Odd isn't the word for the talents and abilities these people manifest, and "awe-inspiring" doesn't even come close.

Savants seem to possess brain functions that are, as of yet, beyond our complete understanding. Theories abound as to what role genetics and reinforcement play in these phenomenal abilities, but the truth is that much of what these people can do, and how they do it, is incredibly perplexing to the scientific and medical establishments.

The most recent cinematic portrayal of an autistic savant was in the 1988 movie *Rain Man,* which starred Tom Cruise and Dustin

Hoffman. In that film, Hoffman played Raymond, a middle-aged autistic who manifested many of the abilities of the savant, including counting, memorization, and calculation. Filmgoers were astounded by what Raymond could do, and many challenged the veracity of the portrayal, but everything depicted in *Rain Man* was scientifically and medically accurate. In fact, as you'll see from the following list of savant abilities, *Rain Man* barely scratched the surface.

1. Musical Abilities

Many savants manifest incredible musical talents. Sixteen-year-old Blind Tom, a blind and severely retarded slave who died in 1908, toured after the Civil War and played the piano at virtuoso level for audiences all over the United States. Tom had a musical repertoire of over 5,000 pieces, and like many savants, could hear a piece of music once and play it perfectly, no matter how difficult or complex the piece. Tom was also somehow capable of assimilating a particular composer's "style." On command, Tom could improvise a musical piece in the manner of any composer he had ever heard, including Beethoven, Bach, Chopin, Verdi, and many others. Tom once performed for President Buchanan. Other documented musical savants include the following:

- A 23-year-old boy with an IQ of 47 who could play the piano by ear and could immediately sight-read sheet music.
- A girl named Harriet who had an IQ of 73 and who hummed perfectly the entire "Caro Nome" aria from Verdi's opera *Rigoletto* at the age of *seven months*. (She was in her crib.) By the time she was four, she could play the piano, violin, trumpet, clarinet, and French horn, but wasn't toilet trained until the age of nine. Harriet also manifested incredible memorization skills and could remember pages of the phone book and minute factual details about hundreds of symphonies. Like Blind Tom, she could also improvise in a composer's style and transpose between keys at will.
- A 38-year-old man with an IQ of 67 who had perfect pitch, could sight-read music, and had an enormous knowledge of facts about composers.
- A 23-year-old girl with an IQ of 23 who could play on the piano any song or melody sung or hummed to her.

2. Calendar Calculating

Calendar calculating is the ability to tell what days dates fall on and when holidays will fall centuries into the future. Probably the most famous savant calendar calculators are twins named Charles and George. Charles's and George's IQs tested between 40 and 70. Some of their most amazing calendar abilities included the following:

- They could tell you on what day of the week any date fell in an 80,000 year span. (They were proficient 40,000 years into the past and 40,000 years into the future.) The twins were able to account for changes in the ways calendars were designed over the centuries when calculating the dates.
- They could tell you in what years during the next two centuries Easter would fall on March 23.
- They could remember and recite the exact weather of every single day of their adult lives.

Although Charles and George could not even do simple math, doctors are convinced that math and complex calculating abilities somehow played a role in the twins' date determinations. Memorization of date tables and calendars also played a part, but scientists are sure that somewhere in the twins' brains an "island of ability" existed that could do high math.

3. Mathematical Calculating

The math skills exhibited by savants include incredibly rapid counting abilities (remember Raymond in *Rain Man* immediately being able to count the number of toothpicks that fell on the floor?), and the ability to do instantaneous complex mathematical calculations in their heads. Some of the things savants have been known to count include the following:

- The hairs in a cow's tail.
- The words spoken in a TV or radio broadcast.
- The number of cars on a highway over a period of time.

Some of the calculations savants have been known to make include the following:

- The number of seconds in a period of time.
- The number of seconds in a person's life.
- The multiplication of 20-digit numbers.
- Square root calculations involving huge numbers.

Some of the calculations performed by savants have taken days, weeks, or even months to do. It seems as though some weird biological computer clicks on when the savant is given the problem and doesn't turn off until the solution is arrived at. Many savants adept at calculating can usually add columns of numbers in seconds *without* paper and pencil (many can't even write for that matter), and they often exhibit the same level of problem-solving proficiency with division, multiplication, and subtraction problems.

4. Incredible Memories

Decades ago, a physician named Dr. Witzman attempted to describe the incredible memory capabilities of some savants. He said that they are often capable of "reproducing at will masses of figures, like railway tables, budget statistics, and entries in bankbooks." Eidetic (photographic) memories are one of the most amazing savant abilities. Anyone who has ever tried to memorize something knows just how incredible a photographic memory actually is. My wife told me that when she was studying for her speech pathology degree, everyone in her class grudgingly acknowledged that the *only* way to learn the necessary anatomical structures the course covered was by rote memorization. Med students have long turned to mnemonics to help them remember complex anatomical features of the human body. (Probably the most common mnemonic device we all used in school was "*E*very *G*ood *B*oy *D*eserves *F*un [or *F*ish, depending on whether it was a Catholic school or not]," which is, of course, the lines of a musical stave.) Here is a look at some of the things individual savants have been reported as remembering:

- The exact configuration of the entire Milwaukee bus system.
- The complete music and lyrics of thousands of songs.
- The daily weather of a person's lifetime.
- Thousands of meticulous details about wars and historical events.

- Word-for-word recollections of complete short stories, and in some cases, entire novels.
- The melodies, page numbers, and complete lyrics of every hymn in a specific hymnal.
- Thousands of addresses, often "industry-specific." For instance, some savants will memorize only the addresses of car dealerships, but they will remember *every one* in an entire city.
- Hundreds of foreign language phrases.
- Detailed and comprehensive biographical details about hundreds of historical personages.
- Decades of obituary records, including next of kin, addresses, and funeral homes.
- The contents of entire newspapers, both forward *and* backward.
- The exact number of bites of food taken during an entire month or longer.
- The precise number of steps walked during a certain period of time.
- The number of hotel rooms in every hotel in dozens of cities.
- The distances between hundreds of cities.
- The seating capacities of dozens of stadiums and arenas.
- Every number seen on every railroad car over an entire lifetime. (And in some cases the savant has been known to not only recall the individual numbers on the trains but keep a running total of their sums.)
- Entire pages from phone directories.
- The times of the comings and goings of hospital staff members over a fifty-seven-year period.
- Voluminous stock market statistical data.
- The transcripts of entire radio and TV broadcasts.

5. Artistic Abilities

Savants with artistic abilities can produce impeccably artistic detailed renderings of something seen only once. Savants have been known to work with drawings and sculptures, and they have created works depicting animals, insects, cats, and other forms of nature.

6. Mechanical Abilities

Savants occasionally are exceptionally good "with their hands."
(In the 1992 film *The Hand That Rocks the Cradle*, the retarded
handyman Solomon seemed to have some savant abilities with
tools and building.) Some recorded mechanical abilities evidenced
by savants include the following:

- One savant once took apart a clock and rebuilt it as a fully
  functioning windmill.
- Savants have been known to build detailed models of cars and
  boats after seeing only a picture of the vehicle.
- Some savants can draw accurately detailed blueprints.
- Some can instinctively repair appliances and other mechanical
  objects.
- Savants have been documented as being able to rebuild and
  modify multi-gear bicycles.

7. Extraordinary Sensory Perception

Some savants have extraordinarily developed senses of sight,
smell, hearing, taste, and touch.

- One blind savant was able to pick out his own clothes and
  shoes by smell alone.
- There is documentation of a savant whose sense of touch was
  so highly developed that he could split a sheet of newspaper
  into two thin leaves, resulting in two sheets of newsprint
  one-half the thickness of the original.

8. ESP

ESP, or *Extra*-Sensory Perception (which is different from *Extraordinary* Sensory Perception), appears to enter the realm of the almost impossible to explain. These abilities have often been
considered paranormal, and yet there are savants who exhibit psychic and other "beyond nature" abilities. Some of the documented
"powers" exhibited by savants include the following:

- A savant being able to hear (and repeat) conversations from
  outside his hearing range.

- A savant apparently being able to read another person's thoughts.
- A savant able to perform "distant viewing": seeing accurately something happening rooms, or sometimes miles, away.
- A savant who was capable of precognition, i.e., being able to accurately predict the future.

Evidence of these paranormal abilities further complicates our understanding of savant syndrome. Or perhaps it clarifies it? Consider this: What if savants are using parts of their brains in bizarre ways that we still cannot understand and their manifestation of psychic abilities is something we might all be capable of, but savants are just tapping into them accidentally? Makes you think, eh?

9. An Extraordinary Sense of Time

Some savants have an incredibly developed sense of the passage of time.

- One savant could tell to the minute the exact time at any time of the day or night, but could not read a clock.
- One savant knew exactly when commercials would begin and end, even when out of range of the TV.
- Savants can tell exactly how much time has passed during a specific period without looking at a watch or clock.

10. Extraordinary Directional Perception

Extraordinary directional perception is sometimes found in savants who have never been out of their house or have never traveled in their lives.

- Some savants can recall exact travel routes of individual trips taken, including every right and left turn made.
- Some savants can memorize maps and precisely reproduce them to scale.
- Some savants can give detailed travel directions to a certain place even if they've never been there and often even if they're blind.

22 "Bad Luck" Playing Cards

Digo, paciencia y barajar.
(What I say is, patience, and shuffle the cards.)
— Miguel de Cervantes, *Don Quixote*

According to the *Encyclopedia of the Unexplained,* the 22 playing cards in the following list are all bad news if they turn up during a fortune-telling card session.

Unlike Tarot reading, with its elaborate spreads and complex, labyrinthian interpretations, fortune telling with the five-card deck of regular playing cards is relatively simple and straightforward. The cards are laid out in a favored pattern, and their meanings are then determined, analyzed, and studied.

As an experiment for this feature, I did my own reading using a regular deck of playing cards and one of the simplest methods known. First, I had to determine my "consulter's" card. Because I am a brown-haired male, my consulter's (or "questioner's") card is the King of Clubs. (Diamonds are for blondes and redheads, hearts for people with light-brown hair, and spades for people with black hair. Males use Kings and women use Queens.)

The divination method I used was to place my consulter's card in the middle and then deal the deck out into three piles, face down. I then turned up the three top cards, twice, "to give a rough indication of the trends of fortune." (You're actually supposed to deal out several sequences of three cards to continue the reading, but I didn't have the time.)

My six cards were the two of spades, the two of diamonds, the three of hearts, the five of clubs, the ace of diamonds, and the two of clubs. According to the *Encyclopedia of the Unexplained,* here's my fortune:

- **The Two of Spades:** "A move; a change or separation, the breakup of a home or the loss of a friend; an operation or a long journey, possibly a death; the card of the wanderer."
- **The Two of Diamonds:** "An unhappy love affair, or an affair opposed by family and friends; take care, something unexpected is in the offing."
- **The Three of Hearts:** "Poverty, shame, imprudence; beware of rash decisions."
- **The Five of Clubs:** "A prudent or wealthy marriage; or news from the country."
- **The Ace of Diamonds:** "An engagement or wedding ring; wealth; a letter brings important news."
- **The Two of Clubs:** "A major disappointment; expect opposition and rely only on yourself."

A bit enigmatic and vague, wouldn't you say? My fortune could be good, or it could be bad. Or it could be both. I guess it all depends on your own state of mind and your own personal interpretation of the reading at the time of the fortune-telling session. If that's the case, then I'll take the wealthy marriage, the wealth, and the news from the country, please. I'll pass on all the others, thank you very much.

All kidding aside, there are many people who place great store in what cards tell them, and I'm sure that there are probably some genuinely intuitive (and perhaps psychic) seers who really try to help people help themselves. Or at least I hope there are.

Here are the miseries attendant to the 22 worst cards in an innocent deck of playing cards. (All fortune descriptions are from the *Encyclopedia of the Unexplained*, published by Penguin USA.)

1. **Ace of Spades:** "A death; illness, bad news, broken relationships, worries, misfortune; cruelty and malice."
2. **Two of Spades:** "A move; a change or separation, the breakup of a home or the loss of a friend; an operation or a long journey, possibly a death; the card of the wanderer."
3. **Three of Spades:** "Tears; quarrels; a broken love affair; failure; a journey over water."
4. **Four of Spades:** "Illness, sadness; a will; sudden loss of money; poverty; envy and jealousy."
5. **Five of Spades:** "Anger, quarrels; try to keep your temper and your patience will be rewarded."

6. **Seven of Spades:** "Loss of money, or loss of a close friend; suffering and sorrow; danger of quarrels."
7. **Eight of Spades:** "Be very careful, danger threatens in connection with some current project; expect opposition and treachery; keep a sharp eye out for damaging errors; consider changing your plans."
8. **Nine of Spades:** "Said to be the most ominous card in the pack, signifying ruin, failure, poverty, sickness and death, hopes and plans frustrated, families broken up; particularly threatening if close to other black cards."
9. **Ten of Spades:** "Bad luck; trouble; disgrace; prison; it cancels the effects of fortunate cards near it; be cautious and trust no one."
10. **Three of Hearts:** "Poverty, shame, imprudence; beware of rash decisions."
11. **Four of Hearts:** "Sadness, anxiety, jealousy, domestic difficulties; a broken engagement or a marriage postponed, or a marriage delayed till late in life."
12. **Seven of Hearts:** "Delusions; dreams that fail to come true; a disloyal or mischief-making friend; a betrayal, broken promises; doubts, puzzlement."
13. **Two of Diamonds:** "An unhappy love affair, or an affair opposed by family and friends; take care, something unexpected is in the offing."
14. **Three of Diamonds:** "Domestic disagreements and unhappiness; possible separation or divorce; legal entanglements."
15. **Four of Diamonds:** "A secret betrayed, or an unfaithful friend; interfering neighbors or relatives; a short journey; a legacy."
16. **Six of Diamonds:** "An early marriage likely to fail or to be ended prematurely; not a favorable card for anyone contemplating marriage; a gift; caution needed."
17. **Seven of Diamonds:** "Minor loss of money, or unfriendly gossip; danger of scandal; lie low and keep quiet."
18. **Eight of Diamonds:** "A late and unhappy marriage."
19. **Two of Clubs:** "A major disappointment; expect opposition and rely only on yourself."
20. **Three of Clubs:** "Discord; a long-lasting marriage or affair, or more than one marriage; or a period of time, three years, months, weeks or days."

21. **Four of Clubs:** "Radical changes, inconsistency, misfortune as a result of some caprice; danger of accident; a land journey."
22. **Nine of Clubs:** "Drunkenness; bad luck; friction with friends."

51 Banned Books and Authors (Including 1 Cartoon Character)

God forbid that any book should be banned. The practice is as indefensible as infanticide.

—Dame Rebecca West

In many ways, this feature is the most frightening one in the entire *Odd Index.* For a writer, the mere thought of book banning strikes terror in the heart. Book banning means blacklisting, book burning, censorship, and the attempt at thought control. The novels *Brave New World* and *1984* come immediately to mind, as does *Fahrenheit 451* and the memory of the Nazi book bonfires.

As you'll see from reading through this compilation, no period in history has been free from the sinister hand of the censor—nor any geographical location. Even ostensibly enlightened places have had their share of notorious censorship and banning incidents.

NOTE: The many and various attempts to repress the following titles include banning, censoring, burning, expurgating, bowdlerizing, forbidding to be imported, confiscating, prosecuting, and/or persecuting for reading and/or owning.

1. *The Odyssey* (9th century B.C.) by Homer
   - 387 B.C., Greece.
   - 35, Rome.
2. *The Sayings of Confucius and His Disciples* (5th century B.C.) by Confucius
   - 250 B.C., China.
   - 213 B.C., China.
3. *The Clouds, The Birds,* and *Lysistrata* (4th century B.C.) by Aristophanes
   - 423 B.C., Athens, Greece *(The Clouds).*
   - 414 B.C., Athens, Greece *(The Birds).*

- 411 B.C., Athens, Greece *(Lysistrata)*.
- 1967, Athens, Greece *(Lysistrata)*.

4. *The Art of Love* (1st century A.D.) by Ovid
  - 8 A.D., Rome.
  - 1497, Florence, Italy.
  - 1928, the United States.
  - 1929, San Francisco, California.

5. *The Bible*
  - 553 A.D., Rome, Italy.
  - 1409, England.
  - 1525–1526, England.
  - 1538, Paris, France.
  - 1551, Spain.
  - 1555, England.
  - 1560, Switzerland.
  - 1611, England.
  - 1624, Germany.
  - 1631, England. (The word *not* was inadvertently left out of the seventh commandment, changing it to "Thou shalt steal" in an edition of 1,000 copies of the Bible. This edition was immediately banned and became known as *the "Wicked Bible."*)
  - 1926, the Soviet Union.

6. *The Talmud*
  - 1190, Cairo, Egypt.
  - 1244, Paris, France.
  - 1264, Rome, Italy.
  - 1490, Salamanca, Spain. (This was during the Spanish Inquisition.)
  - 1926, the Soviet Union.

7. *The Koran*
  - 1926, the Soviet Union.

8. *The Divine Comedy* (c. 1310) by Dante Alighieri
  - 1318, Lombardy, France. (Burned.)
  - 1497, Florence, Italy. *(The Divine Comedy* was one of the works burned by Savonarola in the notorious censorious "bonfire of the vanities.")
  - 1559, Rome, Italy.
  - 1581, Lisbon, Portugal.

9. *The Decameron* (1353) by Giovanni Boccaccio
   - 1497, Florence, Italy. (Also burned in the "bonfire of the vanities.")
   - 1559, Rome, Italy.
   - 1922, the United States.
   - 1926, the United States.
   - 1927, the United States.
   - 1933, Australia.
   - 1934, Detroit, Michigan. (The criteria was that the book was "salacious.")
   - 1935, Boston, Massachusetts.
   - 1953, England.
   - 1954, Swindon, England.

10. *The Sistine Chapel* (1508–12) by Michelangelo
    - 1933, the United States. (An art book of plates of the ceiling of the Sistine Chapel was confiscated by U.S. postal authorities because one of the plates, "The Last Judgment," had naked people in it. The Postal Service was so ridiculed and reviled by both the press and the American people that they rescinded their confiscation and suspended pending prosecution.)

11. *Works* (1517) by Martin Luther
    - 1517, Wittenberg, Germany.
    - 1521, France.
    - 1521, Rome, Italy.
    - 1521, Germany.
    - 1930, Rome, Italy.

12. *William Shakespeare*
    - 1597, England. *(The Tragedy of King Richard II;* political reasons.)
    - 1788–1820, England. *(The Tragedy of King Lear;* political reasons.)
    - 1931, the United States. *(The Merchant of Venice;* objection by Jewish groups to the character Shylock.)

13. *Dialogo sopra i due Massimi sistemi del Mondo* (1632) by Galileo Galilei
    - 1616, Rome, Italy. (Banned by Pope Paul IV for defending the Copernican theory that the planets did not revolve around the earth.)
    - 1633, Rome, Italy. (Ditto, by Pope Urban VIII. The Vati-

can did not get around to recanting their position on Galileo and officially apologizing until 1993.)

14. *Robinson Crusoe* (1719) by Daniel Defoe
    - 1720, Spain.
15. *Gulliver's Travels* (1726) by Jonathan Swift
    - 1726, England.
16. *Fanny Hill* (1748) by John Cleland
    - 1749, England.
    - 1821, Boston, Massachusetts. (This was the first known obscenity case in the United States.)
    - 1965, Illinois.
17. *Tom Jones* (1749) by Henry Fielding
    - 1749, Paris, France.
18. *Critique of Pure Reason* (1781) by Immanuel Kant
    - 1827, Rome, Italy.
    - 1928, the Soviet Union. (*All* of Kant's writings were banned.)
    - 1939, Spain. (Kant was considered a "disgraceful" writer.)
19. *The History of the Decline and Fall of the Roman Empire* (1776–88) by Edward Gibbon
    - 1783, Rome, Italy. (Banned because its scholarship conflicted with church teachings.)
    - 1826, England. [Only a bowdlerized edition was allowed to be published. (See the sidebar on Thomas Bowdler, M.D.)]
20. *Faust* (1790) by Jonathan Wolfgang von Goethe
    - 1808, Berlin, Germany.
    - 1939, Spain. (Goethe was considered a "disgraceful" writer.)
21. *Justine* (1791) by the Marquis de Sade
    - 1791, France.
    - 1948, Rome, Italy.
    - 1955, Paris, France.
    - 1962, London, England.
22. *The Age of Reason* (1793) by Thomas Paine
    - 1797, England.
23. *Wonder Stories* (1835) by Hans Christian Andersen
    - 1835, Russia.
    - 1954, Illinois. (This book was stamped "For Adult Readers" by the authorities to make it "impossible for children to obtain smut.")

24. *The Scarlet Letter* (1850) by Nathaniel Hawthorne
- 1852, Russia.

25. *Uncle Tom's Cabin* (1852) by Harriet Beecher Stowe
- 1852, Russia.
- 1855, the Papal States, Italy.

26. *Leaves of Grass* (1855) by Walt Whitman
- 1881, Boston, Massachusetts.

27. *Madame Bovary* (1856) by Gustave Flaubert
- 1857, Paris, France.
- 1864, Rome, Italy.
- 1954, the United States.

28. *On the Origin of Species* (1859) by Charles Darwin
- 1859, Cambridge, England.
- 1925, Dayton, Tennessee. (This book banning prompted the famous Scopes evolution trial in which teacher John Scopes was found guilty of teaching evolution by using Darwin's book in his classroom. He was fined $100 for his "crime." The verdict against him resulted in an actual law on Tennessee's books that prohibited teaching anything in the state's classrooms except creationism. This law stood for 42 years, until 1967, before it was repealed. [See the feature on "Creationists' Arguments" in this volume.])

29. *Les Misérables* (1862) by Victor Hugo
- 1850, Russia. (All of Hugo's works were banned.)
- 1864, Rome, Italy.

30. *Alice's Adventures in Wonderland* (1865) by Lewis Carroll
- 1931, China. (The reason Chinese censors cited for banning this children's classic was that "animals should not use human language.")

31. *The Adventures of Huckleberry Finn* (1885) by Mark Twain
- 1885, Concord, Massachusetts.
- 1905, Brooklyn, New York.
- 1930, the Soviet Union.
- 1957, New York City. (The frequent use of the word *nigger* prompted the ban in 1957.)

32. *Tess of the D'Ubervilles* (1891) by Thomas Hardy
- 1891, England.

33. *The Adventures of Sherlock Holmes* (1892) by Sir Arthur Conan Doyle
- 1929, the Soviet Union. (The Soviet censors banned

Holmes because of the many references to "occultism" and "spiritualism" in his *Adventures*.

34. *Sister Carrie* (1900) by Theodore Dreiser
   - 1900, New York City.
   - 1958, Vermont.

35. *Man and Superman* (1903) by George Bernard Shaw
   - 1905, New York City.
   - 1929, Yugoslavia. (All works by Shaw were banned in Yugoslavia.)

36. *The Call of the Wild* (1903) by Jack London
   - 1929, Italy.
   - 1929, Yugoslavia.
   - 1932, Germany. (*The Call of the Wild* was banned by the Nazis).

37. *The Jungle* (1906) by Upton Sinclair
   - 1929, Yugoslavia. (All of Sinclair's works were banned.)
   - 1933, Germany. (*The Jungle* was burned in the Nazi book bonfires.)
   - 1956, Berlin, East Germany. (All of Sinclair's works were banned.)

38. *Ulysses* (1922) by James Joyce
   - 1922, the United States. (Confiscated copies were burned.)
   - 1922, Ireland. (Copies were burned.)
   - 1922, Canada. (Copies were burned.)
   - 1923, England. (Copies were burned.)
   - 1929, England.
   - 1930, New York City.

39. *Desire Under the Elms* (play, 1924) by Eugene O'Neill
   - 1925, New York City.

40. *Lady Chatterly's Lover* (1928) by D.H. Lawrence
   - 1929, the United States.
   - 1930, Washington, D.C.
   - 1932, Ireland.
   - 1932, Poland.
   - 1953, England.
   - 1960, Montreal, Canada.

41. *Elmer Gantry* (1927) by Sinclair Lewis
   - 1927, Boston, Massachusetts.
   - 1931, Ireland.

42. *Mickey Mouse* (1932) by Walt Disney

- 1932, the United States. (One of Mickey's cartoons was banned because there was a scene in it in which a cow was seen in a pasture reading Elinor Glyn's book *Three Weeks.*)
- 1937, Belgrade, Yugoslavia. (A Mickey Mouse cartoon was banned for its alleged "anti-monarchical" plot line.)
- 1938, Rome, Italy. (Mickey was deemed "unsuitable for children.")
- 1954, East Berlin, Germany.

43. *Tropic of Cancer* (1934) and *Sexus* (1949) by Henry Miller
- 1934, the United States *(Tropic of Cancer).*
- 1950, France *(Sexus).*
- 1956, Norway *(Sexus).*

44. *Ernest Hemingway*
- 1929, Italy *(A Farewell to Arms).*
- 1930, Boston, Massachusetts *(The Sun Also Rises).*
- 1933, Germany. (The Nazis burned many of Hemingway's works in their book bonfires.)
- 1939, Ireland *(A Farewell to Arms).*
- 1953, Ireland *(The Sun Also Rises).*
- 1960, San Jose, California *(The Sun Also Rises).*

45. *The Grapes of Wrath* (1939) by John Steinbeck
- 1939, St. Louis, Missouri.
- 1939, Kansas City, Missouri.
- 1939, California.

46. *Lolita* (1955) by Vladimir Nabokov
- 1956, Paris, France.
- 1960, New Zealand.

47. *From Here to Eternity* (1951) by James Jones
- 1951, Holyoke, Massachusetts.
- 1951, Springfield, Massachusetts.
- 1951, Denver, Colorado.
- 1953, Jersey City, New Jersey.
- 1954, the United States. *(From Here to Eternity* was placed on the disapproved list of the National Organization of Decent Literature.)
- 1955, the United States. (The Postal Service declared the book "unmailable" even though it had been a bestseller for *four years.)*

48. *Naked Lunch* (1959) by William Burroughs
- 1959, Boston, Massachusetts. (How times change: The

1992 film version of Burroughs's *Naked Lunch* didn't even raise an eyebrow in Boston.)

49. *Tennessee Williams*
  • 1965, Portugal. (All of Williams's work was banned.)
50. *Soul on Ice* (1968) by Eldridge Cleaver
  • 1969, California. (The book was banned from California schools.)
51. *The American Heritage Dictionary* (1969 edition)
  • 1978, Missouri. (The dictionary was banned because it contained 39 "objectionable" words.)

━━ ■ ━━ ■ ━━ ■ ━━ ■ ━━ ■ ━━ ■ ━━

Thomas Bowdler, M.D.: Thomas Bowdler (1754–1825) was a man whose name is now irrevocably associated with censorship. (His descendants must be *so* proud!) Apparently, Dr. Bowdler felt that parts of some of the works of the immortal William Shakespeare were too dirty for most (especially children) and thus took it upon himself to remedy this deplorable situation. In 1818, at the age of 64, Bowdler published *The Family Shakespeare,* an edition of the Bard's works that had been sanitized, purified, refined, sterilized, and generally chopped to smithereens by this renowned, self-defined literary critic and moral guardian. Upon tackling this sacred project, Bowdler decided to omit "those words and expressions which cannot with propriety be read aloud in the family." To this day, to "bowdlerize" is synonymous with the abhorrent practice of expurgating literary works.

━━ ■ ━━ ■ ━━ ■ ━━ ■ ━━ ■ ━━ ■ ━━

The 27 Beatles Songs That Were the Only Compositions Actually Written by John Lennon and Paul McCartney As a Team

John Lennon and Paul McCartney agreed from day one that anything that was released as a Beatles song would be credited to them both, regardless of who actually wrote the song. In only 27 cases did John and Paul actually collaborate on songs. (In a recent interview, McCartney lamented the fact that not only did John not have anything to do with Paul's legendary song "Yesterday," Paul didn't even get first listing in the song's credits when it was released.)

This feature lists the 27 songs (of the over 175 recorded Beatles songs) that Paul and John worked on as a team.

1. "And I Love Her"
2. "Baby, You're a Rich Man"
3. "Baby's in Black"
4. "Birthday"
5. "Can't Buy Me Love"
6. "A Day in the Life"
7. "Drive My Car"
8. "Eight Days a Week"
9. "Eleanor Rigby"
10. "Every Little Thing"
11. "From Me to You"
12. "Hold Me Tight"
13. "I Wanna Be Your Man"
14. "I Want to Hold Your Hand"
15. "I'll Get You"
16. "In My Life"
17. "It's for You"

The 10 Biggest Garbage-Producing Countries on the Planet

I guess we're not the slobs we think we are.

This table lists the ten countries that have the highest per capita production of garbage in the world. As you can see, the United States doesn't even make the top three. Nonetheless, any and all attempts at reducing solid waste output and increasing recycling must continue apace, or we'll all be crawling through crud and dog-paddling through detritus before long.

Country	Pounds of Waste per Capita per Year
1. Australia	1,533
2. New Zealand	1,460
3. France	1,460
4. Canada	1,351
5. United States	1,205
6. Norway	1,059
7. Netherlands	949
8. Denmark	949
9. Finland	949
10. Bahrain	876

4 Bizarre American Cults of Death

The American Heritage Dictionary defines a cult as a group of persons sharing an obsessive devotion to a person or ideal. American history is unfortunately stained with the bloody explosions of cults gone bad. These are just four of the worst to have flourished in the United States.

1. The Symbionese Liberation Army

Leader: Donald "Cinque" DeFreeze.
Date: Friday, May 17, 1974.
Place: Los Angeles, California.
Method of Death: Gunfire.
Body Count: Six SLA members, including DeFreeze. They all died during a violent, bloody shootout with five hundred Los Angeles cops. The SLA kidnapped heiress Patty Hearst on February 4, 1974, and after incessant brainwashing and thought control, she joined their organization and helped them rob a bank. She eventually was captured in 1975 and ended up serving twenty-two months in prison for her part in the robbery.

2. The People's Temple

Leader: Jim Jones, who claimed to be God.
Date: Saturday, November 18, 1978.
Place: Jonestown, Guyana, South America.
Method of Death: Mass suicide by drinking cyanide-laced punch.
Body Count: 913 followers, including Jim Jones. All his

"worshippers" committed suicide at Jones's request. Parents fed the poison to their children.

3. MOVE

Leader: John Africa.
Date: Monday, May 13, 1985.
Place: Philadelphia, Pennsylvania.
Method of Death: Fire.
Body Count: Eleven MOVE members. Their West Philadelphia row house (and sixty-one other houses in a two-block radius) burned to the ground after police dropped a bomb from a helicopter in an attempt to destroy a MOVE rooftop bunker.

4. The Branch Davidians

Leader: David Koresh, who claimed to be Jesus Christ.
Date: Wednesday, April 19, 1993.
Place: Waco, Texas.
Method of Death: Fire.
Body Count: Eighty-six, including David Koresh and an estimated two dozen children. After a 51-day standoff, the Branch Davidians that were still holed up in a three-story compound outside Waco apparently set fire to the place when FBI agents used tanks to knock holes in the building and insert tear gas canisters in an attempt to force them to come out. Four Federal agents were killed on February 28, 1993, when the FBI attempted to serve a search warrant on Koresh, who reportedly had $200,000 worth of arms and ammunition in the compound.

4 Bizarre Laws Pertaining to Women's Feet

Which women's body parts would you consider to be blatantly sexual?

Most men (and women, for that matter) would include the breasts, the buttocks, the pubic region, and the bare legs on the short list of parts that, while they have other functions to be sure, are major erotic turn-ons for most.

But how about feet?

For centuries, women's feet have been considered sexual parts in many cultures, and laws pertaining to their exposure have been written and enforced.

There are magazines dedicated to this interest (see the feature on *Leg Show* magazine), and fringe companies have come into being whose sole purpose is to satisfy the interest of foot freaks. One company even offers a disembodied woman's foot made of a soft, flesh-like material. You can dress it in nylons or shoes, paint its toenails, or, I suppose, just use it as a paperweight.

One of the most mainstream acknowledgments of this somewhat odd fetish was in the 1989 movie *War of the Roses*. In that black comedy, Danny DeVito's character, a high-priced lawyer, was a foot freak who even went so far as to get a "foot job" (his girlfriend masturbated him with her foot under the table while he massaged her toes with oil) during a dinner party with Michael Douglas and Kathleen Turner. Another pop culture foot scene was in the Steve Martin film *Leap of Faith,* in which Liam Neeson gives Debra Winger a sensual bare foot massage while they're having a conversation.

1. **Laos:** There is a foot law in Laos that decrees that a woman cannot show her toes in public.
2. **China:** There is an interesting interpretation of nudity and er-

oticism "on the books" in rural China. The law there prohibits any male from looking at the bare feet of another man's wife. Men are allowed, however, to see anything else they want, including the woman's completely nude body if so desired. But if a neighbor or relative catches a glimpse of her toes, the offended husband has to kill him.

3. **Europe:** During the Rennaisance, painters could not show a woman's toes or bare feet in their works. The women could be stark naked if the artists desired, but feet were verboten.

4. **Europe:** In nineteenth-century Europe, female stage performers were banned from showing their feet. Almost anything else could be flashed, but again, toes were considered indecent exposure.

6 Bizarre Laws Pertaining to Having Sex with Animals

Nothing can be more obvious than that all animals
were created solely and exclusively for the use of
man.—Thomas Love Peacock, *Headlong Hall*

I find a delicious irony in a quotation about animals existing for
the use of man, written by a guy named Thomas *Love Peacock,* leading off a feature on laws having to do with sex with animals. Don't
you?

Human beings have had carnal knowledge of their fellow species
for eons. And societies have tried to regulate and legislate such behavior for almost as long.

1. **Peru:** It is against the law for males to copulate with a female
   alpaca.
2. **Middle Eastern Islamic Countries:** It is a sin and a crime to
   eat any lamb you've had sex with.
3. **Lebanon:** It is a sin and a crime to have sex with any *male* animal. Sex with female animals is allowed.
4. **Bangkok, Thailand:** Any male who rapes a dog is charged
   with cruelty to animals.
5. **Krakow, Poland:** It is a crime for humans to have sex with animals. Extremely horny, three-time offenders are shot in the
   head.
6. **Ancient Rome, Italy:** Anyone caught having sex with an animal had to pay a tax.

17 Bizarre Similarities in the Lives and Assassinations of Abraham Lincoln and John F. Kennedy

Some people would say that all things are predestined; that there is a master plan into which everyone and every event fits like the pieces of a jigsaw puzzle. And there are also people who assert that there is meaning in all things, and that things happen for a reason, and often to send a message.

What does it mean that there are all these similarities between Abraham Lincoln and John F. Kennedy? Is it nothing but coincidence, or is there some divine game plan being fulfilled here? It's your call. This feature looks at the eerie commonalities in the lives and deaths of two of America's most beloved Presidents.

1. Abraham Lincoln and John F. Kennedy were both concerned with civil rights and the problem of racism.
2. Lincoln was elected president in 1860. Kennedy was elected president in 1960.
3. Lincoln's secretary was named Kennedy. Kennedy's secretary was named Lincoln.
4. Lincoln's secretary advised Lincoln not to go to the theater. Kennedy's secretary advised Kennedy not to go to Dallas.
5. Lincoln was slain on a Friday in the presence of his wife. Kennedy was slain on a Friday in the presence of his wife.
6. Lincoln was shot in the head from behind. Kennedy was shot in the head from behind.
7. Lincoln's assassin, John Wilkes Booth, was born in 1839. Kennedy's assassin, Lee Harvey Oswald, was born in 1939.
8. John Wilkes Booth was a Southerner. Lee Harvey Oswald was a Southerner.

9. John Wilkes Booth and Lee Harvey Oswald both espoused controversial, radical, unpopular ideas.
10. Lincoln's successor was Andrew Johnson, a Southern Democratic Senator. Kennedy's successor was Lyndon Johnson, a Southern Democratic Senator.
11. Lincoln's wife, Mary Todd Lincoln, had a child who died while her husband was in the White House. Kennedy's wife, Jacqueline Kennedy, had a child who died while her husband was in the White House.
12. John Wilkes Booth shot Lincoln in a theater and ran to a warehouse. Lee Harvey Oswald shot Kennedy from a warehouse and ran to a theater.
13. The name Lincoln contains seven letters. The name Kennedy contains seven letters.
14. The name of Lincoln's successor, Andrew Johnson, contains thirteen letters. The name of Kennedy's successor, Lyndon Johnson, contains thirteen letters.
15. The name of Lincoln's assassin, John Wilkes Booth, contains fifteen letters. The name of Kennedy's assassin, Lee Harvey Oswald, contains fifteen letters.
16. John Wilkes Booth was killed before being brought to trial. Lee Harvey Oswald was killed before being brought to trial.
17. Lincoln's successor, Andrew Johnson, was opposed for reelection by Ulysses S. Grant, whose last name begins with the letter G. Kennedy's successor, Lyndon Johnson, was opposed for reelection by Barry M. Goldwater, whose last name begins with the letter G.

12 Body Parts People Pierce

Body mutilation has always been popular. Tatoos, piercings, brandings, and other forms of casually violent adornment have been common cultural rituals since man and woman have walked upright.

This feature looks at a dozen body parts into which people willingly put holes—and then jewelry. The parts are listed in order of bodily descent, and for certain parts I also offer some tidbits on who favors each particular mutilatory site. (See also Odd Sexual Bondage Practices and Sexual Blood Sports.)

1. The Ears

Of course. Countless women and many men have pierced ears. Having your ears pierced is a rite of adolescence for most teen or pre-teen girls and many have a girlfriend do it with an ice cube, a needle, and a piece of cork. What's elevating pierced ears into the realm of oddness is the current très chic self-mutilation craze that requires the piercee to pierce the entire length of the ear—even up into the quite thick (and very sensitive) cartilage.

2. The Eyebrows

The eyebrow is pierced from top to bottom and either a hoop or stud earring can be worn. In the fall of 1993, *Entertainment Weekly* magazine reported that pierced eyebrows were especially popular on the campuses of Brown University in Providence, Rhode Island; the University of Kansas in Lawrence, Kansas; and Syracuse University in Syracuse, New York.

3. The Nose

The most common question asked of people with pierced noses (either nostril wall is pierced and either a hoop or a stud earring is worn) is "What do you do when you get a cold?" The answer is the same as for people with *nonpierced* noses: You blow your nose. Apparently, your virus-ridden body fluids just slide right on by the post and clutch arrangement of the earring.

4. The Septum

The septum is the wall of cartilage that separates your right and left nostril. It is usually pierced horizontally through the wall, and a hoop earring is worn so that it hangs onto the upper lip.

5. The Cheeks

I'm talking about the "northern exposure" cheeks here, folks. This type of piercing involves wearing an earring in either facial cheek, with the earring clutch inside the mouth. This seems to appeal to mutilation aficionados, the people who pierce their tongues (see below) and really go nuts with tattoos. In fact, it isn't uncommon to find heavily tattooed people sporting both tongue *and* cheek earrings.

6. The Tongue

As with cheek piercing, this appeals to tattooers and cheek piercers. The tongue is pierced approximately halfway up its length, and the earring is worn on the top of the tongue, with the clutch underneath. Recipients claim it is not painful, and that it does not interfere with eating. (Okay, I'll accept their word about the pain, but I'll bet that lo mein or spaghetti will once in a while get wrapped around the earring post and have to be manually removed. And we won't even bring up bean sprouts.)

7. The Lower Lip

When this site is pierced, usually a hoop earring is worn so that the earring goes through the front and back of the lip. Perhaps stud earrings are also worn here, but it would seem that the clutch on the back of the earring might scrape the lower teeth and make it quite uncomfortable, not to mention remove enamel.

8. The Nipples

This is a favorite of many gay men and lesbian women, as well as people into the S&M/bondage/discipline sex scene. The only type of earring I've seen being worn through the nipple is a hoop, either by itself or with something hanging on it. Buffalo Bill, the serial killer in *Silence of the Lambs,* wore a little charm on the hoop he had through his nipple.

9. The Navel

Lately, it's been quite popular for people with "outies" to put an earring through it. Ouch. But then again, Madonna must know what she's talking about when she says that she gets an immediate and overpowering sexual thrill when she puts her finger into her belly button. Just clean out the lint first, okay?

10. The Fingernails

This is the only "non-flesh" body part included here, but it is listed because it seems to be gaining in popularity. Women with long, natural nails drill a hole in the nail and either wear a hoop or a stud through the hole. I suppose press-on nails can also be used, but I wonder how the plastic-like material would hold up to drilling and piercing.

11. The Labia

The labia majora (the external lips of the female vagina) are also used as a piercing site. This is quite a turn-on for many people, although for heterosexuals the male must be careful not to cut himself.

12. The Penis

Yes, there are men who actually pierce the head of their penis, and also the entire length of the organ. When piercing the head, it's usually done above the urethra and traverses the head from side to side. When the body of the organ itself is done, the earrings can run the entire length of the penis. These types of piercings are most popular among those into S&M, and among primitive tribesmen who do it as a form of ritual adornment. These types of piercings have *got* to hurt, no matter what anyone tells you. (It should be noted that scrotum piercing, which seems like an especially dangerous form of invasive adornment, is also popular.)

6 Celebrity UFO Sightings

I have seen a UFO. It happened back in 1988, when I was still working full-time as the manager of a family jewelry business. I was headed for work, traveling east on Route 1 in East Haven, Connecticut. I stopped for a red light and just happened to look up into the northeastern sky. There I saw an oval-shaped silver object that was moving rapidly in a perfectly straight line in a northerly direction. At first I thought I was seeing a high-flying jet. We do live near a major airport and seeing (and hearing) all kinds of aircraft in our area at all hours of the day and night is not an uncommon experience. But then things got weird. The flying thing I was watching suddenly stopped in mid-air, reversed course, traveled in the opposite direction for a few seconds, and then disappeared. The light turned green and I drove on to work. I still, to this day, do not know what I saw, and thus, I must call it a UFO, since it definitely fits the description.

This feature looks at UFO sightings by a few people whose names are household words. I guess I am in good company.

1. **Muhammad Ali** The champ admits to having seen two UFOs. One was "cigar-shaped" and it appeared over the New Jersey Turnpike. The other looked like "a huge electric light bulb," which he saw in Central Park.
2. **Jimmy Carter** Former President Carter claims to have seen a UFO on January 6, 1969. He was governor of Georgia at the time. He said the object changed colors and was as big as the moon. There is conjecture today that what he saw was actually the planet Venus.
3. **Jamie Farr** Corporal Klinger ("M*A*S*H") claims to have seen an erratically flying light in Yuma, Arizona. He says it stopped in mid-air above his car.
4. **Jackie Gleason** The Great One was extremely interested in the paranormal and the occult and claimed to have seen UFOs in London and Florida.

5. **Dick Gregory** According to Gregory, he saw three red and green lights dance in the sky for close to an hour one night.

6. **William Shatner** You'd almost think he was joking but, no, Shatner was serious when he reported that a silver spacecraft flew over him in the Mojave Desert as he pushed his inoperative motorcycle. He also claims to have received a telepathic message from the beings in the craft advising him which direction to walk. The least they could have done was give him a jump-start, no?

The Church of Satan's 9 Satanic Statements

The United States Government recognizes Anton LaVey's Church of Satan as an official church, entitled to all the protection and rights of any other structured religious establishment in America.

The Church of Satan worships Satan.

They hold Black Masses, which are rituals that use the body of a naked virgin as the altar, and which include inserting the name of Satan into prayers where God or Christ is mentioned. They often also include defilement of "sacred" artifacts such as the Host and wine.

In his writings, Anton LaVey has defined his Church's beliefs and goals and has coalesced their tenets into nine "Satanic Statements," which speak for themselves.

1. Satan represents indulgence instead of abstinence.
2. Satan represents vital existence instead of spiritual pipe dreams.
3. Satan represents undefiled wisdom instead of hypocritical self-deceit.
4. Satan represents kindness to those who deserve it instead of love wasted on ingrates.
5. Satan represents vengeance instead of turning the other cheek.
6. Satan represents responsibility to the responsible instead of concern for psychic vampires.
7. Satan represents man as just another animal—sometimes better, more often worse than those that walk on all-fours—who, because of his "divine spiritual and intellectual development," has become the most vicious animal of all.
8. Satan represents all of the so-called sins, as they all lead to physical, mental, or emotional gratification.

9. Satan has been the best friend the Church has ever had, as he has kept it in business all these years.

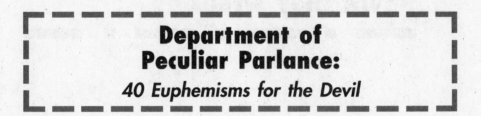

Department of Peculiar Parlance:
40 Euphemisms for the Devil

We have many ways of naming the darkness. Here are 40 of those ways.

1. The Arch Fiend
2. The Author of Evil
3. Beelzebub
4. The Black Gentleman
5. The Black Spy
6. The Black Man
7. The Black Prince
8. The Dark One
9. Dickens
10. The Evil One
11. The Fallen Angel
12. The Father of Lies
13. The Gentleman in Black
14. Goodman
15. His Satanic Majesty
16. Lord Harry
17. Lucifer
18. Mephistopheles
19. The Noseless One
20. Old Billy
21. Old Dad
22. The Old Driver
23. The Old Gentleman
24. The Old Gooseberry
25. Old Harry
26. Old Horny
27. The Old One
28. Old Roundfoot
29. Old Scratch
30. Old Split Foot
31. The Prince of Darkness
32. Queed
33. The Ragman
34. Saint Nicholas
35. Sam Hill
36. Satan
37. Scratch
38. Skipper
39. Toast
40. The Wicked One

28 Computer Viruses and the Havoc They Wreak

Item: Computer programs written for the space shuttle are checked *line by line* before they are transmitted from Houston to the orbiting shuttle.

Paranoid overreaction?

No siree bob.

Actually, to be *really* safe, the programs should be checked *character by character* (and maybe they are now), and you'll understand why after reading through this feature, which looks at 28 ubiquitous computer viruses, the damage they wreak on their host computers, and the torment they inflict on their host computers' poor owners' minds.

When a virus has a name, it is supplied. When a formal moniker was not given to the virus when it was written, then I assign a name to it based on its mischievous characteristics.

1. **The Alameda Virus** This 1988 IBM PCs (and compatibles) virus was written at Merritt College in Oakland, California, and infects a computer during a software reboot. Slow booting, system crashes, and loss of data are its trademarks.
2. **The Cascade Virus** This Russian virus (known in the Soviet Union as **Falling Tears)** makes all the characters on a computer screen fall to the bottom of the screen and pile up. Other than this somewhat horrifying effect *(especially* for a freelance writer), all other features of the infected application work fine.
3. **The ChinaTalk Virus** This 1992 Macintosh Trojan Horse [a program that appears to be harmless (a game or INIT) but contains a nasty bit of business that kicks in at a predetermined time] is an INIT that claims to provide a female voice for MacinTalk. What it actually *does* do is completely delete

the contents of your disk drive when your computer is restarted.

4. **The "Christmas Card" Virus** This was an innocent virus that was actually nothing more than a Christmas message sent by a student in West Germany on December 11, 1987. Called an electronic "pesky chain letter," this Christmas greeting was designed to go to everyone on the recipient's electronic mailing list. Somehow it got into IBM's worldwide network and clogged computer traffic, necessitating a global shutdown of IBM's system for three hours.

5. **The Code 252 Virus** This 1992 Macintosh virus is cruel and mean-spirited, but relatively innocuous: Upon activation, the user is given an onscreen message telling him or her that the contents of their hard drive are being destroyed. After the message is displayed, however, the virus commits suicide and no actual damage results.

6. **The CyberAIDS Virus** This is a nasty and destructive virus named after our current modern Black Plague and written by a guy who calls himself The Plague. Massive destruction of data is its calling card.

7. **The Dark Avenger Virus** This virus (also known as The Eddie Virus—named after the heavy metal band Iron Maiden's skeleton mascot) is named after its creator, the notorious Dark Avenger, a Bulgarian computer programmer who is bold enough to sign his superhero name to the viruses he creates. The Dark Avenger virus randomly destroys sections of an infected hard disk, wiping out whatever happens to be residing at that section of the disk.

8. **The Desert Storm Virus** Believe it or not, this was a very clever virus written by the United States Government and used during the Persian Gulf War against the Iraqis. Our own National Security Agency wrote the virus and installed it on a computer chip that was then clandestinely installed into a French-built computer printer shipped to an Iraqi military computer center in Baghdad. The virus was designed to disable the Iraqis' mainframe computer by attacking it through the peripheral printer, bypassing Iraq's frontline computer security measures. What the virus did was cause everything on a computer screen to disappear whenever a computer operator opened a new "window," a

common interface feature found in most sophisticated programs today. One for us, eh?

9. **The Disk Killer Virus** I'll bet you can guess what this baby does. That's right. This one *does* live up to its name. When activated, it wipes clean your hard disk.

10. **The FluShot4 Virus** This virus was originally written as a vaccine program *against* viruses but got sabotaged before it hit the street. The modified program trashed users' hard disks.

11. **The "4 Numbers" Virus** This virus scans the computer screen once every minute looking for four contiguous numbers. If it finds four digits in a row, it scrambles them. As you can imagine, this can wreak unimaginable havoc if the number scrambled was something critical, such as the length of an airplane wing or a company financial projection.

12. **The "Gotcha" Virus** This is an early virus that did nothing but flash the word *Gotcha!* on the screen at a predetermined time.

13. **The INIT 1984 Virus** This 1992 Macintosh virus activates only on Friday the 13ths. It randomly destroys files and changes the names of files, folders, and attributes to meaningless garbage.

14. **The Internet Virus** Not really a virus, this notorious worm (a program that endlessly copies itself) spread worldwide through the Department of Defense's computers in November of 1988 and ultimately crippled over 6,000 computers. It was written by a Cornell student named Robert Morris, Jr.

15. **The Israeli Virus** This 1987 IBM PCs (and compatibles) virus, written in Jerusalem, makes programs disappear on any Friday the 13th. It also causes a dark spot to appear in a corner of the computer screen and either floppies or hard disks can become infected.

16. **The "Laundry" Virus** British Telecom was once infected with a computer virus that made all their monitors randomly transform themselves into front-loading washing machines. The computer screen would suddenly, and with no warning, magically appear to be the window of a suds-filled, spinning washing machine.

17. **The Lehigh Virus** This 1987 IBM (and compatibles) virus was named for its place of birth, Lehigh University in Bethlehem, Pennsylvania. This is a nefarious bug that activates af-

ter only four restarts, and thus is extremely difficult to detect. When activated, it destroys all system data, and loss of other data is likely.

18. **The LoveChild Virus** This is a quiet, cruel, and devastatingly patient Russian virus that upon activation begins counting down from 5,000 each time the infected computer is used. When it reaches zero the virus becomes The Terminator and completely eradicates the host hard disk.

19. **The "Mac II" Virus** This benign Macintosh virus did one thing, and one thing only: On March 2, 1988, the anniversary of the "birth" of Apple's Mac II Macintosh computer, a message appeared on users' screens that read, "Richard Brandow, Publisher of MacMag, and its entire staff would like to take this opportunity to convey their Universal Message of Peace to all Macintosh users around the world."

20. **The Michelangelo Virus** This is perhaps the most famous of all computer viruses. On March 6, 1992, Michelangelo activated. What was supposed to happen was that all data on both the floppy and hard disks of infected computers would be erased. Michelangelo's fame came from the worldwide panic that occurred when it was rumored that an unthinkable 80 percent of the world's computer population had somehow been infected with the bug. Whether or not this rumor was true will never really be known because the paranoia that set in during the weeks prior to M-Day resulted in an unprecedented surge of "preventative medicine": Anti-Virus software sold off the shelves and many users refused to even turn their machines on on March 6. Consequently, Big M was a dud. Nonetheless, this kind of response on the part of computer users to what was perceived as a global threat effectively illustrated just how dependent the world is on computer data, and just how vulnerable its caretakers feel about its safety.

21. **The Mutating Engine** This is a relatively new, unspeakably deadly virus currently traversing our electronic highways. The Mutating Engine (also sometimes called the Mutation Engine) was created in Eastern Europe. What strikes fear in the hearts of network users everywhere is that the Engine can be "designed" to do any number of nefarious deeds and yet it is, for all intents and purposes, completely undetect-

able. All that expensive anti-virus software you bought for peace of mind won't do diddly until something occurs that isolates a vulnerable or identifiable characteristic or feature of the virus. Clones of the Mutation Engine include viruses called Coffee Shop, Cryptlab, Fear, Groove, Little, and Pogue.

22. **The nVIR Virus** This 1987 Macintosh virus was written in Hamburg, Germany, and is vicious in its ability to infect any and all applications and other programs in a computer within minutes. You know you're in trouble when you experience frequent system crashes, a beep when an application is opened, and the mysterious disappearance of files. If the talking application MacinTalk is installed and you're infected by nVIR, your computer will treacherously tell you, "Don't panic." Don't listen to it. Panic.

23. **The Pakistani Brain Virus** This 1986 IBM PCs (and compatibles) virus was written in Pakistan and replicates itself (shades of *Blade Runner!*) onto any bootable floppies inserted into the computer. This virus actually proudly identifies itself with a message that reads "Copyright © Brain Label" when a disk becomes infected. Troubles include very slow restarts and reboots and a great deal of floppy disk activity for what should be quick and simple tasks. This virus could almost be considered immortal: It will live through a software reboot.

24. **The Scores Virus** This 1987 Macintosh virus infects any application, creates bogus Note Pad and Scrapbook files in the System Folder, and seeks and destroys specific files by name. Symptoms include a general sluggishness and printing problems. System crashes are common.

25. **The Stoned Virus** This ubiquitous virus causes the computer screen to display a message that reads, "Your computer is now stoned. Legalize marijuana." Even though it was not designed to do any damage, it can accidentally destroy or foul up some files.

26. **The T4-A Virus** This 1992 Macintosh virus was first discovered in a game called GoMoku. It randomly damages system files and applications.

27. **The T4-B Virus** This is a "new and improved" version of the T4-A Virus.

28. **The Yankee Doodle Virus** This musical virus first appeared

in 1989 in a United Nations computer in a game called Out-run. It programs computers to play the song "Yankee Doo-dle" at a predetermined time. Several versions of this virus exist, each of which tell the computer when to trigger the "performance." Version 44, for instance, when activated, plays the tune at 5:00 P.M. every day for eight days.

The Contents of the 9 Envelopes in a Sealed Police Rape Kit

When a rape victim is brought to a hospital emergency room, a very strict investigatory protocol is followed. Before the victim is physically examined, the police are summoned. When the police officer or detective arrives, the victim is questioned as to the circumstances of the rape and what he or she can remember about the assailant.

The sealed police rape kit the police have brought with them is then opened by the attending physician in the presence of the police. The attending doctor and nurse then perform the physical examination and the collection of evidence from the victim's body.

The rape kit contains nine envelopes for evidence, sealed cotton swabs, tubes for blood, a comb, and legal forms.

After each envelope is filled, the doctor seals, signs, and dates the envelope. When the examination is complete, the doctor seals, signs, and dates the kit and turns it over to the police. Once it is in the hands of the police it is official legal property.

Here is a rundown of what goes into each envelope.

1. **Envelope No. 1:** This envelope holds combings from the victim's pubic hair. A paper towel is placed beneath the victim's buttocks and the pubic hair is combed. The paper towel with the collected material on it and the comb are both placed in the envelope.
2. **Envelope No. 2:** This envelope holds scrapings and debris from the victim's clothing and/or body. Common detritus found include glass, sand or dirt, gravel, dried blood, and tar particles.

3. **Envelope No. 3:** This envelope holds scrapings from beneath the victim's fingernails and cuttings of the fingernails themselves.

4. **Envelope No. 4:** This envelope holds twelve hairs from the victim's scalp.

5. **Envelope No. 5:** This envelope holds twelve of the victim's pubic hairs.

6. **Envelope No. 6:** This envelope holds a sample of the victim's sputum.

7. **Envelope No. 7:** This envelope holds cotton swabs which have been used to wipe around the external genitalia and the vulva on a woman, or the anus of a man.

8. **Envelope No. 8:** This envelope holds cotton swabs that have been used to take internal smears of the victim's vagina, anus, and mouth.

9. **Envelope No. 9:** This envelope holds a 10 cc vial of the victim's blood drawn during the examination.

The 20 Countries with the Lowest Life Expectancy in the World

You think you've got troubles? Imagine living in one of *these* places.

This feature lists the countries in the world where merciless poverty, almost nonexistent health care, horrible nutrition, rampant violence, and epidemic crime all contribute to a life expectancy almost half of what the luckier countries enjoy.

Country	Life Expectancy
1. Sierre Leone, Africa	41
2. Guinea-Bissau, Africa	42
3. Afghanistan, Asia	42
4. Guinea, Africa	43
5. The Gambia, Africa	43
6. Mali, Africa	44
7. Ethiopia, Africa	44
8. Angola, Africa	45
9. Niger, Africa	45
10. Somalia, Africa	45
11. Chad, Africa	46
12. Mauritania, Africa	46
13. Benin, Africa	46
14. Equatorial Guinea, Africa	46
15. Mozambique, Africa	47
16. Djibouti, Africa	47
17. Malawi, Africa	47
18. Burkina Faso, Africa	47
19. Senegal, Africa	47
20. Burundi, Africa	48

16 Creationist Claims and Why Both the Creationists Themselves *and* Their Spurious Pseudoscientific Claims Are Unequivocally Wrong

The following list of sixteen creationism debunking arguments originally appeared in Dr. Tim M. Berra's brilliant 1990 book *Evolution and the Myth of Creationism*. In his lucid, reasoned, and *enlightened* preface, Dr. Berra said:

> Creationists, for the most part, are fundamentalist Christians whose central premise is a literal interpretation of the Bible and a belief in its inerrancy.
>
> The creationists are determined to force their will on society and the schools, through the courts if possible. Their strategy—ironically enough, considering the moral precepts of Christianity—is founded in deception, misrepresentation, and obfuscation designed to dupe the public into thinking that there is a genuine scientific controversy about the validity of evolution. No such controversy exists, but it is difficult for the lay public to distinguish the scientists, who often disagree on the nuances of evolutionary theory (but not on evolution's existence), from the creationists, who stick together and cloak absurd claims in scientific terminology.

Some Creationist Claims: Do They Raise Any Legitimate Doubts?
by Dr. Tim M. Berra

1. **The Claim:** *Evolution violates the second law of thermodynamics. Entropy (disorder) is always increasing. Since order does not arise out of chaos, evolution is therefore false.*
   The Truth: These statements conveniently ignore the fact that you *can* get order out of disorder if you add energy. For example, an unassembled bicycle that arrives at your house in a shipping carton is in a state of disorder. You supply the energy of your muscles (which you get from food that came ultimately from sunlight) to assemble the bike. You have got order from disorder by supplying energy. The Sun is the source of energy input to the earth's living systems and allows them to evolve. The engineers in the CRS (Creation Research Society) know this, but they permit this specious reasoning to be published in their pamphlets. Just as the more structured oak tree is derived from the less complex acorn by the addition of energy captured by the growing tree from the Sun, so sunlight, via photosynthesis, provides the energy input that propels evolution. In the sense that the Sun is losing more energy than the Earth is gaining, entropy is increasing. After death, decay sets in, and energy utilization is no longer possible. That is when entropy gets you. What does represent an increase in entropy, as biologists have pointed out, is the diversity of species produced by evolution.

2. **The Claim:** *The small amount of helium in the atmosphere proves that the Earth is young. If the Earth were as old as geologists say, there would be much more helium, because it is a product of uranium decay.*
   The Truth: Helium, used to suspend blimps in air, is a very light gas and simply escapes into space; like hydrogen, it cannot accumulate in Earth's atmosphere to any great extent.

3. **The Claim:** *The rate of decay of the Earth's magnetism leads to the calculation that the Earth was created about 10,000 years ago.*

The Truth: The Earth's magnetic field does indeed decay, but it does so cyclically, every few thousand years, and is constantly being renewed by the motion of the liquid core of the Earth. The "fossil magnetism" recorded in ancient rocks clearly demonstrates that polar reversals (shifts in the direction of the Earth's magnetic field) have occurred both repeatedly and irregularly throughout Earth history; the calendar of these reversals was established over two decades ago, and quickly became the linchpin in the emerging theory of plate tectonics and continental drift.

4. **The Claim:** *If evolution were true, there would have to be transitional fossils, but there were none; therefore evolution did not occur.*
   The Truth: There are many transitional fossils, including the ape-human transitional form, Australopithecus. Eusthenopteron shows marvelous intermediate characteristics between the lobe-finned fishes and the amphibians. The transitional fossils between amphibians and reptiles are so various and so intermediate that it is difficult to define where one group ends and the other begins. Archaeopteryx is clearly intermediate between reptiles and birds. In spite of such reptilian affinities as a long bony tail, toothed jaws, and clawed wings, creationists declare that because Archaeopteryx had feathers, it was a bird, not a transitional stage between reptiles and birds. Having no explanation of their own, the creationists attempt to deny the transitional fossils out of existence.

5. **The Claim:** *Fossils seem to appear out of nowhere at the base of the Cambrian; therefore, they had to have been created.*
   The Truth: The earliest microfossils date back, in fact, to the Precambrian, about 3.5 billion years ago. A variety of multicellular life appears in the fossil record about 670 million years ago, which is 80 million years before the Cambrian. The Cambrian does seem to explode with fossils, but that is simply because the first shelled organisms, such as the brachiopods and trilobites, date from the Cambrian; their resistant shells fossilize far more readily than their soft-bodied ancestors of the Precambrian. What is more, Precambrian rocks are so old that they have been subjected to a great deal of deformation. We are thus fortunate to have *any* Precambrian fossils of soft-bodied animals. Still more fossils

are discovered every year, and each one further weakens the creationist position.

6. **The Claim:** *All fossils were deposited at the time of the Noachian flood.*
   The Truth: There is not a shred of evidence in the geological record to support the claim of a single, worldwide flood. Geological formations such as mountain ranges and the Grand Canyon require millions of years to form, and the fossil record extends over several billion years. The time required for continents to have drifted into their present positions is immense. These things cannot be accounted for by a single flood lasting a few days or years.

7. **The Claim:** *There are places where advanced fossils lie beneath more primitive fossils.*
   The Truth: Earth movements such as faulting and thrusting produce these discontinuities; the older rock has simply been pushed over on top of the younger rocks, as we sometimes see even along highway cuts. These places are easily recognized and explained by geologists. They cannot be explained away by the creationists' belief that all fossils are the result of the Noachian flood. Thus the creationists' attempt to fault evolutionary theory by these means ends up demolishing one of their own pet claims.

8. **The Claim:** *The chances of the proper molecules randomly assembling into a living cell are impossibly small.*
   The Truth: Simulation experiments have repeatedly shown that amino acids do not assemble randomly. Their molecular structure causes them to be self-ordering, which enhances the chances of forming long chains of molecules. Simulation experiments also demonstrate that the formation of prebiotic macromolecules is both easy and likely and does not require DNA, which is a later step in the evolution of proteins. The stepwise application of cumulative natural selection acting over long periods of time can make the improbable very likely.

9. **The Claim:** *Dinosaur and human footprints have been found together in Cretaceous limestone at Glen Rose, Texas. Therefore, dinosaurs could not have preceded humans by millions of years.*
   The Truth: This Fred Flintstone version of prehistory is one

of the most preposterous and devious claims that the fundamentalists make, and they have made it in both books and films. The "man-tracks" seen by creationists stem from two sources. One is wishful imagination, whereby water-worn scour marks and eroded dinosaur tracks are perceived as human footprints. The other source is deliberate fraud. Creationist hoaxers obscure the foot pads of dinosaur tracks with sand and photograph what remains, the dinosaur's toe impressions. When reversed, the tip of the dinosaur toe or claw becomes the heel of a "human" print. These prints are shown in poor-quality photographs in creationist literature and films. Because the stride length (7 feet) and foot length (3 feet) exceed any possible human scale, the fundamentalists call these the giants mentioned in Genesis. In addition to doctored dinosaur tracks, there are other hoaxed prints circulating in this area of Texas. In fact, carved footprints were offered for sale to tourists in curio shops during the Great Depression. These caught the eye of the paleontologist Roland T. Bird, who recognized them as fakes, but they eventually led him to the legitimate dinosaur footprint at Glen Rose. This area has since been extensively studied by paleontologists, and numerous species of reptiles and amphibians have been catalogued. No genuine human tracks exist there, but by leading to genuine new discoveries, the hoax became a boon to science.

10. **The Claim:** *Biologists have never seen a species evolve.*
    The Truth: On a small scale, we certainly have. Using allopolyploidy and artificial selection, scientists have manufactured crop plants and horticultural novelties that are reproductively isolated from the parental stock. In addition, one can see stages of incipient speciation in nature by looking at clinal variations and subspecies; that is, gradual change in the characteristics of a population across its geographical range. Major evolutionary changes, however, usually involve time periods vastly greater than man's written record; we cannot watch such changes, but we can deduce them by inference from living and fossil organisms.

11. **The Claim:** *Evolution, too, is a religion, and requires faith.*
    The Truth: Creationists are beginning to admit that their "science" is not science at all, and that it depends on faith;

but, they are quick to add, so does evolution. Not so. Biologists do not have to *believe* that there are transitional fossils; we can examine them in hundreds of museums around the world, and we make new discoveries in the rocks all the time. Scientists do not have to *believe* that the solar system is 4.5 billion years old; we can test the age of Earth, Moon, and meteoritic rocks very accurately. We do not have to *believe* that protocells can be easily created from simple chemicals in the laboratory; we can repeat the experiments, with comparable results. We can also create artificial species of plants and animals by applying selection, and we can observe natural speciation in action. That is the big difference between science and religion. Science exists *because of* the evidence, whereas religion exists upon faith—and, in the case of religious fundamentalism and creationism, *in spite of* the evidence.

12. **The Claim:** *The numbers of humans today would be much greater if we have been around as long as evolutionists say we have.*
    The Truth: This notion makes some very naive assumptions about birth and death rates, and the fecundity of early humans, and assumes that populations are always growing when in fact most animal populations are at a level somewhat lower than the carrying capacity of their environment. Such stable populations remain stable for long periods of time, held in check by environmental constraints. It is only our own species' recently acquired ability to modify our environment that has allowed our numbers to get dangerously out of control. Ironically, it is our ability to master the environment—as the Bible commands us to do—that may yet do us in.

13. **The Claim:** *The current rate of shrinkage of the Sun proves that the Earth could not be as old as geologists say, because the surface of the Sun would have been near the Earth's orbit just a few million years ago.*
    The Truth: This simplistic view neglects the fact that stars, such as our Sun, have life cycles during which events occur at different rates. The characteristics of a newly formed star are quite different from those of stars near death. Astronomers can see these differences today by observing young, middle-aged, and old stars. By now, we know a great deal

about the Sun, and we know that it has not been shrinking at a constant rate.

14. **The Claim**: *A living freshwater mussel was determined by Carbon 14 dating to be over 2,000 years old; therefore Carbon 14 dating is worthless.*

    The Truth: When used properly, Carbon 14 is a very accurate time-measuring technique. The mussel in this example is an inappropriate case for C-14 dating because the animal had acquired much of its carbon from the limestone of the surrounding water and sediment. These sources are very low in C-14, owing to their age and lack of mixing with fresh carbon from the atmosphere. Therefore, a newly killed mussel in these circumstances has less C-14 than, say, a newly cut tree branch. The reduced level of C-14 yields an artificially older date. The C-14 technique has no such problems with the tree branch that gets its carbon from the air, or with the campfire sites of ancient peoples. As with arc welding or Cajun cooking, one must understand the technique to use it properly. This is another example of the self-correcting nature of science.

15. **The Claim:** *The influx of meteoritic dust from space to Earth is about 14 million tons per year. If the Earth and Moon were 4.5 billion years old, there should be a layer of dust 50 to 100 feet thick covering their surfaces.*

    The Truth: This estimate of dust influx is simply out of date. Space probes have found that the level of dust influx from space is about 400 times less than that. Creationists are aware of the modern measurements, but they continue to use the incorrect figure because it suits their purpose. Such is their honesty and scholarship. Do these people believe that the astronauts would have been allowed to land on the Moon if NASA thought they would sink into 100 feet of dust?

16. **The Claim:** *Prominent biologists have made statements disputing evolution.*

    The Truth: The out-of-context quote is one of the most insidious weapons in the creationists' arsenal, and reflects the desperation of their position. Biologists do not deny the *fact* of evolution. We do, however, debate its *mechanisms* and *tempo.* The debate reflects the vigorous growth of a major scientific concept; it is what goes on routinely in all healthy, growing branches of scholarship. Creationists dishonestly portray this as a weakness of the theory of evolution.

These 16 points are just a few of the creationists' arguments. There are others, but they are all of the same character—scientifically inaccurate, willful, or devious.

Reprinted from *Evolution and the Myth of Creationism: A Basic Guide to the Facts in the Evolution Debate* by Tim M. Berra with the permission of the publisher, Stanford University Press, © 1990 by the Board of Trustees of the Leland Stanford Junior University.

16 Crucified Saviors Other Than Jesus Christ

We can believe what we choose.
We are answerable for what we choose to believe.
—Cardinal Newman

It is always easier to believe than to deny.
Our minds are naturally affirmative.
—John Burroughs, *The Light of Day* (1900)

In 1875, religious scholar and historian Kersey Graves published a book that gave the Christian clergy nightmares.

It was called *The World's Sixteen Crucified Saviors, or Christianity Before Christ,* which claimed to prove—calmly, rationally, and with seemingly impeccable scholarship—that Christianity was essentially based on legends and myths from centuries past, and that the "legend" of Jesus Christ bore dozens (in some cases, hundreds) of similarities to pagan gods from as far back as the year 2000 B.C.

Graves began the book with an "Explanation":

The World's Sixteen Crucified Saviors. What an imposing title for a book! What startling developments of religious history it implies! Is it founded on fact or fiction? If it has a basis of truth, where was such an extraordinary mine of sacred lore discovered? Where were such startling facts obtained as the title of the work suggests? [M]any of the most important facts collated in this work were derived from Sir Godfrey Higgins' *Anacalypsis,* a work as valuable as it is rare—a work comprising the result of twenty years' labor, devoted to the investigation of religious history. . . . With the facts and materials derived from this source, and two hundred other unimpeachable historical records, the

present work might have swelled to fourfold its present size. . . .
The recently opened fountains of historic law [irrevocably dis-
prove] the divine origin of the Christian religion, or the divinity
of Jesus Christ.

Graves then detailed the common elements of many ancient religions and pagan gods, including such things as being foretold by
prophets; a virgin birth; being born on December 25th; a sin-
atoning crucifixion (often between two thieves); rising from the
dead after three days buried; physical ascension into heaven; the
presence of magi, or "wise men"; being considered part of a divine
trinity; and being referred to as Savior, Redeemer, Messiah, and
the Son of God.

Graves also claimed evidence that at least twenty ancient religions had holy books that had Old and New Testaments, and that
the Christian Bible can easily be traced to heathen, rather than divine, sources. Reading *The World's Sixteen Crucified Saviors* is an
amazing experience, and is must reading for anyone interested in
the origins of our sociocultural and religious belief systems.

Disclaimer: I must make the point that this feature is solely based
on the research and material found in Graves's 1875 book. I have
not attempted to duplicate his research nor do I vouch for it. I include this feature here for the sake of intellectual advancement
and to stimulate discourse. (I reject the old adage about never discussing religion or politics.) If you are interested in reading first-
hand Kersey Graves's astonishing assertions, then I recommend
you buy his book. It can be ordered from Loompanics. (See their
address in this volume.) Interestingly, when I was finishing up this
chapter, I received a Barnes & Noble catalog in the mail. On page
20, they offered a book called *Pagan Christs* by J. M. Robertson.
The blurb for the book read, "A bold piece of scholarship, first
published in 1903, that argues that alleged historical events on
which Christianity is based never occurred and that the founder of
the religion never existed." Also, I have been told that The Jesus
Seminar, a research endeavor to determine *factual* information
about the life of Jesus Christ, has uncovered some startling, unexpected information about Jesus' life and times, which they published in a book in December 1993. The information, however,
seems to be of interest only to religious scholars and theologians.
The faithful remain so.

1. Chrishna (India)

- His presence on earth and his death were to atone for the sins of Man.
- He was crucified to appease God.
- He was worshipped by his disciples *as* God.
- He has often been depicted in drawings as having a divine halo over his head.
- He has often been depicted in drawings as having a "Sacred Heart."
- The cross became a religious symbol and icon after his death.
- His full name was Chrishna Zeus, which some spelled as Jeseus.
- He performed miracles, including healing the sick; curing lepers; restoring sight, sound, and speech; raising the dead; and casting out demons.
- A "divinely inspired" book *(The Bhagavad-Gita)* told of his coming and his miraculous works.
- He was born of a virgin, and the mother and newborn child were visited by shepherds.
- He spent a period of reflection in the desert.
- He was baptized in the River Ganges. (Christ was baptized in the River Jordan.)
- He once miraculously enabled his hungry followers to catch many nets full of fish.
- He taught by parable and sermon.
- There is similarity in the two names, Chrishna and Christ.
- The name of Chrishna's mother was Maia, which is similar to Mary.
- Chrishna was born on December 25th.
- He had an earthly adoptive father.
- He proclaimed to his followers, "I am the Resurrection."
- He had a last supper with his disciples before being crucified.
- He was crucified between two thieves.
- He was crucified around the age of 33.
- He rose from the dead after three days buried.
- He physically ascended into heaven.
- He taught, "Seek and ye shall find."
- He spoke of the "blind leading the blind."
- He regarded carnal and earthly pleasures as evil.
- He taught that "Faith can move mountains."

- He taught his followers to love their enemies.
- He prophesied his return to earth, which he called a "Second Coming."
- He taught, "It is better to give than to receive."

2. Sakia (Hindu)

- His emblem was a cross.
- One of the crimes for which he was crucified was that he illegally plucked a flower. (One of the charges against Christ was that he plucked an ear of corn on the Sabbath.)
- Legend has it that he was born to atone for man's sins.
- After he was crucified, Sakia was buried for three days, and then rose from the dead.
- He physically ascended into heaven.
- His titles included Savior of the World, and Light of the World.
- His mother was known as The Holy Virgin, Queen of Heaven.
- He was once tempted by the devil.
- He healed the sick and performed miracles.
- He preached "commandments" that included "Thou shalt not kill," "Thou shalt not steal," "Thou shalt not commit adultery," and "Thou shalt not lie."
[The dates for the remaining 14 saviors are approximate.]

3. Thamuz (Syria)

- He was called The Risen Lord and The Savior.
- He was crucified to atone for man's sins.
- He rose from the dead after being buried.

4. Wittoba (Telingonese)

- He was crucified for man's sins.
- He was usually depicted in drawings as having nail holes in his hands and in the soles of his feet.
- His icon was a cross.

5. Iao (Nepal)

- He was known as The Savior.
- He was crucified on a tree.
- He was accepted by his followers as God incarnate.
- Iao (or Jao) is thought to possibly be the root of *Jehovah*.

6. Hesus (Celtic Druid)

- He was crucified with a lamb on one side and an elephant on the other. The elephant was thought to represent all the sins of the world, and so we have the "Lamb of God" dying to take away the sins of the world.

7. Quexalcote (Mexico)

- He was crucified on a cross to atone for man's sins.
- He was crucified with two thieves.
- He rose from the dead after three days buried.
- He was born of a virgin mother from an "immaculate conception."
- He endured forty days of temptation and fasting.
- He rode a donkey.
- He was purified in a temple.
- He was anointed with oil.
- He forgave sins.
- He was baptized in water.

8. Quirinus (Rome)

- He was called Savior.
- He was immaculately conceived and born of a virgin.
- His life was threatened by the reigning king.
- He rose from the dead after being crucified and buried.
- He physically ascended into heaven.

9. Prometheus (Greece)

- He was nailed to a cross.
- His critical theological precept was that of "blood atonement."
- The earth shook when he died.
- He was known as Our Lord and Savior.
- He rose from the dead.

10. Thulis (Egypt)

- He was crucified at the age of twenty-eight.
- He rose from the dead after his crucifixion.
- He physically ascended into heaven.
- His death was supposed to benefit mankind.

11. Indra (Tibet)

- He was known as God and Savior.
- He was nailed to a cross.
- His side was pierced.
- His mother was a virgin.
- He had to die to atone for man's sins.
- He rose from the dead.
- He physically ascended into heaven.
- He could walk on water.
- He knew the future.
- He was believed to be eternal.

12. Alcestos (Greece)

- Alcestos was the only female god who was crucified to atone for mankind's sins.
- She was part of a divine trinity.

13. Atys (Phrygia)

- He was believed to be the Messiah.
- He was crucified to atone for man's sins.
- He rose from the dead after being buried.

14. Crite (Chaldea)

- He was known as The Redeemer.
- He was also known as The Ever-Blessed Son of God, The Savior of the Race, and The Atoning Offering for an Angry God.
- The earth is alleged to have shaken when he was crucified.

15. Bali (Orissa)

- He was believed to be God, as well as the Son of God.
- He was crucified in atonement.
- He was the second part of a divine trinity.

16. Mithra (Persia)

- He was crucified to take away the sins of the world.
- He was born on December 25th.

The 11 Deadliest Airline Disasters

Death in an airline disaster is a frightening thought. Fliers have to face the fact that whether you're the president of a monolithic global corporation or a grandmother on her way to see her new grandchild doesn't mean zilch when your plane is headed nose-down into the Atlantic Ocean.

Everyone who has ever gotten on a plane has had to surrender (albeit unwillingly) part of their destiny to luck.

I know the statistics: Plane travel is safer than riding in a car. But at least when you're involved in a motor vehicle accident, the only sharks you have to contend with are the ambulance-chasing lawyers who occasionally offer to "help" you with your "case." This feature looks at the eleven most disastrous airline disasters.

1. **Number of Dead:** 582.
   Date: Sunday, March 27, 1977.
   Type of Aircraft: A KLM 747 and a Pan American 747.
   Location and Circumstances: These two planes collided on the runway at Tenerife, Canary Islands. This catastrophe has the highest death toll of any airline disaster, although Disaster No. 2 has the notoriety of being the worst *single plane* disaster in history.

2. **Number of Dead:** 520.
   Date: Monday, August 12, 1985.
   Type of Aircraft: A Japan Air Lines Boeing 747.
   Location and Circumstances: This plane crashed into Mt. Ogura, Japan.

3. **Number of Dead:** 346.
   Date: Sunday, March 3, 1974.
   Type of Aircraft: A Turkish DC-10 jet.

Location and Circumstances: This plane crashed at Ermenonville near Paris, France.

4. **Number of Dead:** 290.
   Date: Sunday, July 3, 1988.
   Type of Aircraft: An Iranian A300 Airbus.
   Location and Circumstances: This commercial plane was shot down over the Persian Gulf by the U.S. Navy warship *Vincennes* when the Iranian pilot did not respond to inquiries and directives from the American battleship. The Vincennes could not identify the plane and thus treated it as a hostile incoming aircraft.

5. **Number of Dead:** 275.
   Date: Friday, May 25, 1979.
   Type of Aircraft: An American Airlines DC-10.
   Location and Circumstances: This plane crashed shortly after takeoff at O'Hare International Airport in Chicago, Illinois.

6. **Number of Dead:** 270 (259 passengers and crew members, and 11 people on the ground).
   Date: Wednesday, December 21, 1988.
   Type of Aircraft: A Pan Am Boeing 747.
   Location and Circumstances: This plane exploded and crashed in Lockerbie, Scotland. In 1993, authorities released their findings that a terrorist's bomb had been planted on the plane.

7. **Number of Dead:** 269.
   Date: Thursday, December 1, 1983.
   Type of Aircraft: A South Korean Boeing 747.
   Location and Circumstances: This plane was shot down by the Russians after it violated Soviet airspace.

8. **Number of Dead:** 261.
   Date: Thursday, July 11, 1991.
   Type of Aircraft: A Nigerian DC-8.
   Location and Circumstances: This plane crashed while attempting to land at Jidda airport in Saudi Arabia.

9. **Number of Dead:** 257.
   Date: Wednesday, November 28, 1979.
   Type of Aircraft: A New Zealand DC-10.

Location and Circumstances: This plane crashed into a mountain in Antarctica.

10. **Number of Dead:** 256.
    Date: Thursday, December 12, 1985.
    Type of Aircraft: An Arrow Air DC-8.
    Location and Circumstances: This plane crashed shortly after takeoff in Gander, Newfoundland. This death toll included 248 members of the U.S. 101st Airborne Division.

11. **Number of Dead:** 223.
    Date: Sunday, May 26, 1991.
    Type of Aircraft: An Austrian Boeing 767-300.
    Location and Circumstances: This plane exploded over rural Thailand.

The 9 Deadliest Dogs

Forty-six people have died from dog attacks since 1990. Of those 46 people, 8 breeds were responsible for 45—almost 98 percent—of those deaths. This list offers the deadliest dogs in America, and the number of people who have died, per breed, from 1990 to 1993.

Is your pooch here?

Breed	Number of Registered Kills
1. Pit bull Snoop Nate Dogg	17 (36%)
2. German shepherd	6 (13%)
3. Chow	5 (11%)
4. Malamute	5 (11%)
5. Husky	4 (9%)
6. Wolf hybrid	4 (9%)
7. Akita	2 (4%)
8. Rottweiler	2 (4%)
9. Doberman pinscher	1 (2%)

The 921 Expletives Eddie Murphy Utters in His Two Concert Films, *Delirious* and *Raw*

Lately, Eddie Murphy has been sheepishly disavowing his earlier sexist, homophobic, misogynistic standup comedy persona as the verbalized rantings and maturing process of a young man in his early twenties. His stated defense is that he believes all American men go through a period in which they think of women as objects and also hate and/or fear gays, among other less-than-desirable attributes, but the difference in his case is that he went through it in public, on stage, wearing a leather suit. (And making millions, it must be acknowledged.) It really seems as though Eddie is slightly embarrassed by some of the things he said as part of his act for his two concert films, *Delirious* and *Raw*.

I screened both concerts back-to-back for this feature and can recognize moments where Eddie might now feel uncomfortable. The "Johnny Carson/zebra bush bitch" routine midway through *Raw* seems incredibly (and genuinely) angry, and comes off now as somewhat anachronistic when considered in the light of Murphy's recent marriage to model Nicole Mitchell. (One source told me that their prenuptial agreement runs more than a hundred pages, so maybe he wasn't kidding about seriously wanting to protect himself.)

All that aside, though, I came away from these two films realizing two things: They are *hilariously* funny, and Eddie Murphy is a world-class curser. His use of profanity fulfills the purpose of valid and justifiable use of swear words: adding impact—be it dramatic or comedic—to art.

This feature looks at Mr. Murphy's enthusiastic and spirited use of expletives in his two concert films. The "colorful" words are listed in order of frequency for each film.

Eddie Murphy—Delirious
(1983)

EXPLETIVE	TIMES UTTERED
1. Shit	132
2. Fuck	94
3. Motherfucker(s)	55
4. Motherfucking	46
5. Ass	17
6. Fucking	16
7. Bitch	14
8. Dick	14
9. Pussy	9
10. Goddamn/Damn	5
11. Fucked Up/Fucked	5
12. Nigger	5
13. Faggot(s)	4
14. Bullshit	1
TOTAL	417 Expletives

Eddie Murphy Raw
(1987)

EXPLETIVE	TIMES UTTERED
1. Shit	103
2. Fuck	92
3. Motherfucker(s)	56
4. Ass	50
5. Fucking	39
6. Dick	33
7. Fucked Up/Fucked	28
8. Pussy	28
9. Motherfucking	22
10. Bitch	18

11. Goddamn/Damn	17
12. Nigger	11
13. Bullshit	4
14. Faggot(s)	3
TOTAL	504 Expletives

TOTAL EXPLETIVES FOR BOTH FILMS: 921

27 Movies with the Word *Hollywood* in the Title

"Hooray for Hollywood"—Song title

You would think that Hollywood would make movies about itself that were flattering and respectful. After all, when you're in the driver's seat, you can pretty much go where you want, right?

But, to judge by these 27 films, Hollywood seems to have a fairly schizophrenic perception of itself. They range from the sublime to the ridiculous and don't really do much for Tinseltown's image. (I don't think *Hollywood Meatcleaver Massacre* could ever be construed as a promotional film.)

Here is a look at how Hollywood seems to see itself. (At least *some* of the time, that is.)

1. **Hollywood** (1979, Documentary)
   A 150-hour British documentary on the history of Hollywood.
2. **Hollywood Boulevard** (1936, Drama; 1976, Comedy)
   1936: Onetime movie star writes his memoirs and changes people's lives.
   1976: Joe Dante's first film. An actress makes a movie for a bunch of losers.
3. **Hollywood Boulevard II** (1989, Thriller)
   Sleazy sex and violence on a movie set.
4. **Hollywood Canteen** (1944, Drama)
   The all-star story of the one millionth soldier to visit the Hollywood Canteen during World War II.
5. **Hollywood Cavalcade** (1939, Comedy/Drama)
   Don Ameche and Alice Faye in Hollywood.
6. **Hollywood Chainsaw Hookers** (1988, Horror)
   Hollywood hookers dismember their customers.

7. **The Hollywood Clowns** (1985, Anthology)
An anthology of film clips about classic Hollywood film comics.

8. **Hollywood Cop** (1987, Action)
An undercover cop against the mob.

9. **The Hollywood Detective** (1989, Comedy)
Telly Savalas parodies his Kojak character.

10. **Hollywood Harry** (1985, Comedy)
A detective and his runaway niece fight crime.

11. **Hollywood Heartbreak** (1990, Drama)
A male writer tries to make it in Hollywood.

12. **Hollywood High** (1976, Comedy)
A lame teenage sex comedy.

13. **Hollywood High, Part II** (1981, Comedy)
Another excuse to show teenage tits and ass.

14. **Hollywood Hot Tubs** (1984, Comedy)
A horny guy works at a spa.

15. **Hollywood Hotel** (1937, Musical)
An aspiring actress wins a Hollywood talent contest.

16. **The Hollywood Knights** (1980, Comedy/Drama)
American Graffiti, the Dark Side.

17. **Hollywood Meatcleaver Massacre** (1975, Horror)
A demon bent on revenge slices and dices people at will.

18. **Hollywood on Parade** (1934, Comedy anthology)
Paramount film clips.

19. **Hollywood or Bust** (1956, Comedy)
A typical Dean Martin and Jerry Lewis offering.

20. **Hollywood Outtakes** (1984, Blooper film)
Bloopers from the 1930s, 1940s, and 1950s.

21. **Hollywood Party** (1934, Musical comedy)
A Jimmy Durante film that exists almost solely as an excuse for lavish musical numbers and guest star appearances.

22. **The Hollywood Revue of 1929** (1929, Variety)
MGM's way of introducing its silent film stars to the audience as speaking thespians.

23. **Hollywood Shuffle** (1987, Comedy)
Robert Townsend's parody of the way Hollywood portrays blacks.

24. **Hollywood Story** (1951, Thriller)
A producer makes a movie about an old murder in an attempt to solve it.

25. **The Hollywood Strangler Meets the Skid Row Slasher** (1982, Horror)
An L.A. psycho takes pictures of women and then strangles them.
26. **Hollywood Vice Squad** (1986, Action)
A hooker/addict teenage runaway in Hollywood's less-than-pleasant areas.
27. **Hollywood Zap** (1986, Comedy)
A hick travels to Los Angeles to find his father.

Department of Peculiar Parlance:
51 Euphemisms for Cocaine

The leaf of the South American coca tree contains cocaine, and natives will chew the leaves all day long to maintain a steady, natural high. The cocaine on American streets, however, is anything but natural, and can, in fact, be quite deadly. Cocaine and crack cocaine are two of the most popular illicit drugs in this country. Here is a listing of 51 ways its lovers speak its name.

1. Angel
2. Blow
3. Bolivian Marching Powder
4. Cadillac
5. California
6. Cornflakes
7. Candy
8. Cane
9. Charley Coke
10. C-Jam
11. Crack
12. Croak
13. Doctor White
14. Florida Snow
15. Frisky Powder
16. Gibraltar
17. Go Powder
18. Happy Dust
19. Hooter
20. Icicles
21. Inca Message
22. Joy Flakes
23. Lady
24. Love Dust
25. Magic Flake
26. Mama Coca
27. Nose Candy
28. Number Three
29. Peruvian Flake
30. Pimp Dust
31. Pogo Pogo
32. Rails

33. Reindeer Dust
34. Rock Candy
35. Snort
36. Snow
37. Soda
38. Spanish Fly
39. Stardust
40. Superblow
41. Superfly
42. Toot
43. Tootonium
44. Tootuncommon
45. Uptown
46. White
47. White Cross
48. White Girl
49. White Mosquitoes
50. White Stuff
51. Wings

17 Poems Published in *Rolling Stone* Magazine That Have the Word *Madonna* in Their Title

Are any of these about the beloved Ms. Ciccone? Only the poets know for sure!

1. "Apple Madonna"
2. "Blue Madonna's Words"
3. "Comma Madonna"
4. "Gypsy Madonna"
5. "Hangover Madonna"
6. "Her Hair Flares Madonna"
7. "Jealous Madonna"
8. "Madonna of the Demolition Derby"
9. "Madonna of Too Many Men"
10. "Madonna Who Is Trying to Write Some Books"
11. "Mango Madonna"
12. "Moon Madonna"
13. "Painter's Madonna"
14. "Politician's Madonna"
15. "Spindrift Madonna"
16. "Stamp Madonna"
17. "Unicorn Madonna"

149 Popular Songs of the Past 75 Years Named After Girls

This feature lists 149 American popular songs of the past seven or eight decades that have a girl's name as the title. The single most common thematic element in American popular songs—outside romantic love, of course—is songs about girls, and of these compositions, many are *named* after girls.

What does it say that most popular songwriters have been male and that there is a real dearth of songs about boys and/or men written by female composers? Songwriting seems to have always (until lately) been a man's world, and nowhere is this more evident than in this list of song titles. Men, it appears, write about what they like, and thus we have these almost 150 songs written about, and named after, girls.

I found researching this feature fascinating not only because of the sheer volume of songs named after girls, but also for the incredible variety in the names chosen to use as the "handle" for a song. I don't know about you, but I have never met anyone named Rolene, yet I'm sure that there are plenty of Rolenes out there and at least one may even know that she has a song named for her. (So *please* don't write me an offended letter, Rolene, because I have never heard of your name. It's a *lovely* name. Honest.)

The entries list the song title, the person or group that popularized or first recorded the song, and the year of their recording. I tried to concentrate on the artists who were best known for the particular song.

In selecting the tunes, I was very specific about my title choices: the song titles had to consist of nothing but a one- or two-word girl's name in order to be included here. (What does "K-K-K-Katy" count as then?) This ruled out such classics as "Lucy in the Sky with Diamonds," "Kathleen Mine," "Long Tall Sally," "Lara's Theme," "Martha My Dear," "Polythene Pam," "Ruby Don't Take Your Love to Town," "Ode to Billy Joe," "Raggedy Ann," "Oh!

Carol," "Oh! Susanna," "Polk Salad Annie," "Minnie the Mooch-er," "Mustang Sally," "Sierra Sue," "Sylvia's Mother," "Rosie the Riveter," "Lovely Rita," and even "Marian the Librarian." And many, many more. I also limited inclusion to one song per name. Thus "Sara" by Fleetwood Mac is listed, but "Sara" by Bob Dylan is not. (How did I choose whose version to include? I tried to go with what I thought was the more well-known or popular version, but in some cases, I just picked my favorite. So Sue me.)

A conclusion I think you'll arrive at while reading this list is that it is almost Zen-like in its lyrical repetition of women's names, and from "Alfie" to "Zsa Zsa," it makes a telling statement about the in-terests of popular songwriters (and therefore of the public in gen-eral) of the twentieth century. (And yes, "Zsa Zsa," the last song on the list, *was* written for and dedicated to none other than glamor queen and pugilist Zsa Zsa Gabor.)

THE SONGS

1. "Alfie" (Dionne Warwick, 1977)
2. "Alison" (Elvis Costello, 1977)
3. "Amanda" (Boston, 1968)
4. "Amelia" (Joni Mitchell, 1976)
5. "Anastasia" (Pat Boone, 1956)
6. "Angelina" (Louis Prima, 1944)
7. "Angie" (The Rolling Stones, 1973)
8. "Anna" (The Beatles, 1962)
9. "Athena" (Don Cornell, 1954)
10. "Aubrey" (Bread, 1972)
11. "Bebe" (Billy Jones, 1923)
12. "Bernadette" (The Four Tops, 1967)
13. "Bernadine" (Pat Boone, 1957)
14. "Beth" (Kiss, 1976)
15. "Bianca" (from *Kiss Me Kate*, 1948)
16. "Brandy" (Looking Glass, 1972)
17. "Candida" (Dawn, 1970)
18. "Candy" (Cameo, 1987)
19. "Carol" (Chuck Berry, 1958)
20. "Carolyn" (Merle Hag-gard, 1971)
21. "Carrie" (Europe, 1987)
22. "Carrie-Anne" (The Hol-lies, 1967)
23. "Caterina" (Perry Como, 1962)
24. "Cecilia" (Simon and Garfunkel, 1970)
25. "Cherie" (Paul Whiteman and His Orchestra, 1921)

26. "Cherry" (Harry James and His Orchestra, 1928)
27. "Chloe" (Paul Whiteman and His Orchestra, 1927)
28. "Clair" (Gilbert O'Sullivan, 1972)
29. "Clementine" (Bobby Darin, 1960)
30. "Coquette" (Guy Lombardo, 1928)
31. "Daisy Jane" (America, 1975)
32. "Dawn" (The Four Seasons, 1964)
33. "Delilah" (Tom Jones, 1968)
34. "Denise" (Randy and the Rainbows, 1963)
35. "Desiree" (Neil Diamond, 1977)
36. "Diana" (Paul Anka, 1957)
37. "Dinah" (Ethel Waters, 1925)
38. "Dolores" (Tommy Dorsey and His Orchestra, 1941)
39. "Dominique" (The Singing Nun, 1963)
40. "Donna" (Ritchie Valens, 1958)
41. "Donna Lee" (Charlie Parker, 1947)
42. "Elena" (from *Kean*, 1961)
43. "Elenore" (The Turtles, 1968)
44. "Elvira" (The Oak Ridge Boys, 1981)
45. "Emaline" (Wayne King and His Orchestra, 1934)
46. "Emily" (from *The Americanization of Emily*, 1964)
47. "Emily" (Hot Chocolate, 1975)
48. "Evelina" (from *Bloomer Girl*, 1944)
49. "Fanny" (The Bee Gees, 1976)
50. "Fifi" (from *Every Day's a Holiday*, 1937)
51. "Georgette" (Ted Lewis, 1922)
52. "Gigi" (Vic Damone, 1958)
53. "Gina" (Johnny Mathis, 1960)
54. "Glendora" (Perry Como, 1956)
55. "Gloria" (Laura Branigan, 1982)
56. "Guenevere" (from *Camelot*, 1960)
57. "Guinnevere" (Crosby, Stills, Nash, and Young, 1969)
58. "Harriet" (Gene Krupa and His Orchestra, 1945)
59. "Irene" (from *Irene*, 1919)
60. "Jamie" (Ray Parker, Jr., 1984)
61. "Jane" (Jefferson Starship, 1980)
62. "Jean" (Oliver, 1969)
63. "Jenny" (Ginger Rogers, 1941)
64. "Jesse" (Roberta Flack, 1972)
65. "Jezebel" (Frankie Lane, 1951)

66. "Jo-Ann" (The Playmates, 1957)
67. "Joanna" (Kool & the Gang, 1983)
68. "Joanne" (Michael Nesmith, 1970)
69. "Josephine" (Les Paul, 1951)
70. "Josie" (Steely Dan, 1978)
71. "Julia" (The Beatles, 1968)
72. "Kate" (Eddy Howard, 1947)
73. "Kathy-O" (The Diamonds, 1958)
74. "K-K-K-Katy" (Billy Murray, 1918)
75. "Laura" (Woody Herman and His Orchestra, 1945)
76. "Laurie" (Dickey Lee, 1965)
77. "Layla" (Derek and the Dominoes, 1971)
78. "Lida Rose" (from *The Music Man*, 1957)
79. "Lilli Marlene" (Marlene Dietrich, 1940)
80. "Lily Belle" (Perry Como, 1945)
81. "Linda" (Buddy Clark, 1947)
82. "Liza" (Al Jolson, 1946)
83. "Lola" (The Kinks, 1970)
84. "Lolita" (from *Lolita*, 1962)
85. "Lorelei" (from *This Year of Grace*, 1928)
86. "Louise" (Maurice Chevalier, 1929)
87. "Lucille" (Little Richard, 1957)
88. "Maggie May (Rod Stewart, 1971)
89. "Mame" (Louis Armstrong, 1966)
90. "Mandy" (Barry Manilow, 1975)
91. "Margie" (Eddie Cantor, 1920)
92. "Margot" (from *The Desert Song*, 1926)
93. "Maria" (from *West Side Story*, 1957)
94. "Maria Elena" (Lawrence Welk and His Orchestra, 1941)
95. "Marianne" (Burl Ives, 1957)
96. "Marie" (The Bachelors, 1965)
97. "Marina" (Rocco Granata, 1959)
98. "Marta" (Arthur Tracy, 1931)
99. "Mary Lou" (Ronnie Hawkins, 1959)
100. "Matilda, Matilda" (Harry Belafonte, 1953)
101. "Maybellene" (Chuck Berry, 1955)
102. "Melinda" (from *On a Clear Day You Can See Forever*, 1965)
103. "Michelle" (The Beatles, 1966)
104. "Mimi" (Maurice Chevalier, 1932)

105. "Mira" (from *Carnival*, 1961)
106. "Mirabelle" (Noel Coward, 1931)
107. "Mona Lisa" (Nat King Cole, 1949)
108. "Nancy" (Frank Sinatra, 1945)
109. "Nikita" (Elton John, 1986)
110. "Nina" (Gene Kelly, from *The Pirate*, 1948)
111. "Nola" (Vincent Lopez and His Orchestra, 1916)
112. "Patricia" (Perez Prado and His Orchestra, 1958)
113. "Peg" (Steely Dan, 1978)
114. "Peggy Sue" (Buddy Holly, 1958)
115. "Ramona" (Gene Austin, 1927)
116. "Rhiannon" (Fleetwood Mac, 1976)
117. "Rolene" (Moon Martin, 1979)
118. "Ronnie" (The Four Seasons, 1964)
119. "Rosalie" (Nelson Eddy, 1937)
120. "Rosalita" (Bruce Springsteen, 1973)
121. "Rosanna" (Toto, 1982)
122. "Rose Marie" (Nelson Eddy, 1924)
123. "Rosetta" (Earl Hines and His Orchestra, 1935)
124. "Rosie" (from *Bye Bye Birdie*, 1960)
125. "Rosie Lee" (The Mello-Tones, 1957)
126. "Ruby" (from *Ruby Gentry*, 1953)
127. "Sadie" (from *Funny Girl*, 1964)
128. "Sally" (from *Sally*, 1920)
129. "Sally G" (Paul McCartney and Wings, 1975)
130. "Sandy" (from *Grease*, 1978)
131. "Sara" (Fleetwood Mac, 1979)
132. "Shannon" (Henry Gross, 1976)
133. "Sheila" (Tommy Roe, 1962)
134. "Sherry" (The Four Seasons, 1962)
135. "Susan" (The Buckinghams, 1967)
136. "Susie Q" (Credence Clearwater Revival, 1975)
137. "Suzanne" (Journey, 1986)
138. "Sylvia" (Oley Speaks, 1914)
139. "Thumbelina" (Danny Kaye, 1952)
140. "Tina Marie" (Perry Como, 1954)
141. "Tracy" (The Cuff Links, 1969)
142. "Valerie" (Steve Winwood, 1987)
143. "Vallerie" (The Monkees, 1968)
144. "Vanessa" (Hugo Winterhalter and His Orchestra, 1952)

145. "Venus" (Frankie Avalon, 1959)
146. "Virginia" (George Gershwin, 1923)
147. "Wendy" (Mary Martin, from *Peter Pan,* 1954)
148. "Windy" (The Association, 1967)
149. "Zsa Zsa" (Bernie Wayne and His Orchestra, 1953)

329 Real Strange Real Names

With a name like yours, you might be any shape, almost.—Lewis Carroll, *Through the Looking-Glass*

This list consists of 329 actual names of people as determined from birth records and other sources over the past century or so. These names are all real, and were actually assigned to children at birth by parents who may or may not have asked themselves later, "What, in the name of Jesus, was I thinking?"

When a single name is given, it is the first name of the person and it is included because of its oddness. (Such as Constipation.) Sometimes a first and middle name are given when the combined form is particularly interesting, such as Immaculate Conception. (I can hear the conversation now: "Uh, Fred, I'd like you to meet Immaculate Conception Malinowski.") When the complete name is given, it is usually because it is strange, funny, or both. (Such as Fuk Eyw.)

87 People Named for Body Parts, Diseases, Medications, Cosmetics, or Something Having to Do with Sex

1. A. Pimple
2. Abolena Sweat
3. Ammonia
4. Angina Keys
5. Appendicitis
6. Aspirin
7. Autopsy
8. Bernard Nicewanger
9. Blanch Kidney
10. Bobby Joe Gothard
11. Castor Oil
12. Charlie Hymen
13. Chlorine
14. Chloroform
15. Citronella
16. Constance Hiccup
17. Constipation
18. Cornelia Tonsil

19. Depression
20. Diaphragm
21. Dichloramentine
22. Dick Wacker
23. Digesta
24. Diptheria
25. Distemper
26. Doloris Puke
27. Douche
28. Duncas Hymen
29. Edward Vagina
30. Esophagus
31. Exczema
32. Fallopian
33. Flu
34. Fred Dilldoe
35. Fuk Eyw
36. Gladys Pantzeroff
37. Glycine
38. Granuloma
39. Halitosis
40. Hang Nails
41. Hernia
42. Hyman Pleasure
43. I. P. Blood
44. Iodine
45. Iona Outhouse
46. Kotex
47. Larry Ovary
48. Latrina
49. Lee Lung
50. Lemaza Hotballs
51. Listerine
52. Maria Piles
53. Meconium

54. Meninges
55. Menses
56. Morphine
57. Mr. Balls
58. Mr. Fuck
59. Nancy Nipples
60. Nausaeous
61. Nausea
62. Ophelia Rotincrotch
63. Penis
64. Placenta
65. Placenta Previa
66. Poopie
67. Positive Wasserman
68. Pregmancy
69. Pyelitis
70. Rectum
71. Sal Hepatica
72. Saline
73. Saliva Brown
74. Smallpox Dingle
75. Steve Spleen
76. Syphillis
77. Thomas Headache
78. Thomas Measles
79. Thyroid
80. Toilet Preparations
81. Twila Anus
82. Urine
83. Uvula
84. Vagina
85. Valve
86. Vaseline
87. Vomita Willis

37 People with Names for Which, I'm Sure, There Are Good Explanations

1. Artificial Flowers
2. Auditorium
3. Beautiful Swindler
4. Bigamy
5. Charity Ward
6. Devotee War
7. Emancipation Proclamation Freedom
8. Fertilizer
9. Gasoline
10. Immaculate Conception
11. Kidnap
12. Larceny
13. Large Smash
14. Laundry
15. League of Nations
16. Let's Stay Here
17. Leverage
18. Libel
19. Limousine
20. Machine
21. Magazine
22. Miscellaneous
23. No Parking
24. Petty Larceny
25. Pictorial Review
26. Refund
27. Sparkplug
28. Sylvania
29. Thermal
30. Tomb
31. Try-em-and-See
32. Victrola
33. Weatherstrip
34. What
35. X.Y.Z.
36. Y.Z.
37. Z.

97 People Whose Names Were Probably a Source of Merciless Torment on the Playground

1. Amazon
2. Average
3. Boozer
4. Bright
5. Charles Smellybelly
6. Constance Stench
7. Critic
8. Crook
9. Cute
10. Darling
11. Delerious
12. Delight
13. Dimples
14. Dream-Child
15. Equal
16. Etta Roach
17. Evil
18. Extra
19. Fairest
20. Famous
21. Fatty
22. Favorite

23. Felony
24. Fertilizer
25. Filthy McNasty
26. Flake
27. Flunkey
28. Fool Head
29. Foreward March
30. Free Love
31. Gift of God
32. Hallowed
33. Handsome
34. Haphazard
35. Hasty
36. Hazard
37. Heathen
38. Himself
39. Honest
40. Hot
41. Hot Shot
42. Ima Goose
43. Ima Rose Bush
44. Ima Valentine
45. John Smellie
46. Jolly
47. Knowledge
48. Largie
49. Lassie
50. Lawless
51. Lawyer
52. Lonely
53. Looney
54. Looney Head
55. Lord
56. Love
57. Love Bird
58. Low
59. Lucifer
60. Lucky Blunder
61. Luscious
62. Margaret Black Butts
63. Midget
64. Modest
65. Normal
66. Old
67. Peculier
68. Perfect
69. Person
70. Pleasant
71. Poor Boy
72. Right
73. Rimmer
74. Roach
75. Rodent
76. Rudolph Goldshitter
77. Silent
78. Soggie
79. Special
80. Strange Odor Andrews
81. Suck
82. Sylvester Smells
83. Tiny Small
84. Too Late
85. Toy
86. Trouble
87. Truly White
88. Tweetie
89. Unexpected
90. Useless
91. Vice
92. Wealthy
93. Weary
94. Willibald Thumbfart
95. Wimpy
96. Wonderful
97. Zero

35 People Whose Names Nicely Fit Their Occupations

1. Albert Palm: Masseur
2. Arthur Blessit: Baptist evangelist
3. Brenda Love: author of *The Encyclopedia of Unusual Sex Practices*
4. Deloris Hearsum: Deaf typist for a deaf social agency
5. Denver Driver: Truck driver
6. Don Tree: Gardener
7. Donald Moos: Washington state official in charge of dairy reports
8. Dorothy Reading: Librarian
9. Filmore Graves: Mortician
10. Frank Deadman: Mortician
11. Gordon Marsh: Biologist
12. Hazel Wolf: Works for the Audubon Society
13. Jack Putz: Golf pro
14. James Bond: Detective
15. James Bugg: Exterminator
16. John Barber: Barber
17. Judge Judge: Judge
18. Ken Priest: Protestant minister
19. Lee Coffin: Mortician
20. Max Money: Tax collector
21. Michael Angelo: Artist
22. Michael Fox: Veterinarian
23. Milo B. High: Elvis's pilot
24. Mr. Brain: Teacher
25. Mr. Bury: Mortician
26. Mr. Sexsmith: Marriage counselor
27. Mrs. Bowman: Archery instructor
28. Mrs. Cook: Baking teacher
29. Muffin Fry: Baker
30. Ronald Drown: Lifeguard
31. Sam Wood: Lumber dealer
32. Storm Field: Weatherman
33. Sweep Hand: Watch repairman
34. Virgil Buryman: Mortician
35. Wake Doom: Mortician

21 Doctors Who Probably Have to Talk About Their Names a Lot

1. Dr. Bees: Veterinary assistant (to Dr. Lyons)
2. Dr. Blood: Hematologist
3. Dr. Brain: Neurologist
4. Dr. Cartledge: Podiatrist
5. Dr. Childs: Pediatrician
6. Dr. Cure: Doctor
7. Dr. Docter: Doctor
8. Dr. Dolphin: Veterinarian
9. Dr. Eather: Anesthesiologist
10. Dr. Head: Neurologist
11. Dr. Heard: Eye, Ear, Nose, and Throat Specialist
12. Dr. Hertz: Chiropractor
13. Dr. Jack Fealy: Gynecologist
14. Dr. Leak: Urologist

15. Dr. Lyons: Veterinarian
16. Dr. Organ: Doctor
17. Dr. Saw: Orthopedist
18. Dr. Sawbones: Doctor
19. Dr. Shrink: Psychiatrist
20. Dr. Will Diddle: Obstetrician/Gynecologist
21. Dr. William Rash: Dermatologist

3 Nurses Who Picked the Right Specialty

1. A. Nurse: Nurse
2. Ida Toomer: Oncology nurse
3. Prue Cramp: OB/GYN nurse

48 People Having Food Names or Names Having Something to Do with Food

1. Apple Cider
2. Baby Ruth
3. Bannana
4. Barbara Beans
5. Champagne
6. Cold Turkey
7. Dill Pickle
8. Gardenia Salad
9. Garlic
10. Hearty Meal
11. Herb Rice
12. Hershey Bar
13. Hominy
14. Ice Cream
15. Jelly Bean
16. Lemon Custer
17. Lemon Freeze
18. Lettuce Fields
19. Liza Cucumber
20. Loin
21. Lunch
22. Margarine
23. Mazola
24. Meat Grease
25. Meat Loaf
26. Oatmeal
27. Oleomargarine
28. Olive Green
29. Orange Jello
30. Orangeade
31. Piece O. Cake
32. Pork Chop
33. Sam Broccoli
34. Sam Omelette
35. Sasparilla
36. Sausage
37. Soda
38. Spicy Fudge
39. Strawberry Commode
40. Summer Butter
41. Turnip
42. Utensil
43. Vanilla
44. Watermellon Patch
45. Weldon Rumproast
46. Wheat Bread
47. Whisky
48. Wine

The World's Longest Last Name

The world's longest last name, according to nomenphiliac (name scholar) Elsdon C. Smith, is *Wolfschlegelsteinhausenbergerdorfvorälternwarengewissenhaftschäferswessenschafewarenwohlgepflegtundsorgfaltigkeitbeschützenvonangreifendurchihrraubgierigfeingdewelchevorälternzwölftausendjahrevorandieerscheinenwanderersteerdemenschderraumschiffgebräuchlichlichtalsseinursprungvonkraftgestartseinlangefahrthinzwischensternartigraumaufdersuchenachachidesternwelchebegabtbewohnbarplanetenkreisedrehensichundwohinderneurassevonverständigmenschlichkeitkonntefortpflanzenundsicherfreuenanlebenslänglichfreudeundruhemitnichteinfurchtvorangreifenvonanderintelligentgeschöpfsvonhinzwischensternartigraum,* Senior (594 letters). The gentleman's 26 first names are *Adolph Blaine Charles David Earl Frederick Gerald Hubert Irvin John Kenneth Lloyd Martin Nero Oliver Paul Quincy Randolph Sherman Thomas Uncas Victor William Xerxes Yancy Zesus* (151 letters). (The 1993 *Guinness Book of Records* lists a girl born in Beaumont, Texas, in 1984 who has a first name with 1,019 letters, and a middle name with 36 letters.)

The 88 Times the Word *Klingon* Is Said in the 6 *Star Trek* Feature Films

"*tlhIngan Hol Dajathlh'a'?*"
"*HISlaH'* "
(Do you speak Klingon?
Yes!)—Overheard at a *Star Trek* convention

On a particularly memorable episode of HBO's brilliant comedy series *The Larry Sanders Show* starring Gary Shandling, Larry (played by Gary) is scheduled to have William "Captain James T. Kirk" Shatner as a guest on the show.

Larry's writers set up a conference call with Shatner to discuss a *Star Trek* skit for the show. At first, Shatner is reluctant to do the skit until Larry jumps into the phone call and tells him he's thrilled about him being a guest on the show *and* he's also delighted with the idea of a *Star Trek* skit.

After Shatner resignedly agrees to do the skit, Larry and his writers deliberately and mischievously try to get Shatner to say the word *Klingon* while on the speaker phone.

Larry asks him who it was he had trouble with during the series and Shatner at first replies that he and DeForest Kelley had their problems, but eventually he does say "the Klingons." Larry thanks him for the call, hangs up the phone, and the room erupts in laughter.

A moment goes by and then Shatner, who, unbeknownst to the Larry Sanders staff is still on the phone, suddenly says, "What's so funny?"

I tell that story to make a point. The Klingon race and, yes, even the word *Klingon* itself have achieved a cult status among *Star Trek* fans that is rivaled only by Vulcans and the Transporter.

There is a Klingon Language Institute, as well as a *Klingon Dictionary* and a "Conversational Klingon" instructional audiotape (featuring Michael Dorn, who plays Klingon Lt. Worf on the *Star Trek: The Next Generation* TV series).

This feature lists every mention of the word *Klingon*, or *Klingons*, in the six *Star Trek* feature films.

Enjoy the following Klingon encounters and live long and prosper. (And yes, I know that's a *Vulcan* salutation, so don't write, okay? When something works, I stick with it.)

Star Trek—The Motion Picture (1979) Directed by Robert Wise: 2 "Klingon"s

I originally reviewed *Star Trek—The Motion Picture* for a local newspaper when it was first released in 1979. I liked it then and I like it even more now. Why? Because the 1980 videotape version has additional footage that enhances and clarifies the film. Sure, the movie has a few problems (most of them caused by an awkward tendency for the film to take itself too seriously), but this *was* the first of the bunch and a lot was riding on it, so it's understandable why they would put a lot of emphasis on special effects and a gussied-up Enterprise. With *The Wrath of Khan,* the focus reverted back to the characters, and the films that followed have been (for the most part) quite enjoyable and much truer to the spirit of the series.

One script flaw I noticed in *Star Trek—The Motion Picture* involved Spock and the Enterprise's attempt to establish communication with V'ger. After the ship is snared by V'ger's tractor beam, Spock reprograms the Enterprise's LinguaCodes to inform V'ger that they were friendly and non-hostile. If Spock could communicate that little piece of info to V'ger, then why didn't he attempt to establish a dialogue with the entity instead of just floating along for what seems like an eternity? It must be assumed that V'ger got the message because the Enterprise was not destroyed, so Spock and Kirk had to know that V'ger was reading them. But if they did begin a dialogue that got them out of the space cloud, then they wouldn't have been able to use all those nifty, expensive computer-generated special effects, now would they?

Also, gaffe expert and author Bill Givens in his book *Son of Film Flubs* (Citadel Press) notes that in the scene where Kirk leaves the Enterprise to go after Spock, you can actually see the sound stage above and behind William Shatner as he stands outside the cargo bay door. Look for it: It's definitely there and it is truly mind-boggling that this blatant screw-up slipped through.

Star Trek II: The Wrath of Khan (1982) Directed by Nicholas Meyer: 7 "Klingon"s

Star Trek II: The Wrath of Khan is an absolutely wonderful *Star Trek* experience. The characters are back, the storyline is fascinating, and the villain is classic. The film is almost operatic in its grand scope and irresistible villains, most notably Khan, played by Ricardo Montalban in a scenery-chewing performance.

Star Trek III: The Search for Spock (1984) Directed by Leonard Nimoy: 9 "Klingon"s

Star Trek III: The Search for Spock was probably the most eagerly awaited *Star Trek* film of all time. As we all well know by now, yes, they did find Spock, and now, four or five films later, he is back firmly ensconced on the Enterprise where he belongs. *The Search for Spock* is notable for the Vulcan rituals and the final fight between Kruge and Kirk on the disintegrating Genesis planet. This is one of the fans' favorite *Star Trek* movies.

Star Trek IV: The Voyage Home (1986) Directed by Leonard Nimoy: 11 "Klingon"s

Kirk and Spock have to save Earth from annihilation by going back in time for two extinct-in-the-future humpback whales, the only species that can communicate with the mysterious space probe that is preparing to blow our planet out of the galaxy. It sounds farfetched, but the storyline works and *The Voyage Home* is one of the more humorous *Star Trek* films. The scenes in which the crew of the Enterprise visit twentieth-century San Francisco are classic—and *very* funny.

Star Trek V: The Final Frontier (1989): Directed by William Shatner: 22 "Klingon"s

Sybok the Vulcan (Spock's half-brother) hijacks the Enterprise and takes it beyond the Great Barrier to meet God. This entry in the film series harkens back to the metaphysically toned episodes of the TV series and is actually quite effective—until we realize that God is not really God, after which the story kind of fizzles out.

Star Trek VI: The Undiscovered Country (1991)
Directed by Nicholas Meyer: 35 "Klingon"s

Captain Kirk and Dr. McCoy find themselves on trial for allegedly murdering the Klingon Chancellor Gorkon. Fans are treated to a trial as well as a traitorous shape-changer played by model (and Mrs. David Bowie) Iman. *The Undiscovered Country* put director Nicholas Meyer *(The Wrath of Khan)* back behind the *Trek* cameras.

A 119-Entry *Wayne's World* Dictionary

I love this movie.

This dictionary offers 119 choices and most excellent moments from *Wayne's World,* the movie. When a word in the definition is in **bold** type, there is a corresponding definition for that word elsewhere in the list.

Party On.

1. **"A Sphincter Says What?"** A rhetorical question that achieves its maximum insult value when the person to whom it is addressed says, "What?"
2. **Amazing** A variant of **Excellent.**
3. **"As If"** Yuhhhh, right.
4. **A Babe Lair** An expensively appointed apartment. (aka "A Fully Functioning Babe Lair")
5. **A Babe Fest** A bar where there are many **babes.**
6. **Babes** Babes.
7. **Babia Majora** Latin for **mega babe.**
8. **Babraham Lincoln** A **mega babe** who gets elected President.
9. **Bacon** A police officer.
10. **"Baking Powder?"** "Beg your pardon?"
11. **"Being Pulled in by Her Tractor Beam"** Being pulled into the sphere of influence of a **psycho hose beast.**
12. **"Bite Me"** Fuck you.
13. **Blow Chunks** Vomit, **honk, hurl, spew.**
14. **Bogus** Lame.
15. **Bolt** Split.
16. **Bonus** An additional **excellent** party element.
17. **Brutal** Cruel.
18. **Buds** Friends.

19. **The Carbohydrate, Sequined Jumpsuit, Young Girls in White Cotton Panties, Waking Up in a Pool of Your Own Vomit, Bloated, Purple, Dead on a Toilet Phase** The final phase (Phase 3) of being a successful rock star.
20. **Cool** Cool.
21. **"Cream of Some Young Guy"** One of Wayne's spurious Chinese food dishes.
22. **"Croolers"** Wayne's pronunciation of crullers.
23. **Damian** A synonym for **gimp**.
24. **Denied** Forbidden.
25. **Dick** A synonym for "nothing," as in "Kids know dick."
26. **"Diddly-Doo, Diddly-Doo"** The sound effect for the wavy lines that precede a flashback.
27. **Double Live Gonzo** Musically excellent.
28. **Dude** A dude.
29. **Dutch Door Action** Swindling one person and then **poking** the swindlee's girlfriend.
30. **Dweeb** A dweeb.
31. **"Ex-Squeeze Me?"** "Excuse me?"
32. **Excalibur** Wayne's name for the pre-CBS Fender corporate buyout 1964 Stratocaster Fender guitar in classic white with triple single-core pickups and a whammy bar.
33. **Excellent** Excellent.
34. **Extreme Close-Up** A rapid, useless, and completely unnecessary camera zoom.
35. **Feeble** Lame, **bogus.**
36. **Fished In** See **snowed.**
37. **Fox** A **mega babe.**
38. **Get Right Out of Town** A variant of **no way.**
39. **Get the Net** Attempt to restrain a girl who is either **mental,** a **psycho hose beast,** or both.
40. **The Get-a-Load-of-This-Guy Cam** An inside-joke-to-the-audience camera shot that serves as a surreptitious mocking of a lame *Wayne's World* guest.
41. **Gimp.** A **dweeb.**
42. **Going Shithouse** A general overall decline in appearance and attitude.
43. **Good** A variant of **smooth.**
44. **Good Call** An excellent choice, suggestion, or insight.
45. **A Gratuitous Sex Scene** A gratuitous sex scene.
46. **"Grrrrr"** "I am sexually aroused."

47. **A Haiku** A piercingly brilliant and insightful comment or observation.
48. **Hand Job** TV studio hand cues.
49. **The Hanging Out with Ravi Shankar Phase** Phase 2 of being a successful rock star.
50. **"He Blows Goats"** One of the insults commonly leveled against a **sphincter boy.**
51. **"He Shoots, He Scores"** Said when something is spit accurately into something.
52. **"Hello?"** A variant of **"Ex-squeeze me?"**
53. **The Help-Me Cam** A camera shot of Garth in some kind of trouble during an episode of *Wayne's World.*
54. **Hock a Loogy** Spit a phlegm ball.
55. **Honk** Vomit, **blow chunks, hurl, spew.**
56. **A Humungoid Giant Star** Phase 1 of being a successful rock star.
57. **Hurl** Vomit, **blow chunks, hurl, spew.**
58. **"I Was Not Aware of That"** This I did not know.
59. **"I'm There"** I will show up at some particular event.
60. **"If a Frog Had Wings He Wouldn't Bump His Ass When he Hopped."** See **"Monkeys Might Fly Out of My Butt."**
61. **Incoming** The approach of a **psycho hose beast.**
62. **Intensity in Ten Cities** Musically excellent.
63. **Interesting** Interesting.
64. **A Joe Job** Mundane, unsatisfying, everyday employment.
65. **Ladies** Another term for **babes.**
66. **Live at Budokan** Musically excellent. (From the Cheap Trick album of the same name).
67. **"Live in the Now"** Get real. (Used as an admonishment regarding something seemingly impossible, such as Wayne's hoped-for purchase of a pre-CBS Fender corporate buyout 1964 Fender Stratocaster guitar in classic white with triple single-core pickups and a whammy bar.)
68. **Magically Babe-a-Licious** The qualities of a **mega babe.**
69. **Marriage** Punishment for shoplifting in some states.
70. **The "May I Help You?" Riff** A piercingly loud guitar riff played in a music store that unfailingly summons a clerk who asks the riffer, "May I help you?"
71. **Mega Babe** An incredible woman, a level (or more) up from a **babe.**
72. **Melon** The human head.

73. **Mental** Crazy.
74. **Milwaukee** Algonquin for "The Good Land."
75. **The Mirth-Mobile** Garth's car, a blue AMC Pacer.
76. **"Monkeys Might Fly Out of My Butt"** A sarcastic way of saying, "It might happen." (The odds are massively against something happening.)
77. **Mr. Donut Head Man** A superhero created by Garth from donuts and **croolers.**
78. **Munchables** Donuts, particularly **croolers.**
79. **"Na-Ho Lang Gha"** Cantonese for "You look pretty" (phonetic pronunciation).
80. **No way** No way.
81. **A No-Honk Guarantee** The assurance that a **partied-out** individual will not **spew.**
82. **"Not"** Used to express a negative or the cancellation of a sentiment after a seemingly complimentary statement. (e.g., "You're a handsome dude. Not.")
83. **"Okay"** Okay.
84. **Partied Out** Borderline comatose from either too much drink, too many drugs, or a combination of both.
85. **"Party On"** Party on.
86. **Party Time** Party time.
87. **Poke** Screw.
88. **A Pork Product** A police officer.
89. **Pralines and Dick** The flavor nefarious TV producer Benjamin would be if he were an ice cream.
90. **Psycho Hose Beast** A young woman obsessed with a particular guy. In Wayne's case, it was Stacey.
91. **Queen's "Bohemian Rhapsody"** A **good call.**
92. **Really Good** Extra **smooth.**
93. **A Robo Babe** A **mega babe.**
94. **Saucy** Confident, poised, and having enough money to buy something prized.
95. **"Schwing"** The sound an involuntary and spontaneous erection makes when it is erecting.
96. **Smooth** Slick.
97. **Snowed** Successfully bullshitted. See **fished in.**
98. **Spew** Vomit, **honk, blow chunks, hurl.**
99. **Sphincter Boy** An asshole.
100. **"Spose"** I suppose.
101. **"Sssssss"** The sound a **mega babe** makes when touched.

(Usually used when touching a fingertip to a photo of the mega babe in question.)

102. **A Stacey Alert** A **psycho hose beast** is approaching.
103. **"Stairway to Heaven"** The Led Zeppelin song **denied** in music stores as a "test song."
104. *Star Trek: The Next Generation* "In many ways it is superior, but it will never be as recognized as the original."
105. **A Tangent Break** An incongruous shift in the conversation.
106. **A Tent Pole** An erection.
107. **"This Man Has No Penis"** One of the insults commonly leveled against a **sphincter boy.**
108. **Twisted** Weird.
109. **"Very High on the Strokability Scale"** Prime masturbation fantasy material; usually used to describe a **mega babe.**
110. **Wail** Sing, usually excellently.
111. **"Way"** The opposite of **no way.**
112. **"We Fear Change"** We fear change.
113. **"We Suck"** See **we're not worthy.**
114. **"We're Not Worthy"** We pale in the shadow of your mega greatness.
115. **Weird** Twisted.
116. **Wicked** A variant of **cool.**
117. **"Yes"** A sign of approval
118. **"Yuhhhhh"** Yeah, right; all right.
119. **"Zeg"** "Excellent" [phonetic pronunciation] in Cantonese.

Death Wishes: 9 Suicidal Sports

The thought of suicide is a great source of comfort: with it a calm passage is to be made across many a bad night.—Friedrich Nietzsche

I have never been able to understand participating in a sport in which death is one possible outcome.

I know, I know, it's the thrill, right?

The cheating of death.

The endorphin rush.

The personal satisfaction of actually *doing* it.

Perhaps.

But the truth is that the deadly risk in and of itself is what turns a lot of people on when it comes to these "sports," and I think that it says something about a person's personality that they really don't feel quite alive unless they're testing fate and daring death to take his (or her) best shot.

These nine activities don't all qualify as sports per se, but they are things that people do that could wind up killing them.

1. **Boxing:** This is a sport where you deliberately fight someone, and willingly allow yourself to be pummelled about the face and body by your opponent. I know that boxing aficionados like to talk about the "technical" aspects of the "game," the reach, the weight differentials, the blows scored, etc. But all that aside, boxing comes down to a sanctioned brawl. Men have died in the ring, and that's what makes this a suicidal sport. It is also not the healthiest thing in the world to have your head bashed repeatedly. For those of you who don't believe boxing can do any lasting harm, I have two words for you: Muhammad Ali.

2. **Bungee Jumping:** This is brilliant. Tie an elastic rope to your

ankles and then jump off a bridge. Remember when your mother used to ask you, "If all the other kids jumped off a bridge, would you?" I guess the answer now is, "Cool! Let's do it, dude!" People have died while bungee jumping when their bungee cord snapped. Lately, air bags have been used when practical, but when the jump takes place over water or rocks, such a precaution is not always possible. Recently, during a trip to Australia and New Zealand, *Good Morning America*'s Joan Lunden and Charlie Gibson bungee jumped off a bridge. Later, they joked that their insurance companies were not advised that they planned on leaping into oblivion. Hmmm. I wonder if David Hartman and Deborah Norville are available?

3. **Car Racing:** Drive around a narrow track in a tiny matchbox car at speeds almost faster than a speeding bullet, with a whole bunch of other guys trying to run you off the road. There's a high concept for you. The accepted wisdom is that everyone goes to car races just to see the crashes. That ought to be a hint to the drivers, don't you think?

4. **Knife Throwing/Arrow Dodging:** Okay, maybe this isn't technically a sport, but I included it here because people actually do it, and there are idiots out there who actually then try to duplicate it at home. At carnivals and circuses, knife throwers hurl blades at an "assistant" (usually a woman) who either holds balloons in her mouth or spins around on a wheel. To give them their due, these guys have pretty good aim. But if they miss even once . . . Another form of this "entertainment" is when archers do a "Robin Hood" and shoot apples or balloons off someone's head. Recently, two young guys tried this themselves. It took quite a while to get the arrow out of the "target's" head, but he did survive. We should be happy he'll be around to contribute to the gene pool, don't you think?

5. **Marathon Running:** What kind of sadistic mind came up with this "sport"? Run 26 miles without stopping. Why? People have died participating in marathons. Those endorphins must be worth it, I guess, because it sure ain't the fabulous prizes.

6. **Mountain Climbing:** Did you see *Cliffhanger*? I rest my case.

7. **Running with the Bulls:** People running through the streets of Pamplona, Spain, are chased by a herd of enraged bulls.

That's the sport. People are gored, trampled, and killed. The "festival" lasts nine days and includes eight bull runs. My only question, again, is, "Why?"

8. **Russian Roulette:** Here's another "game" that convinces me that we're nearing the end of civilization. *People actually play this.* Participants put one bullet in a revolver, spin the chamber, hold the gun to their head, and pull the trigger. The guy who blows his brains out is the loser. He won't miss them because he obviously wasn't using them, right?

9. **Sky-diving:** Let's go up in an airplane and jump out. That is the essence of the sport of sky-diving. Sometimes the parachute fails to open. Then you die. But at least your loved ones get a refund.

16 Devices, Tools, Artifacts, and Practices Used for Sexual Enhancement and Diversity

Humankind as a species has spent a lot of time trying to improve its sex life. This feature takes a look at 16 sexual enhancements, many of which are genuinely creative innovations in human sexuality. (Ben Wa balls and the Sybian come immediately to mind.) And then again, some are not.

As with any sexual activity, the most important concern is the practice of safe sex. This means meticulous care with any activity in which bodily fluids are exchanged or skin is broken.

As of right now, AIDS is still a death sentence. Do your part to stay HIV negative, okay?

1. **Artificial Vaginas** Known as the "Bachelor's Friend" in ads in men's magazines, artificial vaginas are hand-held latex or rubber masturbation tools that look exactly like a female vagina, complete with clitoris and pubic hair. Some of these ersatz orifices can be filled with warm water to give them a fleshlike feel, and some are battery-powered and vibrate as well. (An image that persistently comes to mind when contemplating the sex product industry is that of the factories that make this stuff. I can't help but picture assembly lines loaded with artificial vaginas and penises stretching endlessly through a giant manufacturing plant. The word bizarre doesn't even come close to adequately describing such a scene.)

2. **Ben Wa Balls** The traditional Ben Wa balls are an ancient and clever oriental sex toy designed for women only. They are two small stainless steel balls that are inserted into the vagina and then left there all day. The balls rub against the

lining of the vagina and cause continual sexual arousal. Many women report constant pleasure from the Ben Was, but orgasm is uncommon because most women need some type of clitoral stimulation to achieve a climax. There is a male version of this enhancement known as Ass Eggs or Ass Weights, but they are less common than Ben Wa balls because the rectum, while possessing great erotic stimulatory potential, is not biologically a sex organ.

3. **Cock Rings** Cock rings are rubber or leather rings that fit around the base of an erect penis and exert just enough pressure to help maintain an erection by constricting blood flow.

A popular model is a leather snap-on job that is "easy on, easy off." Others are available that also have straps that fit around the scrotum and enclose the testicles.

The pirate high school disk jockey (played by Christian Slater) in 1990's *Pump Up the Volume* (who went by the name of Hard Harry) used to boast that he was wearing nothing but a cock ring during his broadcasts. No one in his high school knew what he was talking about.

4. **Condoms** Rubbers have come of age. By necessity. A product that used to feel like the inside of an inner tube wrapped around your turgid love python now feels . . . not totally detestable. Let's face it, the old adage that using a condom is like taking a shower wearing a raincoat did not come into being because of the gloriously erotic stimulation experienced by cloaking your little friend in a rubber tube. The glans penis is sensitive for a reason: it is meant to be stimulated by the vaginal walls. Condoms, no matter how thin and lubricated, do decrease some of that sensitivity.

But . . .

We all know that condoms are not only still necessary for birth control, but are now serving as a reasonably effective front-line defense against sexually transmitted diseases, the most deadly of which, of course, is AIDS.

So condom manufacturers have heeded the call for increased sensitivity and now make prophylactics in a variety of super-thin materials and in many colors and sizes. (One for big boys is called the Magnum.)

These in and of themselves are not technically sexual enhancements unless you count the lessening of inhibitions that can come with the absence of a fear of pregnancy. The ones that *are* enhancements are designed in somewhat creative ways, the most well-known of which is the French Tickler, which has knobby bumps up and down its length—the better to tickle your innards with, m'dear.

5. **Dildos** Dildos are fake penises. They come in a variety of extremely lifelike shapes, sizes, and colors, and many have a scrotum, complete with individual testicles, attached. They are used by women for masturbation and to mount another woman in lesbian intercourse, and by both men and women to mount a male in anal intercourse. They are also used by impotent men as a means of satisfying their partners. They can be strapped on with a waist belt or used by hand. Two-headed penises are available for mutual lesbian intercourse. Some male porno stars have sat for plaster castings of their erections and testicles and then marketed the dildo under their own brand name. Women in X-rated films are often seen fellating dildos. They pretend to enjoy this, but the primary purpose of such activity is visual stimulus.

6. **Electric Shock** Electric shock is used during sex to stimulate the genitals and other organs. Battery- and AC-powered prods and devices are used to apply small electrical charges to the penis, testicles, vagina, clitoris, and anus. These devices are never used on the nipples (or anywhere above the waist for that matter) because the electrical current could interfere with the heart's normal rhythm and cause arrhythmia, palpitations, and in some cases, heart attack and death. There have been reported cases of electrocution when devices were used improperly or fell into water. Advocates claim electric shock intensifies and prolongs sexual arousal and orgasm.

7. **Erotica** Erotica *could* be defined as anything that gets you horny. Today, erotica comes in a variety of forms, including nudie magazines, hardcore sex magazines, sex paperbacks, sex letters magazines, fantasy magazines, X-rated videos, X-rated amateur videos, and erotic cable channels.

Newsstand photo magazines This group consists of mainstream softcore magazines—the type sold on most newsstands and by subscription. *Playboy* is the most accepted of these publications (no pink), with *Penthouse* (almost) right behind it. This category also includes non-explicit (no penetration) magazines such as *Hustler* and others of its ilk that show almost-erect penises and frontal vaginal shots but no actual genital or oral/genital contact. Everything is feigned in these magazines. (*Penthouse* also runs sexual encounter photo spreads, but they're usually lesbian or bondage themed.) This group of magazines is essentially for people who like looking at naked bodies and staged sex scenes.

Hardcore photo magazines This group of magazines and photo "books" is usually sold in adult theaters and sex shops, or can be mail-ordered from ads in the back of magazines such as *Hustler.* They feature photographs of everything you see take place in X-rated films, and in many cases the photos were actually taken during the shooting of a porno movie. Every taste, interest, fantasy, and fetish is available in these magazines. Some magazine titles I turned up in my research included *Giant Clits, The Zoo Slut, First Masturbation, Blacks and Blondes,* and *Anally Yours.* Bondage and discipline, golden showers, and enemas are some of the other topics available in photo magazines.

Paperback novels These are novels loaded with explicit and graphic sex scenes. They tend to be formulaic in both plot and tone and any attempt at a story usually exists for the sole purpose of having the characters (usually gorgeous, handsome, irresistibly erotic and ridiculously oversexed) engage in scads of sex. By the way, these books are always text only; the only photograph is on the cover.

What is the difference between a sex scene in a mainstream novel and one in an adult sex novel? The difference is the level of explicitness and the use of graphic and lascivious language to describe a sexual encounter. A mainstream romance novel (or even some other type of novel that includes a sex scene or scenes) uses euphemisms and imagery to describe sexual activity and passion. A penis might be described as "his throbbing manhood," a vagina as "my fiery center." Breasts "heave" and lips "burn."

In a hardcore paperback sex novel the sex is cruder and more blatant. Penises are invariably "giant purple-headed cocks" that thrust and "spurt gallons of thick cum"; nipples are always thick and long, and they spend a great deal of time lustfully throbbing and poking; tongues are hot and wet and spend most of *their* time sucking and licking one body part or orifice or another. Every sex scene is intended to arouse the reader rather than advance the story, so such encounters usually take place every few pages. In the throes of passion and/or orgasm these human sexual dynamos often shriek things like "Ohhhh-ohh!" and "Yeahhhhhh!" and OHHHH-wow!" Subtle they're not.

The writing in many of these novels is often atrocious. Also, the editing usually leaves something to be desired, and it is not uncommon to find several typos on one page of text. These books are mass-produced, and ironically, some are written under phony names by well-known writers who do them for quick money. In some cases an occasional well-crafted sentence or lyrical image or line of dialogue will shine through. But these writers are being paid for the sex scenes, so the art of fiction mostly has to take a backseat to friction.

As with all the other types of adult erotica, paperback novels have something for everyone. Popular topics include lesbian/gay stories, orgies, bondage and discipline, three-ways, incest, oral sex, anal sex, fetishes, and most other types of sexual interests. These types of novels are usually not sold in mainstream bookstores such as B. Dalton. You will find racks of them, though, in adult bookstores, and in some instances, the publishers will repackage two similarly themed novels (lesbians, teen sex, orgies, etc.) into one "value-priced" volume. More orgasms for your money. Is this a great country or what?

Letters magazines Letters magazines came into being because of the popularity of the letters sections of men's magazines such as *Penthouse* and *Genesis*. In these sections, readers write in and describe their favorite (and entirely imagined?) sexual encounters. There's a very funny "letters" scene in the 1985 Rob Reiner film *The Sure Thing*, which starred John Cusack and Daphne Zuniga. Cusack's perpetually horny roommate is writing a totally bogus sex letter to *Penthouse* and wants to know from Cusack if *Penthouse* will know that "scoops of flesh" means breasts. Cusack looks at him and asks him what *else* could it *possibly* mean? Today's letters magazines are usually digest size (so they're easier to hold with one hand?) and broken into sections such as orgies, lesbians, voyeurism, amputees, and golden showers.

Fantasy magazines Fantasy magazines are like letters magazines (many of them also have letters sections) except that they run supposedly first-person, true-life articles about people's sexual encounters. Some of them even break their tables of contents into sections: Group Sex, Masturbation, Mother/Daughter, Analingus, Exhibitionism, and so on. These magazines are also digest size and usually have erotic photos and illustrations scattered throughout.

X-rated videos Remember when X-rated movies were only available on 8-mm film? If a bunch of guys wanted a film for a stag party, they'd have to either order one or find someone who had one hidden in a drawer somewhere, dig up a projector and screen, and then hope that the film didn't jam and allow the projector bulb to burn a hole in the thin celluloid.

Things are a little different today. X-rated videotapes are available in almost every neighborhood video rental store and in many of the chain operations. Many video stores limit their adult video selections to straight and bisexual pro and amateur tapes, although there are stores that carry extensive offerings of gay, bondage, and kinky tapes.

X-rated videos have flooded the market since the VCR became almost as ubiquitous in American homes as the omnipresent TV. Lately, the production values have improved, and you don't see too many mike booms in the shots or flashbulbs going off as the still photographer takes shots for magazines. (See "Hardcore photo magazines above.")

Many videos are rented by couples and used as a high-tech aphrodisiac. I know a lesbian couple and a heterosexual couple who both rent X-rated tapes regularly to spice up their respective sex lives.

The titles of many X-rated videos are often puns on titles of popular mainstream films, television shows, or songs. Here is a sampling of some of the funnier ones I noted on a recent visit (pencil and legal pad at the ready) to the adult room of my friendly local video purveyor.

- *The Anus Family*
- *The Bad News Brats*
- *The Best Rears of Our Lives*
- *Club Head*

- *Dougie Hoser, M.D.*
- *Fatliners*
- *Fresh Tits of Bel Air*
- *Full Metal Bikini*
- *The Goddaughters*
- *Hard Rider*
- *Hill Street Blacks*
- *I Cream of Genie*
- *Leave It to Cleavage*
- *Life Is Butt a Dream*
- *The Naked Bun*
- *A Pussy Called Wanda*
- *Rain Woman*
- *Sexual Instinct*
- *A Shaver Among Us*
- *Sinderella*
- *The Stepsister*
- *A Tale of Two Titties*
- *Tinseltown Wives*
- *2 Hung 2 Tung*
- *Valley of the Sluts*
- *Wilde at Heart*
- *Young and Restless*

Then there are the "special interest" tapes. These are videos aimed at those interested in very specific sexual acts, such as cunnilingus, fellatio, or anal sex. And finally, there are those tapes whose titles are intended to save time. They are, ahem, what you might call "to the point."

- *Girls Who Love Big Black Cock*
- *Girls Who Love Big White Cock*
- *Hard Dicks & Slick Holes*
- *The Hard Core Cafe*
- *White Bunbusters*
- *Wide Open Spaces*
- *You Said a Mouthful*

Adult tapes are also available by mail order, and *Playboy* magazine recently began offering a line of sex instruction tapes that are educational as well as erotic.

Mail-order videos You can order stuff you sometimes can't find in video rental stores by mail from ads in the backs of erotic magazines. Tapes exist for the most specific and narrow of interests. Recent tapes advertised in an issue of *Hustler,* for instance, included titles focusing on really large penises, shaved vaginas, bestiality, feet, transsexuals, and older women.

X-rated amateur videos In a way, X-rated amateur movies are sort of like what old-fashioned stag films used to be. Ever since the video camera became relatively affordable, people have been making and starring in their own porno movies. And because everyone is curious about what's *really* going on next door, companies have sprung up to buy and market these efforts. Some of them are so primitive they're laughable. I saw one once that began with a naked guy setting up a video camera on a tripod facing the side of his bed (we actually saw him adjusting the camera's focus). The Mrs. was already lying on the bed with her legs spread and her vagina facing the camera, looking like she's waiting for a Pap smear. A less erotic scene cannot be imagined. The guy then walked in front of the camera, his erection bouncing like a see-saw, mounted his wife, and proceeded to hump away for about twenty minutes. He has an orgasm, gets off his wife, and leaves her there in the same position in which we first saw her. The End.

What is often fascinating about these films is the glimpse we get into people's homes. One amateur tape my video dealer recommended consisted of a woman masturbating with a vibrator on her sofa for about a half hour. After the first couple of minutes, I found my attention wandering and started looking around their house, almost all of which was visible in the shot. I saw that they used Dawn dishwashing liquid (it was on their sink); they read the newspaper at the dining room table (it was still open to the sports section); someone collected ceramic frogs (they were visible in a hutch in the living room); and they may have owned a Harley-Davidson motorcycle (they had a Harley mirror in the hallway). All the while I'm snooping around their house, the lady of the manor is lying naked on the sofa with a fourteen-inch black vibrator jammed up her vagina, moaning and writhing to beat the band, while a Steely Dan song played on a radio in the background.

Weird experience, lemme tellya.

Erotic cable channels These are relatively new pay channel services that offer soft-core porno films that show simulated sex and loads of nudity. The *Playboy* channel is the most popular, and others include Spice. Some have to be subscribed to, although new addressable cable converters are allowing many cable companies to now offer by-the-day "rental" of these adult services.

8. **Footware** Foot fetishism is an industry unto itself. Marla Maples' ex-manager Chuck Jones had one, as did Danny DeVito's character in *War of the Roses*. [See the features on Foot Laws and *Leg Show* magazine.] Legs, feet, and toes have long been esteemed as sex objects, even though they have absolutely no connection with the genitals whatsoever (although foot reflexologists will argue that point). I guess this proves that the most powerful sex organ *is* the brain.

   A big part of foot fetishism is footware, which includes all types of shoes, as well as legware such as nylon stockings, garter belts, socks, and panty hose. The big favorite, of course, is high heels. These shoes have a devoted, occasionally fanatical following. High heels even have their own magazines and movies.

   There are several theories as to why high heels are so popular, one of which is that men like the way women have to walk when they're wearing heels. The shoes' construction (especially the *really* high heels, 3 inches or more) change a woman's gait so that the hips sway more, the calf and thigh are emphasized, and the buttocks are prominent. This might be partially true, but it does not explain the popularity of magazines in which women are posed in a reclining position wearing nothing but high heels. Sure, the nudity is a factor, but the shoes themselves tend to be the focus of attention in these photos.

   Some psychologists claim that the potential threat of the stiletto-like heel of the shoe is a turn-on to men who have latent masochistic and submissive tendencies.

9. **Glory Holes** Glory holes are three-foot-high holes in walls in bars, adult theaters, and sex shops. Men stick their erect penises through the holes and are sucked or masturbated to orgasm by someone they never see.

10. **Handkerchiefs** Handkerchiefs worn on the clothing are

used more as a sex signaling device than an enhancement, but they do play an important role for S&M aficionados and in the gay population, so they're worth a look.

Sexual Interest	Handkerchief Color
Anal Sex	Dark Blue
Anything	Orange
Bondage	Gray
Breasts/Breast Milk	Pink
Catheters	Lemon
Corsets/Garters, etc.	White Lace
Costumes/Military	Olive Drab
Feces	Brown
Fisting	Red
Food Games	Mustard
Group Sex	Lavender
Heavy S&M	Black
Light S&M	Robin's Egg Blue
Novice	White
Oral Sex	Light Blue
Piercing	Purple
Prostitution	Green
Urine	Yellow
Vampirism/Menstruating/ Blood	Maroon

Also, handkerchiefs worn on the left side indicate a dominant type; those worn on the right side mean submissive. However, because the meanings of the color codes vary from coast to coast, embarrassing faux pas have occurred.

11. **Love Dolls** Love dolls, being what they are, get absolutely no respect. Let's face it, these things are innately funny. Love dolls are inflatable dolls that have open mouths, vaginas, and anuses. Men use these dolls as surrogate sex partners. Some can be filled with water and made to feel extremely lifelike. Dolls are sold in sex shops and by mail order. Some X-rated film actresses have modeled for dolls marketed under their own brand name. Love dolls are almost always female. Women turn to dildos and vibrators for masturbation because an inflatable doll cannot provide an erection adequate for sexual stimulation. On top of that, the dolls

can't move by themselves. Inflatables work just fine for men, though.

12. **Male Masturbators** These are latex tubes into which the erect penis is inserted. When stroked up and down an erection, the tubes are supposed to simulate fellatio. Some come with squeeze balls that expand and contract the chamber, and most are used with some type of lubricant. (SLIK is popular.) Models advertised include the Ejacumatic (which is also battery-powered) and the Stroker (which includes a supply of lubricant).

13. **Penis Pumps** Penis pumps are different from male masturbators because they are not usually used for masturbation. These are essentially vacuum tubes that the flaccid penis is inserted into and then the air is sucked out of (electrically or with a squeeze ball), causing an erection by the suction effect on the penis. These products are occasionally advertised as "penis enlargement" devices and technically that's what they are. But the ads make you think that the pump will make a penis bigger and longer than it actually is. They won't. What they *will* do is make a flaccid penis bigger and longer by *inducing an erection*. But then again, for many men, a copy of *Playboy* would probably do the same thing. I suppose, though, that pumps could be helpful for men who have trouble achieving erection but are all right once they get one. Models advertised include the Hyperemiator, the Sizemaster, and the Matrix.

14. **Phone Sex Lines** "Make the call—we'll make you cum." That's how one phone sex service advertises itself. (You've got to admire their frankness, don't you think?) Phone sex lines are 800 or 900 numbers customers call and have "operators" talk "dirty" to them. Users masturbate during the two-way (or more) conversation. Phone sex has boomed in the Age of AIDS and, as a variant of masturbation, is looked to as one of the ultimate forms of safe sex. Phone sex lines are now a multimillion-dollar business. Phone sex is expensive. Charges range from flat fees of ten to fifty dollars for a fixed amount of time to by-the-minute charges that can add up rapidly. One service I saw advertised "only $3 a minute for as long as you need." A twenty-minute conversation quickly becomes a sixty-dollar phone bill.

But these services are popular, and what is helping them

proliferate is the use of credit cards rather than phone line charges. Many services now allow users to charge their fee to a Visa or Mastercard, both of which are revolving credit cards. This means that there are people out there still paying for the orgasm they had six months ago. (I personally know of a case in which a friend's house guest rang up close to ten thousand dollars' worth of 900-line sex calls in a three-month period. The guy was only making two or three calls a night, but he was staying on the phone for twenty or thirty minutes at a time.)

Phone sex lines are as varied as the range of human sexuality. In one issue of *Hustler* magazine the following twenty 900 services were among the hundreds advertised:

- "Amateur Phone Fantasies"
- "Ass Licking"
- "Beach Bunny"
- "Big Busty Babes"
- "Bondage Bliss"
- "Bound to Please"
- "Cornhole Connie"
- "Cum Fill My 3 Holes"
- "Danish Delights"
- "Double Your Pleasure"
- "Geisha Girls"
- "I Love to Talk Dirty While I Play with Myself"
- "Kinky 2-Girl Orgies"
- "Live Group Action"
- "Man-to-Man Action"
- "Older Women Phone Fantasies"
- "Ride the Orient Express"
- "She-Male Phone Fantasies"
- "Slap and Tickle"
- "Susie's School of Sex & Orgasm"

The phone sex services usually try to acquire a phone number that can convert to suggestive letters. They like the last four digits to spell out something salacious. I have seen services whose phone numbers end in LUST, LIPS, WILD, SEXX, MORE, CUNT, SUCK, TITS, ORGY, TRAMP, COCK, XTACY, HOTT, SEXY, TABU, and GUYS.

A recent well-known talk show looked at the phone sex business and had on the panel actual phone sex "operators." One of these operators described her fantasy character. We were told that what her customers wanted was a short, dusky Latin type with small breasts, huge dark nipples, and a willingness to engage in oral sex. So "Maria" (not the character's real name) was born. The "operator," however, was a short Jewish guy named "Bernie" (not his real name), who happened to have a voice that could easily be swallowed (no pun intended) as that belonging to someone just like "Maria." Other "operators" included middle-aged grandmothers and working housewives who talked all *kinds* of trash on their watch.

"Hot Phone" (as one service describes itself) could someday become as big as the X-rated video business if they moderated their prices. There are a lot of lonely, masturbating people out there to whom a live erotic fantasy conversation would be a very welcome substitute for the usual videos and magazines, but who now shy away from the calls because they're so expensive.

15. **String of Pearls** This is a sex toy consisting of a string that has between six and twelve small rubber balls threaded on it at ½- to 1-inch intervals. All of the balls are inserted into a partner's rectum and left there. The string is left hanging out of the anus. The lovers then go about their business, be it vaginal intercourse or something of the oral variety. At the moment of the man's orgasm, the balls are pulled out of his rectum. This enhances and prolongs the orgasm by stimulating the sensitive rectal nerves and prostate gland. Women often use this toy as a sexual enhancement not related to orgasm. A String of Pearls, for obvious reasons, is a "one-owner" plaything.

16. **Vibrators** Vibrators are penis-shaped electrical (AC or battery) devices used to stimulate the genitals, anus, and nipples. Women often insert a vibrator into the vagina, and men use it to penetrate the anus. Some frequently advertised models include the Corkscrew, Black Beauty, the Equalizer, Superdong, the Invader, Fill 'Er Up, Big Brother, and Mr. Satisfier.

There are other types of vibrators that do not look like penises but vibrate electronically and are used for stimulation but not penetration. One model seen advertised in magazines was named to cash in on a particularly notorious episode of the TV series *L.A. Law.* The episode centered around a sexual technique known only as the "Venus Butterfly," which was never actually defined. A company now markets a hand-held Venus Butterfly Massager that vibrates against and stimulates the clitoris.

One other vibrator worth mentioning is the Sybian, although it is more like a piece of exercise equipment than a sex toy you can hide in a drawer. The Sybian is barrel-shaped and has a vibrator sticking up out of its back. A woman gets on the Sybian, inserts the vibrator into her vagina, and then turns the "ride" on. The Sybian bucks like a bronco while the faux erection vibrates inside the woman. The artificial boner also rotates as well. The rider has complete control of the vibrations, and as you can imagine, multiple orgasms are quite common.

Department of Peculiar Parlance:
30 Euphemisms for Being Sexually Aroused

It is only appropriate to follow a feature on sexual enhancements with a listing of euphemisms for being sexually aroused. This, then, is a compendium of 30 ways to indicate an increase in certain volatile hormone levels, *without* going for a complete blood workup.

1. To Be Affy
2. To Be Blotty
3. To Be Mustard
4. To Be on Blob
5. To Be Constitutionally Inclined to Gallantry
6. To Be Dripping for It
7. To Feel Fuzzy
8. To Feel Hairy
9. To Be Het Up
10. To Be Hot and Bothered
11. To Be Hot Assed
12. To Be Hot Blooded
13. To Be Hot in the Biscuit
14. To Be Hunky
15. To Be in Season
16. To Be in the Mood
17. To Have Itchy Pants

18. To Be Juicy
19. To Be Mashed
20. To Be On for One's Greens
21. To Have Peas in the Pot
22. To Be Primed
23. To Be Proud
24. To Be Randy
25. To Be Ranting
26. To Be Rooty
27. To Be Rusty
28. To Be Touchable
29. To Be Turned On
30. To Be Wet

7 Way Cool Superhero Superpowers

"Look! Up in the sky! It's a bird! It's a plane!"

It was none of the above, of course. It was Superman!

Who didn't watch Superman growing up? Clark Kent was terminally laid-back in his double-breasted suits and black horn-rimmed glasses, and no one, especially Jimmy Olsen and Lois Lane, saw the resemblance between Clark and Superman. Those glasses were some disguise, eh?

Superheroes have always been very appealing fantasy characters. They can do all the things we can't, and thus, by reading about them or watching them in movies or on TV, we can vicariously leave our limitations behind and imagine what it's like to be able to fly or freeze a lake with our breath or stretch ourselves so super-thin that we can slide through keyholes.

This feature looks at 7 mega-cool superpowers.

1. **Flaming** "Flame on!" is The Human Torch's battle cry, and what it does is turn him into a human torch and give him flying power. He literally becomes a flaming, flying crime fighter. (It's always a surrealistic treat to see the Human Torch's face hidden in flames after he flames on.)

2. **Flight** Brainiac 5 possesses a flight ring that allows him to fly at will; The Green Lantern can use his Power Ring to fly; The Human Torch can fly when he ignites; Mighty Mouse, Underdog, and Superman can all fly at will (although early on Superman only leaped enormous distances); and Doc Strange (the poor man's Superman) has incredible leaping power

which falls just short of actually flying. (Wonder Woman needs her invisible plane to fly.)

3. **Force Fields** Captain America's main strength is the possession of a force field that is impervious to hot and cold temperatures, all manner of projectiles, and a variety of rays, including heat and death. Also, Jedi Knight Luke Skywalker can access The Force, an invisible power that surges through all living things in the universe. With The Force at his command, Luke manifests astonishing super strength, is telekinetic (he can move huge objects, including enormous spacecraft, with his mind), precognitive (he can see the future), and can miraculously heal with his hands and mind.

4. **Power Ring** The Green Lantern's power ring lets the lantern do *anything he wants to do.* By invoking the ring's power he can fly, become invulnerable or invisible, and call upon any superpower he needs at the moment. Unlike other superheroes' powers, with their specific limitations and vulnerabilities, The Green Lantern's powers are limitless. I always found that thought intoxicating.

5. **Stretching** Mr. Fantastic is a member of the Fantastic Four and can stretch himself to super thinness, thus making himself invulnerable to bullets, knives, and all types of destruction.

6. **Super Speed** The Flash is capable of physical movement at super speeds, which allows him to actually travel invisibly because he can move faster than the eye can follow. This also permits him to travel through time, since he can move faster than the speed of light.

7. **X-ray Vision** Mighty Mouse, Superman, and Underdog all possess this extremely desirable superpower. Superman's X-ray vision is blocked by lead, though, and Underdog needs special Energy Pills to access *all* his superpowers, including his X-ray vision.

Special Award for Astonishing Superhero Deeds by a Mere Mortal: Batman

Batman is one of the most-loved superheroes of all time, due in part to the "Dark Knight" *Batman* graphic novels of the 1980s that were aimed at an older audience, and the Batman series of movies, which acknowledged the icon's dark side and did not play his character for laughs the way the Superman movie series did at times.

Batman is not a supernatural being but just a wounded man who witnessed the murder of his parents and who has dedicated his life to fighting crime. He is smart, wealthy, and in great physical condition. He is also one of the coolest superheroes who has ever lived. Nowhere is this more evident than in the scene in the first Batman movie when Michael Keaton glares at a crook and tells him, "I'm Batman." (Acknowledging the Dark Knight's incredible presence and the influence of the character on popular culture, David Letterman *always* refers to Keaton as Batman when he is a guest on his show. For instance, he will offhandedly ask bandleader Paul Shaffer whether he knows that they have Batman on the show that night.)

Batman has at his disposal an enormous variety of tools, gadgets, weapons, and vehicles. His vehicle inventory includes, of course, the BatMobile, as well as the BatBoat, BatCopter, BatCycle, BatPlane, BatRocket, BatWings, Bat Jetpack, and the Whirly-Bat.

Batman also wears a Utility Belt that contains any number of amazing devices and paraphernalia. The belt contains an infrared flashlight, a two-way radio, a gas mask, a "Bat-a-rang" boomerang, a Bat Rope, tear gas pellets, smoke grenades, a laser torch, and a camera.

Batman works out of stately Wayne Manor (Bruce Wayne, Batman's alter ego, is a millionaire entrepreneur), and in the Manor's basement there is a complete crime lab and a state-of-the-art computer.

Bruce Wayne's longtime butler Alfred knows that his employer is Batman. The elderly gentleman is well versed in the Dark Knight's legend, as well as in the logistics of Batman's crime-fighting endeavors.

The 6 Types of Devils, As Indexed in the *Compendium Maleficarum*

In 1608, Friar Francesco-Maria Guazzo wrote a book called *Compendium Maleficarum* in which he attempted to document the six types of devils that exist in our world.

Apparently, these six types of devils all work to serve Lucifer (the head honcho) and his sixteen servants, from Beelzebub (the patron devil of pride) to Iuvart, a devil who is on hiatus, so to speak. (In 1612, Iuvart was trapped in the body of a nun at Louviers Convent.)

This feature provides a listing of these six devilish types and describes their main body of interest.

1. **Fire Devils** These fiends are the upper management of devils. They reside in our upper atmosphere and supervise the nefarious doings of the other five demons.
2. **Aerial Devils** These guys are everywhere. They live in the very air that surrounds us. These are considered the most dangerous and malefic type of demons because they are so ubiquitous.
3. **Terrestrial Devils** These villains are your basic "back-to-nature" devils. They live in the forests and the rural areas of our world.
4. **Aqueous Devils** These rogues are into water sports, residing in the lakes, oceans, and rivers of Mother Earth. They are said to be responsible for catastrophes at sea.
5. **Subterranean Devils** As you might guess, these troglodytes are your cave-dweller types. They live beneath mountains and in caves.
6. **Heliophobic Devils** Remember the vampire legends? One of

their most recognizable characteristics was their fear and "allergy" to light, right? It is possible that vampires were (are?) a form of heliophobic devil because these chaps are the demons who appear only after sunset and who hate the light.

33 Display and Classified Ads from One Issue of *Soldier of Fortune* Magazine

Soldier of Fortune magazine has an agenda: It is a right-wing, pro-weapon, anti-crime, jingoistic publication that has a loyal and fervent (although currently declining) readership. Citing an "incredible amount of negative publicity," a survey in the March 1993 issue offered four alternate names for the magazine and asked readers to choose one. The "new" titles were *Soldiers of Freedom, The Professionals, Worldwide Military Review,* and *Global Military Journal.* I'll bet that nine out of ten *Soldier of Fortune* subscribers are also members of the National Rifle Association (NRA). (That's a personal guess and I do not have the statistics to support my contentions *but* the fact that the NRA took out a four-page, full-color, glossy paper ad in the March 1993 issue of *Soldier of Fortune* must mean *something*.)

Two recent *SOF* cover stories were "Banned in the U.S.A.: Clinton's Surprises for Gun Owners" and "Saddam's Revenge: American Soldiers Poisoned by Oilfield Arson."

It has always been my belief that one of the ways you can get an accurate and insightful assessment of a periodical's readership is by studying the ads that run in the magazine.

The editorial staff of *Soldier of Fortune* magazine recognize that some of their display and classified ads (and some of their articles for that matter) can be construed as inflammatory and, in the case of offering weapons for sale across state lines, possibly illegal. For that reason, they run this disclaimer in each issue:

There may be products in the magazine of which sale, possession, or interstate transportation may be restricted, prohibited or subject to special licensing requirements in your state. Purchasers should consult local law enforcement authorities in their area. All data in this publication, technical or otherwise, is based upon personal experience or individuals using specific tools, products, equipment and components under particular conditions and circumstances, some of which may not be reported in the article and which *Soldier of Fortune* has not otherwise verified.

(One reason for this disclaimer might be the fact that *Soldier of Fortune* recently lost a lawsuit that almost bankrupted them. The suit involved a mercenary who was hired through one of their classified ads.)

Soldier of Fortune's editorial "departments" (the names of which speak volumes about the magazine's interests and readers) include Vietnam Veterans Affairs, Military History, Unconventional Operations, Military Affairs, Paramedic Operations, Explosives and Demolitions, Aviation, Africa, Outdoor Affairs, Latin America, Battle Blades, and Gun Rights.

Here is a sampling of some of the display and classified ads that ran in a recent issue of *Soldier of Fortune* magazine. (The company name is listed in **bold** type and the products they offer follow in plain text. If any of these items or services interest you, contact the magazine for back issues.)

1. **Paladin Press:** Paladin Press had three full-page ads in the magazine. Paladin offers books for the discriminatingly paranoid. Titles they offer include the following:
   - *Barroom Brawling*
   - *Drug Smuggling*
   - *Handgun Stopping Power*
   - *How to Avoid Electronic Eavesdropping and Privacy Invasion*
   - *How to Beat the Credit Bureaus*
   - *How to Get Anything on Anybody*
   - *Instinct Combat Shooting*
   - *Manual of the Mercenary Soldier*
   - *101 Sucker Punches*
   - *Pocket Medic*
   - *Righteous Revenge*
   - *Street Lethal: Unarmed Urban Combat*
   - *Survivalist's Medicine Chest*

- *The Ultimate Sniper*
- *Winning a Street Knife Fight*

2. **Dutchguard:** For $66, a "Telephone Voice Changer" that works on any two-piece phone offered "Sixteen Different Programmable Voice Masking Levels!"

3. **Sonic Technology:** Six different model stun guns, as well as pepper-spray defensive aerosols.

4. **Your Supply Depot, Ltd.:** A "Ninja" pistol crossbow and a .22-caliber tear-gas pistol.

5. **Steve Arnold's Gunroom:** "Professional Locksmithing Tools," including "Double Sided Disk Tumbler Picks."

6. **Law Enforcement Supply Co.:** "Authentic, Professional, Full Size Badges."

7. **Executive Protection Products, Inc.:** "Israeli Instinctive Combat Shooting" video.

8. **Collector's Armoury:** Counterfeit guns, including a phony Uzi submachine gun.

9. **Genesis:** An "Air Assault Course" taught by the "Kaibil" Special Forces of Guatemala. Course includes Tactical Rappeling, Insertion/Extraction Techniques, use of a UH-1-H Helicopter, and a Badge and Certificate of Completion from the Guatemalan Army.

10. **Doctor Center:** A "Secret Gunbelt" for "ultimate concealment."

11. **Michigan Body Armor:** Body armor that can stop a .44 magnum bullet.

12. **Intelligence Incorporated:** "Extraordinary" surveillance and investigation aids, including the "Amazing Mule Tool" that can open 95 percent of all locks made.

13. **SOF-Nancy:** T-shirt decals, including one that shows a U.S. flag and reads, "If You Don't Love It . . . LEAVE!"

14. **Margarita Tours:** A "Jungle Survival and Leadership Course" in the "Tropical Amazon River Jungle Forest." The course includes accommodations in Indian villages and all survival food while in a training area.

15. **The Pilot's Shop:** German WW II army helmets.

16. **Celestial Enterprises:** An "Ammo Watchband." It has six compartments for bullets (from .22-caliber to 9-mm cartridges) and it puts "Fire Power at Your Finger Tips."

17. **NIC Law Enforcement Supply:** Photo identification cards

for every profession, from Bail Enforcement Agent to Certified Parachutist.

18. **Omega Group, Ltd.:** A "Bullet" pen and pencil set made from "actual NATO expended brass shell casings with copper bullet tips."

19. **E.C. International:** Nazi MP40 submachine guns.

20. **Bud K World Wide:** Solid brass "paper weights" that have four holes and a wide oval open base that make it easy to pick up with your fingers.

21. **NIC, Inc.:** KGB ID folios.

22. **J.W. McFarlin Company:** A .625 magnum blowgun, the "World's Most Powerful."

23. **Aerotek:** Homemade rocket motors.

24. **W.W. #2 Ltd.:** Nazi generals' caps.

25. **SARCO, Inc.:** M17A2 gas masks, German MP40 Schmeisser submachine gun magazines, 98 Mauser bayonets, East German AK 47 magazines, a U.A. sniper scope M84, and a bazooka rocket projectile.

26. **Classified Ad:** A poster that read, "When you absolutely have to have it destroyed overnight—call in a ranger."

27. **Classified Ad:** "Oriental Ladies Want Husbands."

28. **Classified Ad:** A book of "Secret Scanner Frequencies."

29. **Classified Ad:** Your own secret FBI, NSA, Justice, and State Department files for only $29.95.

30. **Classified Ad:** "Second Identity" passports.

31. **Classified Ad:** Home videos of the L.A. riots.

32. **Classified Ad:** Videos of "Young Voluptuous Models" from 37 countries.

33. **Classified Ad:** For Sale: Smoke Balls, Cartridges, Candles, Bombs, Pots, and Grenades.

8 Distressing and Unexpected Facts About the Pentagon

On May 12, 1993, the Pentagon celebrated its fiftieth anniversary. That same day, newspapers throughout the country highlighted some of the alarming problems with the "world's largest office building." A ten-year, $1 billion repair and renovation program is tentatively scheduled to begin in 1994, but Pentagon insiders are not optimistic. Funds for the Pentagon fall under the umbrella of "defense spending," and with the cutbacks in this area of federal funding, the Mammoth may have to do without some of the improvements it desperately needs.

1. **Asbestos** The Pentagon has asbestos in the floor tiles and on the ceilings. Asbestos was also used for insulating pipes and for the construction of heating and cooling air ducts. It's all gotta go.
2. **PCBs** This deadly chemical is present in many of the Pentagon's lighting fixtures.
3. **Sewage Pipes** Many of the Pentagon's sewage pipes are almost completely corroded through. One report claims that many of the pipes are so rotted they can be punctured with a pencil.
4. **Leaking Fuel Tanks** Some of the eight underground fuel tanks on Pentagon property are leaking.
5. **Missing Sprinklers** The Pentagon does not have installed sprinkler systems.
6. **Smoke Control** The Pentagon does not have an implemented comprehensive smoke control plan.
7. **Disabled Access** Ironically, access for the disabled to the Pentagon, one of the Federal Government's largest buildings, is at best limited, and nonexistent in some areas.
8. **Security Problems** This item is probably the most alarming,

considering the building in question. Apparently, security at loading docks is haphazard, and some Pentagon windows are easily accessible to (and able to be opened by) nonauthorized personnel.

Dr. Ese's 11 Signs of Demonic Possession

Dr. Ese, a noted medieval researcher of the paranormal, came up with the following eleven indications that a person might be possessed by a demon or by Old Scratch himself. Some of these are scary: Centuries past, living alone and being ugly were enough to convince people that you were possessed. With those criteria, it wouldn't be too difficult today for an awful lot of people to qualify for discount exorcisms. [This list is derived from information in *An Encyclopaedia of Occultism* by Lewis Spence (University Books, 1960)].

1. Imagining yourself possessed.
2. Leading an evil life.
3. Living alone.
4. Chronic ailments, unusual symptoms, a deep sleep and/or the vomiting of strange things (although no specifics are offered as to what exactly the suspected possessee had to vomit in order to qualify).
5. Blaspheming and/or making frequent reference to the Devil.
6. Making a pact with the Devil.
7. Being controlled by spirits.
8. Having a face that inspires horror and fear. (This meant that you were suspected of being possessed by the Devil if you were ugly.)
9. Being tired of living and giving up all hope. (Depression qualified too, it seems.)
10. Being enraged and/or being violent.
11. Making the cries and noises of a beast.

5 Early Movie Roles Big Stars Would Probably Like to Forget

Mighty things from small beginnings grow.
—John Dryden, *Annus Mirabilis*

Even big stars had to start somewhere. This feature looks at five early film roles that are an embarrassment to their perpetrators today. But they are fun to watch, are usually funny when they are not intended to be, and are genuine cinematic curiosities. If you are a fan of Arnold, Sly, Kevin, Jessica, or Madonna, these five movies have to be put on the top of your "must rent" list.

1. **Arnold Schwarzenegger in *Hercules in New York* (1969):** No one would have ever guessed that the "Arnold Strong" in this lame fantasy/comedy would someday be the highest paid and biggest box-office draw in the movie business.

   This film, Arnold's first, was pre-*Conan*, pre-*Terminator*, and pre-Maria (Shriver, of course). It begins with a dramatic narrative about vengeful gods, which is shown over scenes of erupting volcanoes and storms. It then quickly atrophies into a pathetic comedy that is badly dubbed and has bad costumes. Arnold plays Hercules, the illegitimate son of the god Zeus.

   We never get to hear "Ahnold" speak because all of his lines were dubbed by some guy with a white-bread, All-American voice. It is hilarious and ludicrous to hear the voice that comes out of Schwarzenegger's mouth. (His very first cinematic spoken line was "I'm bored," although it wasn't his voice. Could he have been talking about making this movie?)

   A young Arnold is pumped up and buffed, and his pecs and lats frequently on display in this movie, which has also been released as *Hercules—The Movie* and *Hercules Goes Bananas*. (In one early scene, Arnold alternately bounces one pectoral muscle at a time. Grotesque.)

Hercules in New York is probably an embarrassment to Arnie now. Nonetheless, it's worth checking out to see what Conan the Barbarian and the Terminator were doing in their early years.

2. **Sylvester Stallone in *A Party at Kitty and Stud's/The Italian Stallion* (1970):** One can only imagine the orgasmic shrieks of glee that emanated from the producers of *A Party at Kitty and Stud's* when they finally realized that the star of their low-budget 1970 porno film was also the star of the film that won the 1976 Academy Award for Best Picture.

A Party at Kitty and Stud's was Sylvester Stallone's first movie role, and in it he is totally nude and simulates sex. *Party* was retitled, repackaged, and re-released in 1985 as *The Italian Stallion.* Apparently, the producers also commissioned some *Rocky*-specific elements for the newly edited film. Rocky Balboa's theme in *Rocky* was "Gonna Fly Now"; in *Stallion,* Stud's song is "Fly with Me," a less-than-memorable tune that mimicked "Gonna Fly Now" 's funky beat and horn riffs.

They also added a ridiculous "Prologue" in which a woman waxed pseudo-sincerely about how admirable Sly was for owning up to the fact that he did, indeed, make *Party* when he was just starting out in the business. (Yeah, I'm sure he's *real* proud.)

So what exactly does Sly do in *Stallion?* Well, basically he rolls around naked a lot. He washes and plays with Kitty's breasts, and he has his big toes pulled. He also never gets an erection, nor has intercourse, although he does simulate the mattress jig in one scene that ends up being hilarious thanks to Stallone's passionate moaning and groaning. He sounds so much like the Rocky of the "Yo, Adrian" period that it strikes one as funny instead of erotic.

Also, in one scene, he poses in front of a mirror while two women, one white, one black, writhe around on a bed while a *Rocky*-like trumpet theme plays on the new soundtrack. Strange.

To give him his due, Stallone's acting in this film is not

bad. He comes across as natural and relaxed and his talent is obvious.

The story, such as it is, revolves around Kitty's continual horniness for Stud, and concludes with a huge orgy that includes everybody, including Sly, holding hands and dancing around in a circle completely naked.

In one scene, Kitty supposedly bites Stud's penis while giving him head, and he takes a belt to her bottom. Stallone gives this scene his trademark crooked leer—that all-purpose facial expression he has often used to simulate passion, rage, confusion, pleasure, and any combination of the above.

In another scene, this one dripping with irony, Stallone looks into a mirror and asks, "When are they going to recognize me?" Kitty replies, "Soon everyone will know who you are."

The rest of the movie is nothing but a series of orgies, most of which Sly participates in and none of which show any real sex. There's constant nudity, but all the balling is bogus.

It's no wonder that Sly lists Woody Allen's *Bananas* (he was a thug) as his first film. *A Party at Kitty and Stud's* is not something I'd want on *my* resume either.

3. **Kevin Costner in *Sizzle Beach, U.S.A.* (1974):** *Sizzle Beach, U.S.A.* was Kevin Costner's first film. This soft porn Troma release (Troma is the same company that has graced us with the *Toxic Avenger* series and others) was shot in 1974 and released on video in 1986. There is almost nothing about this film even approaching mediocrity, such is its exquisite wretchedness.

It begins with a cheesy ballad playing over the credits, which include "Special Guest Star" Kevin Costner. If this was his first film, how could he already be a star? But let's move on, shall we?

The story centers around three bimbettes, Dit, Cheryl, and Janice, who all share Dit's cousin Steve's beach house where they take off their clothes. A lot.

Janice plays the guitar and writes and sings horrible folky-type songs. (All of the songs in this movie suck. One song on the soundtrack called "Agin' Babies" contains the lines,

"Agin' babies roll their hair/Agin' babies like to swear/ Agin' babies, they don't care.")

Cheryl is a phys-ed instructor who likes to ride her exercise bike topless, and Dit is a horseback rider who meets Costner's character, John Logan, at his Rocky Mountain Riding Stables. (She picked his stable out of the yellow pages because she was originally from Colorado and the name seduced her.)

Costner's first-ever scene has him oiling a leather saddle strap as Dit calls him from outside. His first line is, "Hello?" (This from a man who would graduate to scenes in *JFK* in which he would speak complex speeches that go on for pages.) After their first meeting, Costner invites Dit out riding, and they eventually end up in front of a fireplace where *his* shirt comes off before her bathing suit top. (How forward thinking!)

Costner owns several stables and has working for him a midget bookie (yes, a midget bookie) who "likes tall women."

As is usually the case with terrifically talented people in horrendous films, Costner is the best actor in the movie. He is the only one who even *remotely* comes close to a natural reading of his lines, and his performance is really the only reason to rent this movie. (Unless, of course, you rent movies by the Joe Bob Briggs rating system: breasts and kung fu. Using Joe Bob's criteria, *Sizzle Beach, U.S.A.* would be a must rent by breast count alone. No kung fu, however.)

Other than the presence of Costner, though, this film is a disaster. The sound is horrible, the story ludicrous, and the acting is the pits. Renowned film critic Leonard Maltin described *Sizzle Beach, U.S.A.* as "ultra-low-budget beach-bimbo junk." I find that apt, and upon reflection, might actually consider the acting in this film some of the worst, if not *the* worst, I've ever seen. It's so bad, it doesn't even qualify as camp.

Renter beware.

4. **Jessica Lange in *King Kong* (1976):** This Dino de Laurentiis remake of the 1933 Fay Wray classic is notable to movie fans for several reasons. First and foremost, of course, is that it marks the film debut of the lovely and talented Jessica Lange. (She plays the bimbo Dwan; you know, like Dawn but

with two letters reversed?) *King Kong* also gives us a very early glimpse of the equally lovely and talented Joe Piscopo and Corbin Bernsen, as well as a thin and hirsute Charles Grodin in a deliriously over-the-top performance as a slimeball oil company exec.

The first Lange screen appearance is a stunning cameo of her left arm. Her limb is glimpsed dangling over the edge of a life raft, and her first spoken line is "Where's Harry and everyone?," which she utters after awakening on the Petrox oil company ship. (She is wearing a low-cut skintight black dress that is almost see-through thanks to the water, and the camera makes sure the audience knows it.)

"Did you ever meet anyone before whose life was saved by *Deep Throat?*" she asks hero Jeff Bridges and the leering crew members. It seems that Dwan refused to watch a below-decks screening of the porno film on the yacht with "Harry and everyone" and was thus on deck when the ship went down. Harry had "discovered me," she explains, and "was gonna put me in a movie he was making in Hong Kong."

Lange then does an almost-nude shower scene and parades around the ship in a variety of scanty "cheesecake" outfits, including hot pants and cut-off T-shirts. The ship is on its way to a fog-bound island that Grodin's character Fred Wilson believes is a huge depository of oil. (This film was released during the energy crisis seventies and thus the search for new sources of fuel was a timely topic.)

The remainder of the story is status quo: Kong falls in love with Dwan; Fred captures Kong for a Petrox circus (he's presented in a giant gas pump); Kong escapes, the big guy finds Dwan, and is later killed by machine-gun wielding helicopters as he leaps from tower to tower of the World Trade Center. (Apparently the Empire State Building was busy.)

This remake of *King Kong* is unintentionally funny when it is attempting to be profound, thus transmuting the film into a camp classic. In one scene, a passionate Jeff Bridges, trying to convince the oil guys that Kong was real, heatedly asks them, "What the hell do you think went through there? Some guy in an ape suit?" (This is funny because yes, it was some guy—effects wizard Rick Baker to be precise—wearing an ape suit.) Also, some of the dialogue is hilariously dated. At one point Lange calls Kong a "chauvinist pig ape," and because Dwan is a big astrology buff, she often waxes sincere about signs and such. Before she's captured by Kong, Lange tells Bridges, "My horoscope said I was going to cross over water and meet the biggest person in my life."

Another memorable line of dialogue is heard when one of the oil guys radios to Bridges the "estimated monkey time to your position." Estimated monkey time? Who *wrote* these lines, the monkey?

It's also hilarious the way the oil company, Petrox, is depicted. In this film, they are the quintessential sleazy, money-hungry, detestable, polluting, stupid, hypocritical, multinational conglomerate. And Charles Grodin's character is the definitive sleazebag. See if you don't cheer when Grodin meets his demise by getting squashed by Kong's six-foot-long foot.

Jessica Lange was flagrantly wasted in *King Kong*. Her talent was hard to miss, though, and she later went on to such classic films (and performances) as *All That Jazz, The Postman Always Rings Twice, Frances, Tootsie, The Music Box,* and *Cape Fear.*

5. **Madonna in *A Certain Sacrifice* (1979):** Madonna is a better singer/dancer than actress. Her only genuinely watchable film roles have been in the documentary *Truth or Dare,* in which she played herself, and in *A League of Their Own,* when she played a toned-down *imitation* of herself. *A Certain Sacrifice* was Madonna's first film role, which was released after she became the media goddess we all know and love. It was a student film shot on 16-mm film and later cleaned up (barely) and transferred to video. Madonna sued (unsuccessfully) to keep this piece of cinematic drek off the market. *A Certain Sacrifice* is unwatchable. It is only worth checking out for the appearance of Madonna. In the film, she dances in a park and gets raped in a loft.

The film seems to have been made without a script and nowhere is this more evident than in a scene that takes place in a diner in which an older guy tries to pick up a young, good-looking guy who is having his breakfast. The dialogue for this scene was so obviously improvised that it's actually embarrassing to watch. This segment makes a movie fan realize just how difficult it actually is to write scintillating film dialogue and how easy it is to spout non-linear non-sense and try to pass it off as screenwriting.

A *Certain Sacrifice* can be purchased on video for about ten dollars. The sound is lousy, the color and picture clarity abominable, and the story nonexistent. But this execrable piece of nonsense *is* a collectible and I suppose that fact says more about popular culture and fame in our society than any shelf-load of books of social commentary.

An Eclectic Selection of 245 *Playboy* Playmate of the Month "Turn-Ons" and "Turn-Offs" from the 1970s Through the 1990s

The *Playboy* Playmates' "Turn-Ons" and "Turn-Offs" can ostensibly be looked upon as a barometer of the interests and concerns of the late-teens, early-twenties female in America at a given moment in our history.

That's why these lists span three "eras": the distant pre-Reagan, late 70s, the materialistic 80s, and the "hard times" 90s. (*Playboy* did not include "Turn-Ons" and "Turn-Offs" in their 60s editions.)

Do the concerns of these young women reflect what was happening in our culture and society in those times? It would seem so. The "Turn-Ons" are mostly indicative of the frothy, playful interests of a young woman of *any* era (although the 80s "Turn-Ons" include an interest in personal gratification and material possessions, a couple of women going so far as to include a 450SL and furs in their lists).

But the "Turn-Offs" *really* point up the differences in our times. In 1979, the turn-offs included braggarts, obnoxious drunks, and fat, an important concern of the pre-feminist young woman who agreed to willingly define herself by body image.

But then, in the 80s and 90s, all hell breaks lose with these young women. Now what's pissing them off includes animal abuse, environmental defilement, dishonesty, hypocrisy, disrespect for women, men's lack of concern for birth control, drug abuse, men who are unfaithful, and race relations. Social and political concerns and worries weigh heavily on their minds, and they are not afraid to speak up when something bothers them.

The times, they are a-changing, eh?

The Turn-Ons
The 1970s

The beach
A big, warm bed on a cold, rainy night
Good food
Good music [mentioned several times]
Ice cream
My boyfriend
Outdoor living
Sailing
Stimulating conversation
Sunshine
Walt Disney

The 1980s

Acting class
Animals
Anything French
Arabian horses
Attending various musicals and ballets
Baby powder
Bach
The beginning of a new relationship
Being a Sigma Chi sister of USC
Big dogs
Camping
The Chicago Bears
Children [mentioned several times]
Christmas
Counting money
Dancing
Delicate jewelry
Diamonds [mentioned more than once]
Drawing
Eating
Exercising
Fast boats

Fast cars
Faster horses
Flying First Class
Foot massages
A 450SL
Fresh snow
Funny people
Furry animals
Furs
The future [mentioned several times]
Gardenias
Good food
Good jokes
A good mechanic
Gymnastics
Happy people
Harleys [mentioned more than once]
High fashion
Hot oil massages
Jesus Christ
Karmann-Ghias
Live entertainment
Massage
Mom's home cookin'
Music [mentioned many times]
The ocean [mentioned more than once]
Old people
Onions
Photographs
Sailing alone at night under the stars
San Sebastián
Sexy lingerie
Sharing enjoyable experiences with those I love
'69 Camaros
Spending money
Sports cars
Star gazing
Stocky men
Tight jeans
Traveling [mentioned many times]
UFOs

Vegetables
Vintage champagne
Warm sunshine on the hot sand
Well-toned bodies [mentioned more than once]
White lace
Wide open country
Witty conversations
Yellow roses

The 1990s

An all-around bad boy
Auto racing
Beach walks
Big cats
Bubble baths for two
Candlelight dinners
Confident men
Cowboys in tight Wranglers
Dirty dancing
Ear kissing
Fast cars [mentioned more than once]
Guitarist Dan Wexler
Harleys [mentioned more than once]
Having doors opened for me
Having my back tickled
Hidden tattoos
Italian style
Jim Morrison
L'Auberge in Sedona
Lots of attention
Men who wear braces
Men with good voices
Mountains
Music [mentioned more than once]
Nintendo
Pasta
A pastrami sandwich at Gross's Deli
Patrick Swayze in *Dirty Dancing*
Pink roses

Police work
Quiet, rugged men in cowboy boots and jeans
Scary movies
Sexy dressing
Strawberries and cream
Sunshine
Surprises
Sweet foods
Taking a long hot shower with my boyfriend
A wicked smile
Wine

The Turn-Offs
The 1970s

Dishonesty
Fat
Having to wait
Jealousy
Litterbugs
Men who like women for their looks
People who brag
People who get obnoxious when they drink
Pushy people
Rude people
Superficial people
Violence

The 1980s

Animal abuse
Asparagus
Being alone
Being sick
Bell peppers
Bleached blond hair
Born-again zealots
Broken promises

Cavities
Closed minds
Conceit
Conformists
Critical people
Crowds [mentioned more than once]
Cruelty to animals
Disco
Dishonesty [mentioned more than once]
Driving in rush-hour traffic
Fast-food restaurants
Gaudy jewelry
Getting up early
Gossipy hairdressers
Grudges
Heartaches [mentioned more than once]
Hovering salespeople
Idolatry
Jealousy
Judgmental people
Junk mail
L.A. freeways at 5 P.M.
Lazy people
Liars [mentioned many times]
Liver
Macho men
Manipulators
Negativism
Pay-toilet stalls
People who are late
People who don't have anything nice to say
People who make promises and break them
People who stereotype others
People who think all pretty girls are dumb
Pessimists
Phony people
Politics
Pollution
Pomposity
Power boats
Pretentious people

Punk rock
Renewing my driver's license
Rude people
The saying, "You're pretty good for a girl."
Screen violence
Smoking [mentioned more than once]
Spiders
Stress
Sunday-morning radio
Tax time
Traffic
Violence
Waiting
War [mentioned more than once]
Wasting time [mentioned more than once]

The 1990s

Animal abuse
Arrogance
Bad grammar
Big egos
Burping
Cold climates
Cold people
Cold rooms
Cynics
Dishonest people
Disloyal friends
Drop-dead looks from snotty (maybe jealous) females
Environmental abusers
Flight delays
Getting sick when there's no male nurse around
Greed
Guys in bikini briefs
Guys who like me just for my looks and not my personality
Hypocrites
Itchy clothes
Jealousy [mentioned more than once]
Liars [mentioned more than once]

Lip smacking
Loud obnoxious men
Meat Loaf
Men who act tall
Men who don't care about using protection
Men who have no respect for women
Men you can't trust
Obsessive body-builders
Overbearing cologne
Overbooked flights
Parking tickets
People who abuse drugs
People who exercise too much
People who lie
People who take up two spaces in parking lots
Racism
Slobs
Slowpokes
Small-town gossip
Smog
Speed bumps
Speeding tickets
Sunday drivers
Traffic
Wrinkled shirts

Department of Peculiar Parlance:
75 Euphemisms for Female Breasts

America has been called the most breast-fixated country on the planet. In Europe, the natives cannot understand the salivating camera-laden American tourists who shoot rolls and rolls of pic-

tures of European women—young, old, thin, and not-so-thin—
gracing the ubiquitous topless beaches.

They think us immature and childish when it comes to our attitudes about sex and nudity. They do have a point, and this list
seems to validate their belief that we, as a culture, are preoccupied
with the female breast. Here are 75 imaginative ways of euphemistically describing the most conspicuous physical distinction between the male and female genders.

1. The Apple Dumpling Shop	33. Globes
2. Babaloos	34. Grapefruits
3. Baby Pillows	35. Grapes
4. Balloons	36. Handwarmers
5. Bazongas	37. Headlights
6. Bazooms	38. Honeydew Melons
7. Bee Bites	39. Hooters
8. Begonias	40. Jelly on Springs
9. Big Brown Eyes	41. Jugs
10. Bodacious Tatas	42. Kajoobies
11. Boobies	43. Kettledrums
12. Boobs	44. Knockers
13. Boulders	45. Lemons
14. Bouncers	46. Love Bubbles
15. Bra Busters	47. Lungs
16. Bubbies	48. Lung Warts
17. Bulbs	49. Maracas
18. Bumpers	50. Marshmallows
19. Butter Bags	51. Melons
20. Charlies	52. Milk Bottles
21. Charms	53. The Milky Way
22. Chestnuts	54. Mosquito Bites
23. Cream Jugs	55. Mountains
24. Cupcakes	56. Muffins
25. Dairies	57. Murphies
26. Dinner	58. Oranges
27. Droopers	59. Pantry Shelves
28. Eyes	60. Peaches
29. Feeding Bottles	61. The Playground
30. Fried Eggs	62. Superdroopers
31. Garbanzos	63. Swingers
32. Gazongas	64. Teacups

65. Tonsils
66. Torpedos
67. The Treasure Chest
68. Tremblers
69. Twin Loveliness
70. The Twins
71. The Udders
72. The Upper Deck
73. The Upper Works
74. Warts
75. Watermelons

39 Egregious Movie Blunders

Movies being the collaborative nightmare that they are, it is not surprising that many supposedly "finished" films are released replete with flaming boo-boos galore. Spotting, noting, and cataloging these big screen bungles has become a much-loved hobby for many film fans, and in a few cases has even turned into a cottage industry unto itself.

Premiere magazine welcomes hearing about movie mistakes from readers and has for years highlighted these slip-ups in a section of the magazine called "The Gaffe Squad." (They humorously conclude most of the month's listing of gaffes with a sentiment akin to, "We're sure the producers regret their errors.")

There are also many magazines and newspaper articles that have been published about movie bloopers, and as feature films continue to be made it's a given that many more such blush-inducers will inevitably appear. (Journalists are an intrepid lot, aren't they, seeing as how they're always so considerately on the lookout for someone else's screw up?!)

But the title "Lord of the Lapse" must go to the stalwart Bill Givens, author and compiler of the *Film Flubs* book series published by Citadel. Bill and his "Sharp-Eyed, Quick-Witted Gaffe Spotter Squad" have taken upon themselves the job of recording cinematic faux pas for posterity, and the result is more fun for a film fan than should be legal. Bill's four *Film Flubs* books contain mistakes from literally hundreds and hundreds of films, and it does an obsessive/compulsive's heart good to know that there are others out there who fixate simply to fixate.

Over the years I too have always greatly enjoyed noting "uh-ohs" in movies. After a while I stopped writing them down, although I do remember that one of the first ones I ever noticed was the camera crew's reflection in a storefront window in Woody Allen's *Take the Money and Run*. (I later wrote a book about Woody and his work called *The Woody Allen Companion* and, of course, forgot to mention the blooper.) Another scene I recall catching immediately was the car make-out scene in *Animal House* in which Otter's date is first braless and then completely covered up when she leaps out the car window.

For those of you who want to OD on movie mistakes, I heartily recommend Bill's *Film Flubs* series. I'll be honest, though, and admit that some of the mistakes his Gaffe Squad uncovers are a bit too esoteric for me. (Such as his comparison of mismatched exteriors and his noting of directional incongruities: Those are not really of much interest to me.) I prefer blatant, obvious errors that are, above all, genuinely funny.

Other excellent sources for film information are Roger Ebert's *Movie Home Companion;* any of the mass-market film guides, including Leonard Maltin's, and Mick Martin and Marsha Porter's; as well as books such as *The Golden Turkey Awards, Film Turkeys, The Phantom's Ultimate Video Guide,* and *Bad Movies We Love.* Also do not overlook magazines such as *Film Threat, Entertainment Weekly, Premiere,* and *Movieline.* These books and publications often reveal errors in continuity and other head scratchers in their reviews and are a goldmine of information for the movie buff.

Here are thirty-nine of my favorite blunders from thirty-seven popular films. (Four of *Gone With the Wind*'s bloopers are thoughtfully provided.)

1. **1939, *Gone With the Wind:*** There are several bloopers in America's favorite film. Here are four of them: (1) there's a light bulb visible in a lamppost years before the invention of the incandescent bulb; (2) when the carriages move up the Twelve Oaks driveway the day of the barbecue, the shadows of the trees do not fall on the vehicles (the trees and the drive were both special effects and the FX team did not have time to paint the shadows onto the carriages); (3) Scarlett's garnet necklace disappears and reappears in the Twelve Oaks nap scene; and (4) when Melanie and Scarlett kneel at the bed of a dying soldier, their shadows do not correspond with their positions or their movements.

2. **1939, *The Wizard of Oz:*** Auntie Em miscounts the chickens in the early barnyard scene.

3. **1941, *The Maltese Falcon:*** Peter Lorre's tie changes from polka-dot to striped.

4. **1954, *Rear Window:*** Jimmy Stewart's cast switches legs in one scene.

5. **1956, *The Ten Commandments:*** A blind man is seen wearing a watch.

6. **1959, *North by Northwest:*** A young boy can be seen covering his ears just before Eva Marie Saint shoots Cary Grant.

7. **1959, *Operation Petticoat:*** A little boy calls Cary Grant "Mr. Grant."

8. **1960, *North to Alaska:*** John Wayne's toupee comes off during a fight scene.

9. **1963, *The Birds:*** The attacking birds cast no shadows on the ground beneath them.

10. **1966, *One Million Years B.C.:*** The cavewomen are wearing false eyelashes.

11. **1966, *The Bible:*** Adam has a belly button.

12. **1966, *The Fortune Cookie:*** Walter Matthau is forty pounds lighter from one scene to the next. Matthau had a heart attack during filming and had to take five months off. Thus the weight loss.

13. **1967, *Casino Royale:*** David Niven's mansion is blown up, then intact, then blown up again.

14. **1969, *Butch Cassidy and the Sundance Kid:*** Sundance fires seventeen shots from two six-shooters.

15. **1969, *Easy Rider:*** Peter Fonda's watch changes from a Rolex to a Timex.

16. **1969, *Take the Money and Run:*** The camera crew is reflected in a store window.

17. **1970, *Love Story:*** The hospital where Jenny dies is across the street from the skating rink from which Oliver and Jenny originally took a cab from to get to the same hospital.

18. **1972, *The Godfather:*** Michael shoots the police chief in the neck but the bullet hole is seen in the guy's forehead.

19. **1977, *Star Wars:*** Mark Hamill calls Princess Leia "Carrie." (Princess Leia was played by Carrie Fisher, remember?)

20. **1979, *Star Trek—The Motion Picture:*** This one is so obvious it's almost unbelievable it slipped through. A soundstage is visible in a scene where Captain Kirk floats away from the Enterprise.

21. **1982, *Star Trek II: The Wrath of Khan:*** This just might be my favorite blooper of all time. When Khan first sees Chekhov in the marooned Botany Bay, he says, "I never forget a face."

He is, of course, referring to the *Star Trek* TV episode "Space Seed" in which Khan and his crew were reanimated. They then tried to take over the Enterprise. Fine. Only one problem: Chekhov was not on the Enterprise (Walter Koenig was not yet part of the show's cast) for the "Space Seed" episode.

22. 1987, *Wall Street:* A reference is made to the explosion of the space shuttle *Challenger,* which took place in January of 1986, but the film takes place in 1985.

23. 1988, *Funny Farm:* Chevy Chase's clothes are dry after jumping in a lake.

24. 1988, *The Last Temptation of Christ:* Christ's robe has a label in it.

25. 1988, *Walker:* I love this one. Someone who can read sign language reported to Bill Givens that in one scene of *Walker,* Marlee Matlin actually signs, "Fuck off," which was apparently not the intended line of dialogue.

26. 1989, *Driving Miss Daisy:* A Styrofoam cup is used years before its invention.

27. 1989, *Indiana Jones and the Last Crusade:* Hitler misspells his own name. He writes "Adolph" instead of "Adolf."

28. 1989, *Pet Sematary:* The flowers on Gage's grave disappear from one scene to the next.

29. 1989, *The Abyss:* A dead guy in the sunken ship blinks.

30. 1989, *The War of the Roses:* Michael Douglas says, "No, no, DeVito," to Danny DeVito.

31. 1990, *GoodFellas:* Ray Liotta's religious medal changes from a Star of David to a cross.

32. 1990, *Presumed Innocent:* A reporter's hand-held tape recorder has no tape in it.

33. 1990, *Pretty Woman:* An usher calls Julia Roberts "Julia" instead of "Vivian."

34. 1990, *Rocky V:* Sylvester Stallone calls Burt Young "Burt" instead of "Paulie."

35. 1991, *Terminator 2: Judgment Day:* Linda Hamilton's running bare feet make the sound of shoes hitting the floor.

36. 1991, *The Doors:* Meg Ryan calls Val Kilmer "Val" instead of "Jim" (Morrison).

The 10 Favorite Sexual Activities Men and Women Prefer for Themselves, According to the *Khan Report on Sexual Preferences*

Are men and women turned on by the same things?

No way, José.

Here is a comparative look at the sexual activities men and women prefer for themselves. Being aware of this information might help your relationship with your lover, so pay attention, willya?

Men's Favorites

1. Oral sex, female on male.
2. Viewing a nude female.
3. Intercourse with the woman on top.
4. Nude male/female petting.
5. Viewing a partially clad female.
6. Three-way sex: Two men and one woman engaged in intercourse and/or oral sex.
7. Female on male sadomasochistic activity.
8. Oral sex, male on female.
9. Intercourse with the man on top.
10. Partially clad male/female petting.

Women's Favorites

1. Oral sex, male on female.
2. Three-way sex: Two men and one woman engaged in inter-course and/or oral sex.
3. Nude male/female petting.
4. Intercourse with the woman on top.
5. Partially clad male/female petting.
6. Intercourse with man on top.
7. Male on female sadomasochistic activity.
8. Viewing a nude male.
9. Oral sex, female on male.
10. Watching a male masturbate to orgasm.

Body Count: U.S. Battle Deaths in 9 Wars

A total of 652,769 Americans have died during battle in nine wars since 1775. In 1993, this averaged out to approximately 3,000 battle deaths for every year of this country's existence, or more than eight per day, every single day that the United States has been in existence.

The reality: One of the costs of keeping America alive is eight human beings a day.

1. World War II (1941–45):   292,131
2. The Civil War (1861–65):   214,938 (both sides)
3. World War I (1914–18):   53,513
4. The Vietnam War (1964–75):   47,356
5. The Korean War (1950–53):   33,629
6. The Revolutionary War (1775–81): 6,824
7. The War of 1812 (1812–15):   2,260
8. The Mexican War (1846–48):   1,733
9. The Spanish-American War (1898):   385

54 Forms of Divination

The Encyclopedia of Psychic Science defines divination as "[A method of] exploring the unknown or the future by scrying practices, dreams, drugs, omens or reading of the stars." And just what exactly is an omen? Well, as you'll see from this feature, an omen can be anything from entrails to arrows, and they are used in ways that go beyond being simply creative. Many of these practices move into the realm of being truly *odd*. Thus, this form of existential musing was a natural for *The Odd Index*.

This listing of forms of divination ranges from aeromancy, which is using atmospheric phenomena such as thunder, lightning, and comets to tell the future, to xylomancy, which is the Slavonic method of telling the future using the position of randomly found small pieces of wood you happen to come across during a journey. Note, for instance, how often fingernails figure into the process.

For brevity, most forms of divination will be defined by the objects used. For instance, for anthropomancy, I will not say "The entrails of men and women are studied to tell the future," but rather, "Male and female entrails."

1. **Aeromancy:** Observation of atmospheric phenomena such as thunder, lightning, clouds, comets, and storms.
2. **Alectryomancy:** A rooster pecked seeds of grain off letters drawn in a circle and spelled out the name of a person.
3. **Aleuromancy:** Messages written on paper were wrapped in balls of flour and then mixed up nine times and distributed. The person's fate was revealed by the flour ball they received. (This seems to have been the ancestral forefather of the Chinese fortune cookie.)
4. **Alomancy:** Salt.
5. **Alphitomancy:** Barley was given to people suspected of crimes. Whoever got sick from eating it was guilty.

6. **Amniomancy:** The flesh "caul" membrane found on the faces of some newborns.
7. **Anthropomancy:** Male and female entrails.
8. **Apantomancy:** Chance meetings, especially with animals.
9. **Arithmancy:** Numbers.
10. **Armomancy:** Examination of the shoulders.
11. **Axinomancy:** An axe or a hatchet.
12. **Belomancy:** Arrows.
13. **Bibliomancy:** A person suspected of being a wizard or sorcerer was weighed. If he weighed less than the local church's Bible, he was innocent.
14. **Botanomancy:** Carved-in questions appeared on burned brier branches.
15. **Capnomancy:** The observation of smoke. (Sometimes smoke from the burning of poppy seeds.)
16. **Catoptromancy:** Use of a mirror.
17. **Causimomancy:** Fire.
18. **Ceraunoscopy:** Examination of the air.
19. **Ceroscopy:** Melted wax disks were read by a magician.
20. **Cleromancy:** The throwing of lots, using black and white beans, bones, stones, and so on.
21. **Clidomancy:** The name of a person who figures into some situation is written on a key then hung on a Bible. The Bible is then hung on the fingernail of the ring finger of a virgin. The direction in which the swaying book turns determines the fate of the person in question.
22. **Coscinomancy:** A sieve, a pair of scissors, and the thumb nails of two people are used in concert to determine innocence or guilt. The sieve is hung by a thread from the shears supported on the thumb nails of the two people in question. The direction of the sieve's spin determines the guilty party.
23. **Critomancy:** Cakes.
24. **Crystalomancy:** Also known as crystal gazing, this form of divination involves a seer looking into a crystal ball or some similar object to tell the future.
25. **Dactylomancy:** Rings.
26. **Daphnomancy:** Throwing a laurel branch into a fire.
27. **Demonomancy:** Turning to demons for occult knowledge.
28. **Eromanty:** The use of air. The Persians devised this method of divination in which they would breathe over a vase filled

with water. Bubbles in the water meant that the objects of their desire would come to them.

29. **Gastromancy:** Seers would hear voices emanate from a person's belly and answer questions. This was often just a fraudulent form of ventriloquism.

30. **Gyromancy:** A small circle was drawn on the ground and the letters of the alphabet were written on its circumference. The person who wanted an answer to a question stood inside the circle and was spun around repeatedly until he was too dizzy to stand up. The letters he stumbled over as he fell out of the circle spelled out his answer.

31. **Hippomancy:** The movement of certain sacred white horses divined the future.

32. **Hydromancy:** This refers to various uses of water as a means of divination, including throwing things into water and suspending things on a string over water.

33. **Kephalonomancy:** This is one of those ancient practices that makes us curious about just how weird those ancients actually were. I mean, who *came up* with these things? This practice involved burning a piece of carbon on the head of an ass (or sometimes a goat) and reciting the name of suspected criminals. If a crackling sound was heard when a certain person's name was mentioned, the guy was guilty as charged.

34. **Lithomancy:** Any number of forms of divination using stones.

35. **Margaritomancy:** A pearl was placed beneath an upside down vase. As in many other forms of divination, the names of suspected bad guys were then recited. When a guilty person's name was mentioned, the pearl would fly upward and shatter the bottom of the vase.

36. **Muscle Reading:** A form of fortune telling in which a seer reads the unconscious muscle movements of a person who is suspected of knowing some truth that needs to be revealed. It was based on the principle that muscles (especially throat muscles) will shape themselves into the position of a name thought of by a person. A qualified seer could then interpret the movements as words.

37. **Myomancy:** The behavior of rats or mice.

38. **Necromancy:** The spirits of the dead reveal the future and answer questions.

39. **Onimancy:** Divination by observation of a manifestation of the angel Uriel after oil of walnuts mingled with tallow is placed on the fingernails of an "unpolluted" boy or a young virgin.
40. **Onomancy:** The spelling of and distribution of vowels and consonants in a person's name.
41. **Onychomancy:** Divination by observing the sun's reflection in a person's fingernails.
42. **Oomantia:** Eggs.
43. **Ornithomancy:** The flight and/or song of birds.
44. **Phyliorhodomancy:** Rose leaves.
45. **Psychomancy:** This is similar to necromancy in that the spirits of the dead are invoked for purposes of divination.
46. **Psychometry:** Telling the future by holding something possessed by a person.
47. **Pyromancy:** Telling the future by reading fire.
48. **Rhabdomancy:** Using a rod or a staff for divination.
49. **Rhapsodamancy:** This method of divination involved opening a book of randomly selected poetry and reading the first verse the eye fell upon.
50. **Spodomancy:** Divination by reading the ashes and cinders of any number of different sacrificial fires.
51. **Stolcheomancy:** A form of **rhapsodamancy** in which the works of Homer or Virgil are used.
52. **Stolisomancy:** The way a person dresses.
53. **Sycomancy:** The leaves of the fig tree.
54. **Xylomancy:** The Slavonic method of telling the future using the position of randomly found small pieces of wood you happen to come across during a journey.

6 Forms of Penis Modification

Penis modification is one of the most extreme forms of strange sexual behavior known to man. (When I say "man," I am, of course, not speaking generically of mankind.)

Why change your penis? As you'll see from the following feature, penis modification is used to enhance the organ for sex. With penis modification, the penis is almost looked upon not as an organ we should be accepting of and pleased with, but rather as a tool that should be improved, if possible.

I personally find the whole idea of changing the organ you were born with a horrifying prospect. Just the pain potential alone is enough to make the average male pale. And yet, as you'll see from the following feature, such surgeries are indeed done.

1. **Bihari Surgery:** During *Bihari Surgery* a ligament in the groin above the penis is surgically severed. This allows what is essentially a dangling erection. This apparently makes men who have the surgery look better endowed than they actually are. It probably also allows for a wider variety of sexual positions, in that the post-surgery penis has a wider range of motion than the normal erection, which is suspended upright from the groin. The procedure was named after an Egyptian doctor.

2. **Foreskin Restoration:** There are two types of *foreskin restoration* currently being done. The first involves stretching the skin of the flaccid penis a little at a time until enough new skin has grown to cover the head of the penis. (Each stretch tears the skin, to which the body responds by growing more.) This process could take years.

   The second—a skin graft procedure—is even more bizarre. Mark Waring, author of the 1988 book *Foreskin Restoration*, describes this procedure, and it is also discussed in

Brenda Love's (yes, that's her real name) *The Encyclopedia of Unusual Sex Practices:*

[The skin graft method] consists of cutting the ring of skin approximately an inch below the glans penis, pulling the top skin forward so that it covers the glans, then cutting two parallel openings into the scrotum that are perpendicular to the penis. The penis is then inserted into this open pocket so that the cut area on the penis is covered, yet the top of the glans still extrudes far enough for urination. The man is sent home and after almost a year returns for the second surgical procedure which consists of detaching the skin surrounding the penis from the scrotum and securing it into place. Complications with this type of surgery include scarring, disfiguring, and possible growth of scrotal hair on the new foreskin.

Foreskin restoration is apparently so popular that it even has its own magazine, *Foreskin Quarterly,* and its own professional organization, Brothers United for Future Foreskins (BUFF).

3. **Meatotomy:** This is one even I couldn't believe when I first read about it. Even though my source book had a black-and-white line drawing of a "meatotimized" penis, this is one of those incredibly bizarre forms of sexual oddness that I would actually pay to see in the flesh. Well, on video, actually. I'm sure that there are some specialized X-rated video dealers who may actually have movies that include this practice, but in my research I have not yet come across a tape that included it. Meatotomy, like penis dividing, is almost unbelievable, but it is done. Meatotomy is the deliberate enlargement of the urethra. The way it's done (and I can sense the males out there cringing already) is by inserting progressively larger and larger diameter catheters into the urethra during masturbation, each time tearing and widening the urethral tube and then allowing it to heal in the larger size. Each time the urethra is torn, new skin grows to fill in the tear until after many deliberate enlargements the urethra is *huge.* There are men, I am told, who have enlarged their urethras so much that they can accept the head of another man's penis into the opening.

4. **Penis Implants:** This modification is not to be confused with the procedure of implanting a rod or inflatable tube in an

impotent man's penis in order to allow him to have intercourse. This type of implanting has as its goal making the
penis look like a French tickler condom. (You know, the
ones with all the bumps?) Men into this type of "improve-
ment" slice open the skin of their penis shaft, insert balls,
stones, beads, pearls, and other solid, hard, usually round
objects into the slits and then allow the incisions to close
and heal. There are some women who greatly enjoy this type
of erection enhancement, although I can imagine it being
somewhat uncomfortable for the "modified" man when he is
not having sex. Especially if he wears BVDs.

5. **Penis Inserts:** This is like piercing (see "Body Parts People
Pierce"), except a bar or a ring is inserted into the head of
the penis, configured so that it enters through the urethra
and comes out beneath the head. Ouch.

6. **Penis Dividing:** This bizarre procedure involves actually cutting the penis in half, from the head to the groin. The organ
is surgically bifurcated lengthwise down the shaft, and when
the surgery is performed properly, the two halves can heal
into two separate (although joined at the base), fully functioning penises. Of course, at the very least, this type of surgery requires a board certified urologist surgeon and a
plastic surgeon. (It's probably not a bad idea to have a psychiatrist involved as well, know what I mean?)

Department of Peculiar Parlance:
195 Euphemisms for the Penis

What is it about we men and our members anyway? We seem to
be so enamored of our "dangling participle" that we not only
treat it like a king but bestow upon it names, names, and more
names.

The following list of euphemisms for the penis runs the gamut
from descriptive (The Baby Maker) and imagistic (The Foaming
Beef Probe), to vulgar (The Honeypot Cleaver) and bewildering
(Zubrick?). As intellectual Woody Allen has been known to admit,

his brain is his *second* favorite organ. This list effectively illustrates why he feels that way. (And I dare you to try to read this list aloud without laughing. I'll bet you can't get through a dozen names before cracking up.)

1. Ass Opener
2. Baby Maker
3. Bald-Headed Hermit
4. Baloney Pony
5. Banana
6. Battering Ram
7. Bean Tosser
8. Beef Bayonet
9. Best Leg of Three
10. Bishop
11. Blow Torch
12. Bone
13. Boy
14. Broom Handle
15. Bug Fucker
16. Bum Tickler
17. Burrito
18. Bush Beater
19. Bushwhacker
20. Candle
21. Carrot
22. Cherry Picker
23. Club
24. Coral Branch
25. Crack Hunter
26. Creamstick
27. Crimson Chitterling
28. Crotch Cobra
29. Cucumber
30. Dangling Participle
31. Dart of Love
32. Ding Dong
33. Dingus
34. Dipstick
35. Divining Rod
36. Dong
37. Donkey
38. Dork
39. Dragon
40. Dribbling Dart of Love
41. Drumstick
42. Eel
43. Eye Opener
44. Fishing Rod
45. Foaming Beef Probe
46. Fool Sticker
47. Frankfurter
48. Gardener
49. Giggle Stick
50. Girlometer
51. Gooser
52. Goose's Neck
53. Gravy Maker
54. Grinding Tool
55. Gun
56. Hair Splitter
57. Hammer
58. Hanging Johnny
59. Holy Poker
60. Honeypot Cleaver
61. Horn
62. Hose
63. Irish Root
64. Jack-in-the-Box
65. Jiggling Bone
66. Joy Stick
67. Kidney Scraper
68. Kosher Pickle
69. A Ladies' Delight
70. Ladies' Lollipop
71. Lance of Love
72. Licorice Stick

73. Life Preserver
74. Live Sausage
75. Lizard
76. Lobster
77. Love Dart
78. Love Muscle
79. Love Pump
80. Love Sausage
81. Lung Disturber
82. Magic Wand
83. Master of Ceremonies
84. Martimonial Peacemaker
85. Maypole
86. Meat Whistle
87. Middle Leg
88. Milkman
89. Mr. Happy
90. Muscle of Love
91. Mutton Dagger
92. Nag
93. Needle
94. Nine Inch Knocker
95. Old Slimy
96. Our One-Eyed Brother
97. One-Eyed Milkman
98. One-Eyed Monster
99. One-Eyed Pants Mouse
100. One-Eyed Trouser Snake
101. One-Eyed Wonder
102. One-Eyed Worm
103. One-Eyed Zipper Snake
104. Peacemaker
105. Pee-Wee
106. Pen
107. Pencil
108. Piccolo
109. Pile Driver
110. Pilgrim's Staff
111. Pink Oboe
112. Pioneer of Nature
113. Pipe
114. Pisser
115. Pistol
116. Plug
117. Plunger
118. Pointer
119. Poker
120. Pole
121. Pork Sword
122. Prong
123. Pump Handle
124. Quim Wedge
125. Ram
126. Rammer
127. Ramrod
128. Raw Meat
129. Reamer
130. Red Hot Poker
131. Rod of Love
132. Rolling Pin
133. Rooster
134. Root
135. Roto-Rooter
136. Rumpleforeskin
137. Rump Splitter
138. Saint Peter
139. Sceptre
140. Schlong
141. Schvontz
142. Schween
143. Screwdriver
144. Serpent
145. Shaft of Cupid
146. Short Arm
147. Silent Flute
148. Skin Flute
149. Small Arm
150. Snake
151. Spigot
152. Split-Ass Mechanic
153. Staff
154. Stallion

155. Star Gazer
156. Stick
157. Stretcher
158. Stump
159. Sugar Stick
160. Sweet Meat
161. Swizzle Stick
162. Sword
163. Tail Pipe
164. Tally Whacker
165. Tent Peg
166. Thingamabob
167. Third Leg
168. Thumb of Love
169. Tickler
170. Tool
171. Torch of Cupid
172. Toy
173. Trigger
174. Tube
175. Tube Steak
176. Tummy Banana
177. Uncle Dick
178. Wand
179. Wang
180. Water Spout
181. Wazoo
182. Weapon
183. Wedge
184. Weenie
185. Whacker
186. Whang
187. Whang Bone
188. Whanger
189. Whip
190. Whistle
191. Whore Pipe
192. Worm
193. Wriggling Pole
194. Yum-Yum
195. Zubrick

7 Freakish and Odd Physical Things That Can Go Wrong with the Human Body

Est modus in rebus, sunt certi denique fines,
Quos ultra citraque nequit consistere rectum.
(Things have their due measure; there are ultimately
fixed limits, beyond which, or short of which,
something must be wrong.)—Horace, *Satires*

Barnum and Bailey used to advertise their freak show as "The Peerless Prodigies of Physical Phenomena and Great Presentation of Marvelous Living Human Curiosities." It might have been hyperbolic, but it sure as hell worked to draw the crowds.

Throughout man's time on this planet, things have consistently gone wrong with the development of the fetus in utero, or later, with growth and/or the health of some particular body part or function. In the past, before modern medicine, often these "freaks of nature" died. In many cases, however, they survived and had to earn their keep by exhibiting their deformities in circus freak shows. (Tod Browning's classic 1932 film *Freaks* chronicles life in a freak show.)

This feature looks at seven of the things that can go wrong with the human body before or after birth. (Often things such as weird abilities or skin disorders don't manifest themselves until later in life.)

We've all seen the new mommy and daddy counting their new baby's toes and fingers. There's good cause for that practice, as you'll see from the following.

1. **Bizarre Eyeball and Ear Abilities:** Some people can pop their eyeballs out of their sockets and blow smoke through their eyes and out of their ears. It's true. I've seen pictures.

2. **Bizarre Skin Disorders:** Strange types of human skin have included alligator-like skin, skin that can be stretched like rubber, and hard, elephant-like skin.

3. **Enormous Testicles:** This is actually a disease called elephantiasis. *The Bantam Medical Dictionary* defines the disease as "a gross enlargement of the skin and underlying tissues caused by obstruction of the lymph vessels, which prevents drainage of lymph from the surrounding tissues. Inflammation and thickening of the walls of the vessels and their eventual blocking is commonly caused by the parasitic filarial worms. The parts most commonly affected are the legs but the scrotum, breasts, and vulva may also be involved. Elastic bandaging is applied to the affected parts and the limbs are elevated and rested."

   Elephantiasis is mostly found in tropical countries. Explicit photos of afflicted natives are common in many books about freaks and human oddities. In some men, their scrotum enlarges to the size of a large watermelon and bigger. In some cases, the scrotum becomes so large it is big enough to be sat upon like a hassock.

   The treatment for elephantiasis is the drug diethylcarbamazine, which kills the worm larvae that are in the bloodstream.

4. **Huge or Extra Breasts:** Extra breasts or nipples is called polymastia or pleomastia. In 1886, two women lived who both had ten breasts each, all of which secreted milk. In eighteenth-century France, a polymastic woman named Madame Ventre lived in Marseilles. Madame Ventre had a fully functioning, lactating breast sticking out of her left thigh just below her waist. In 1894, a case was reported of a man who possessed eight breasts. In modern times, one of the most visible victims of polymastia is rapper Marky Mark, who has three nipples. The third nipple is airbrushed out of his underwear ads.

   Huge breasts is another condition involving women's mammary glands. (Enlarged breasts in males has its own name: gynecomastia.) One case involved a woman whose breasts weighed 44 pounds and measured 33 inches in circumference. I have seen a photo of this woman topless and her breasts looked like two huge sacks of grain extending from the middle of her chest, across her lap, and all the way down to her knees.

5. **Huge Buttocks:** This is called steatopygia, characterized by the accumulation of *huge* amounts of fat in the buttocks. It is also called the "Hottentot Bustle," named after the Hottentot Tribe of Africa where this condition was first noted. Today, this grotesque enlargement of the buttocks is thought by the medical establishment to be possibly an evolutionary development that allows the storage of large amounts of body fat without impeding heat loss from the rest of the body. Another characteristic of steatopygia is long labia minor that hang down between the knees.

6. **No Arms:** People born without arms become incredibly adept at doing things with their feet and toes. Some astonishing abilities manifested by these armless wonders include painting, playing the violin, shooting a rifle, driving a carriage, writing "longfoot," driving a car, playing the mandolin, playing cards, and doing carpentry work. One British man with no arms was such a talented foot pianist that he performed on concert tours and earned his living as Tommy Toes Jacobsen.

7. **Siamese Twin Syndrome:** Siamese twins are twins born joined together at some body part, and sometimes sharing common internal organs. The term *Siamese twin* came from the twins Chang and Eng, who were born conjoined at the stomach in Siam in 1874. Two terms used to describe conjoined twins are *Sephalopagi,* which means joined at the top of the head, and *ischiopagi,* meaning joined at the groin. Sometimes the twin is alive and functioning; sometimes the twin is just a parasitic non-viable appendage that juts out from somewhere on the host's body.

Here is a rundown of 17 notable Siamese twins:

Betty Lou Williams: Betty Lou had a twin growing out of her waist that had buttocks and a pair of legs.

Bill Durks: Bill was two-faced. Literally. He possessed two noses and two eyes and, for commercial purposes, painted a third eye in the middle of his forehead. Bill's mouth was split at the middle of his upper lip and looked like two mouths.

Daisy and Violetta Hilton: These conjoined girls were stunningly beautiful and both were talented musicians. They were joined at the hips and yet both had very active sex lives. They claimed to be able to separate themselves mentally when the other was having sex.

Donni and Ronnie Galyon: These two males were joined at the stomach.

Edward Mordrake: I wonder if this guy was called "Ed the Head"? Mordrake had a second face on the back of his head that could laugh and cry but not eat or speak.

Frank Lentini: Frank was born in 1889 in Sicily and had three legs and two complete sets of sex organs. Photographs exist of Frank showing the camera his extra leg and two penises.

Laloo: Laloo was a Hindu who was born in Oudh in 1874. He had a headless twin attached to his body at the neck. The twin had two arms and two legs, and a functioning set of genitals. The twin could urinate and get an erection.

Liou-Tang-Sen and Lious-Seng-Sen: Two males who were joined by a thin strip of skin at the stomach.

Macha and Dacha: These guys had two complete upper bodies and two heads, and shared one lower body.

Margaret and Mary Gibb: These girls were joined at the buttocks and refused to separate even though doctors believed the operation would be successful. They died together in 1967.

Margarete Clark: She had a twin growing out of her belly. It looked as though the twin's head was stuck in Margarete's belly, face down, with the buttocks facing away from Margarete's body.

Millie and Christina: These were conjoined slave girls who were born in 1851 in North Carolina. Their father was an American Indian, and their mother was a mulatto slave. They were joined at the back.

Myrthe Corbin: Myrthe Corbin, a woman from Clebourne, Texas, had a twin growing out from between her legs. Myrthe had four legs, twenty toes, and two vaginas. She married in 1882 and during her life had five children, four girls and one boy. Three of her children were born from one body, and two were born from the other. Myrthe's husband usually had intercourse in the twin's vagina.

Pasquel Piñon: Pasquel was born in Mexico in 1917 and had a extra head on his forehead.

Rita and Christina: These Siamese twins were born in 1829

in Sassari, Sardinia, and had a double body above the waist. They had two heads, four arms, four lungs, two hearts, two stomachs, one bladder, and two legs.

Rosa and Josepha Blazek: These twins were born in Bohemia in the late eighteenth century and were joined at the waist. They had one anus, but two vaginas. In 1910, Rosa got pregnant and had a baby. Josepha claimed not to have been aware of her sister having sex, although many Siamese twins claim that their nervous systems are somehow linked to their twins and that they feel what the other feels.

The Tocci Brothers: These Italian twins were born in 1877 and had two heads and two upper torsos, but shared one set of legs.

The 36 Highest-Cholesterol Foods Known to Man

I read an article in *USA Today* the other day that meat is making a comeback.

Apparently, people are indulging again in big thick steaks (as well as ice cream and fried foods) when they eat out in a restaurant. The meat industry is eagerly preparing for the beginning of the next ten-year "red meat" cycle. Meat consumption peaked in 1976 and 1986. The next peak year should be 1996, and cattle ranchers can't wait.

This feature looks at one of the drawbacks of meat consumption: cholesterol. Cholesterol is a fatty substance found only in animal protein. Cholesterol clings to your artery walls like the thick brown gunk that lined the walls of people's houses in the Midwest after the 1993 Mississippi River floods finally receded. (The Midwesterners call the stuff "gumbo.") The difference, however, is that cholesterol can't be scraped off your arteries all that easily, and if enough of it builds up, it's goodbye, Charlie.

The medical establishment would like us all to have cholesterol levels of 200 or lower. This means that, as a rule, you would have to restrict your daily cholesterol intake to 100 mgs or less. One hard-cooked egg, at 274 mgs., shoots your wad for the day.

Here are 36 foods and dishes that, if partaken of on a regular basis, will make your cardiologist shake his head and start talking about the wisdom of "pre-need" funeral planning.

Bon appetit!

Food	Cholesterol Content (mg.)
1. 3 oz. cooked pork brains	2,169
2. 3 oz. cooked beef brains	1,746
3. 1 cup stabilized dry eggs	1,714

4. 1 cup plain dry eggs 1,615
5. 6 oz. cooked beef sweetbreads 1,560
   [thymus]
6. 1 cup egg salad 1,124
7. 7 oz. braised lamb sweetbreads 932
8. 1 cup stewed chicken liver 884
9. 1 cup stewed turkey liver 876
10. 6 oz. braised pork spleen 856
11. 1 cup scrambled eggs 854
12. 1 whole fried chicken with skin, batter- 810
    dipped
13. 2 slices braised beef kidney 750
14. 1 whole duck, roasted with skin 640
15. 1 jar Gerber's Egg Yolks Baby Food 622
16. 6 oz. braised pork liver 604
17. 1 2-egg omelet 536
19. 3 oz. cooked pork kidney 408
20. 1 cup braised beef heart 398
21. 2 cup cheese soufflé 392
22. 3 oz. fried beef liver 372
23. 1 cup stewed turkey gizzards 336
24. 1 serving chicken giblets, floured and 335
    fried
25. 1 cup stewed turkey heart 328
26. 2 slices Quiche Lorraine (9″ pie) 318
27. 12 oz. roasted turkey breast with skin 310
28. 4 tablespoons Hollandaise sauce 298
29. 1 hard-cooked egg 274
30. 6 oz. cooked pork tongue 248
31. 6 oz. cooked pork chitterlings 244
32. 1 raw duck liver 227
33. 1 6-oz. pork fritter 222
34. 1 cup turkey fat 209
35. 8 oz. eggnog 150
36. 1 cup cooked pork sausage 124

Department of Peculiar Parlance:
33 Euphemisms for Defecation

We all have to do it, and strangely, it is something many of us are quite embarrassed about. From such chagrin do euphemisms blossom. Here are almost three dozen ways of describing the body's way of taking out the garbage.

1. Bury a Quaker
2. Ca-Ca
3. Capoop
4. Chuck a Turd
5. Deposit
6. Dispatch your Cargo
7. Do a Job
8. Drop a Load
9. Drop Turds
10. Drop Your Wax
11. Dump
12. Ease Nature
13. Fill Your Pants
14. George
15. Go Potty
16. Go to the Bathroom
17. Go to the Library
18. Grunt
19. An Irish Shave
20. Make a Deposit
21. Pick a Daisy
22. Poop
23. Poo-Poo
24. Post a Letter
25. Relieve Yourself
26. See John
27. Shit
28. Smell the Place Up
29. Soil Your Linens
30. Squat
31. Squeeze Cheeks
32. Take a Crap
33. Take a Dump

25 Horrific Tortures and Punishments Through the Ages

This feature details some of the ways humans have devised to inflict pain upon fellow humans. What is it about certain people that causes them to be so creative and inventive when it comes to finding new ways to get to Agony Plaza? Is it a brain chemistry kind of thing? Or is it purely environmental?

The guy having his testicles removed by having them tied off and "strangulated" probably doesn't really care that much about how his castrator came to his dream career. Some of these vile acts are still being practiced today.

1. **Bamboo Under the Fingernails** This Chinese torture was agonizingly painful and would often guarantee the confession the torturers wanted. Long thin shoots of sharp bamboo would be inserted beneath the fingernails of the victim, usually all the way back to the cuticle, and then left there. If the prisoner resisted surrendering the wanted information, another finger was done. And another. And then another. If all ten fingers didn't do the trick, there were always the toenails.

2. **The Brank** This was a mean one. Here we have an English device designed to punish women who talked too much. The Brank, also known as the Scolder's Bridle, consisted of a steel cage worn on the head like a helmet. Inside the cage was a protruding steel plate that either had sharp spikes on it or which was cruelly sharpened. This plate was placed in the offending woman's mouth so that if she even moved her tongue she would do major damage to her mouth and tongue and experience excruciating pain. The woman had to wear this contraption in and about town. Occasionally a

chain was attached to the front of the Brank so that she could be led around like a dog on a leash.

3. **Castration** A wire or cord was wrapped around the base of the victim's scrotum and the testicles were either cut off or pulled off. Guys, you may exhale now.

4. **The Chinese Water Torture** We all remember this one from old spy movies, don't we? A prisoner was tied to a table and his head was strapped in place so that he couldn't move anything but his eyes. Water was then dripped onto his forehead, one inexorable drop at a time. Apparently this was absolutely maddening, and after a period the victim would reveal the secret, confess to the crime, or agree to do anything his or her captors requested to get them to stop the drip, drip, drip. This doesn't sound as if it would be too hard to take, but reports from people who have undergone it confirm it to be devilishly effective. This was particularly favored in circumstances where torture was necessary, but no evidence of physical damage could show.

5. **Disemboweling** This could ostensibly be considered a form of execution, in that not too many people can survive having their upper and lower transverse colons and their stomachs surgically removed (without anesthesia of course) and not put back. I've included it here because disembowelment was often used as a means of torture/punishment during which the victim just happened to die. Victims of this horrible torment were usually tied to a post or a tree. Their abdomen was then sliced open and their innards pulled out and either left hanging or cut out completely and thrown on the ground. Sometimes the victim was forced to watch his guts set on fire while he was still alive. Needless to say, because of the violent trauma to the body, it did not take long for this form of torture to turn into an execution. Vlad the Impaler was a big fan of disembowelment.

6. **The Drunkard's Cloak** If an Englishman was found guilty of public drunkenness, he was often obligated to wear a Drunkard's Cloak, which was essentially a huge, heavy barrel that covered the offender from knees to neck, and from which only his arms, legs, and head protruded. Sometimes weights were hung off the barrel or off the wretch's wrists to make it even more difficult to walk about. This was consid-

ered one of the most humiliating forms of punishment that could be inflicted on an evil-doer.

7. **The Ducking Stool** This was mainly used to punish "scolding women" and women of "bad repute" in England and Scotland, although brewers of bad beer and bakers of bad bread were also punished in this manner. The ducking stool device was either on wheels and mobile or permanently erected by the side of a river. An arm chair (which was usually actually quite comfortable) was fastened to the end of a long (twelve to fifteen feet) wooden beam attached by a bolt in the center of the beam to a cross bar so as to allow the arm to be raised and lowered at will like a see-saw. A rope was hung off the shore end of the bar and the "guilty" woman was repeatedly lowered into the cold water for varying amounts of time "to cool her immoderate heat." Sometimes the man in charge of administering the punishment (and it was *always* a man) would get carried away and leave the woman beneath the water too long and accidentally drown her. The ducking stool was being used as recently as the late 1700s both in England and the colonial United States.

8. **The Finger Pillory** This was what it sounds like: a minipillory designed for one or more fingers. The oak top bar would be closed tightly at the knuckle onto a finger bent into a right angle pointing down. There was no way for the finger to be removed until the bar was opened. As you can imagine, after a short time, the pain was excruciating.

9. **Foot Roasting** This one must have hurt like a bastard. Foot roasting was one of Tomás de Torquemada's favorite Spanish Inquisition tortures and was greatly feared. The procedure for this torment consisted of exactly what its title says: a prisoner's feet were covered with lard and then slow-roasted over a fire for hours. Ouch.

10. **The Garotte** Is it possible that our word *garrote,* meaning strangle or choke, came from this painful Spanish Inquisition torture? You be the judge: The garotte torture involved binding a prisoner to a rack and tying ropes around his arms and legs. The rope was then slowly tightened and tightened until it ate through first skin, then layers of muscle, until it finally reached the bone. If a person was left tied up long enough on the rack, gangrene and blood poisoning

would often set in. But by the time that happened the guy was usually either in shock or dead.

11. **The Garrucha** This was one of the three most-favored Spanish Inquisition tortures. A prisoner's hands were bound behind his back and he was then picked off the floor by his wrists by a chain suspended from the ceiling. When his body reached a certain height, his captors would begin slowly lowering him to the floor with jerky, bouncy pulls on the chain. By the time the victim reached the floor, both of his arms were usually pulled out of their sockets.

12. **Hacking to Pieces** Depending on what and how many body parts were hacked off determined whether this was a torture/punishment or a form of execution. If a hand or a foot (or more than one) was lopped off with a sword or an ax, the victim might survive. Runaway slaves in pre-Civil War America were often hobbled by having one foot chopped off if they were caught. (Remember *Roots?*) Larcenous workers in African diamond mines were also punished in like manner. (Remember *Misery?*) Some Far Eastern countries (Iraq and Iran, in particular) still use amputation of the hands as punishment for certain crimes, especially stealing.

13. **Hat Nailing** Vlad the Impaler, the inspiration for the *Dracula* legend, came up with this one. Two Italian ambassadors once refused to take off their hats in his presence. Their punishment was having their hats nailed to their heads.

14. **Impalement** Impalement was a particular favorite of Vlad the Impaler. This form of torture/execution involved impaling people on wooden spikes and leaving them to die a horrible and painful slow death. The impalement was often done up the rectum, or sometimes through the stomach or heart. Occasionally, for variety, Vlad would impale people upside down through the skull. Sometimes just the head was impaled, but this was more a form of decorating than torture because the owner of the head was usually long dead by the time he was put on display. In Cambodia, Pol Pot's barbarous Khmer Rouge was particularly enamored of head impaling.

15. **The Jougs** This English device was nothing more than an iron collar that opened in the back and had a ring for a padlock in front. The jougs were usually attached by chain to a public site such as a church door or a pole or tree in

the town center. Its primary purpose was to serve as a means for public humiliation, but, as was often the case with our oh-so-inventive forefathers, additional torments were often added to confinement in the jougs.

16. **The Pillory** The pillory was a form of standing stocks. A seventeenth-century historian named Holloway described the pillory at Rye, England: "It measures about six feet in height, by four in width. It consists of two up-posts affixed to a platform, and has two transverse rails, the upper one of which is divided horizontally, and has a hinge to admit of the higher portion being lifted, so as to allow of the introduction of the culprit's head and hands." Offenders were put into the pillory for public humiliation. Often the evidence of the crime (bad meat, stolen bread, and so on) was hung around their neck. Some towns combined a pillory with stocks and a whipping post, providing convenient one-stop punishment. The pillory in and of itself wasn't too bad, but it was the "add-on" punishment that turned this into a genuine torture. Citizens convicted to stand in the pillory often had to also endure having their ears nailed to the pillory, having their ears sliced off after their sentence was served, and having their noses slit open and then burned with a hot iron.

17. **Rape** Women have always known that rape is not a crime of sexual passion but a crime of violence, and throughout the ages the rape of women has been used as a particularly heinous and devastating form of torture. The Serbs are the latest to use rape as a weapon of war. There are reports that Serb troops have been ordered to rape Muslim women at will, even going so far as to chain young girls in "rape rooms" where entire battalions of soldiers gang-rape them in numbing succession. Variations on rape as a form of torture include using sexual congress as the ultimate form of humiliation: after the invading soldiers have had *their* way with the women, fathers are forced to rape their daughters while the mothers watch; sons are forced to rape their mothers; brothers are forced to have sex with their pre-adolescent sisters. Aside from the blatant degrading factor of being raped, another, more insidious reason for the practice is that it contributes to "ethnic cleansing." The raped women often give birth to children sired by the invading soldiers, thus essentially diluting the enemies' blood line.

18. **The Repentance Stool** This old form of Scottish punishment wasn't very violent, but it was considered especially humiliating in that it was carried out in a church before all the other worshipers. The repentance stool was an elevated stool with a foot rest. Persons guilty of adultery were forced to sit on the stool in the front of the church during services and be gazed upon by all the other holier-than-thou parishioners. Sometimes a black hood was put over the person's head.

19. **Riding the Stang** This was a particularly ridiculous form of punishment that once again resorted to public humiliation for maximum deterrent effect. If a man was suspected of beating his wife *or* being henpecked (and modern men think *they're* misunderstood!), his fellow townsfolk would ride the stang for three consecutive nights. Riding the stang basically involved making fun of the suspected husband. The wittiest man in the town would be carried through the streets on a chair carried on the shoulders of some of the other local males. He would beat a drum and make up insulting rhymes about the husband. One (rather humorous) rhyme from Yorkshire, England, went as follows (the language has been modernized for reading ease):

> Heigh dilly, how dilly, heigh dilly dang,
> It's neither for your part nor my part
> That I ride the stang;
> But it is for Jake Soloman—
> His wife he does bang.
> He banged her, he banged her,
> He banged her indeed;
> He banged the poor woman,
> Though she stood him no need.

Do you get the feeling that our forefathers had too much free time on their hands?

20. **Scalding** This consisted of pouring large quantities of boiling water onto a victim's bare skin. One of the most notable sufferers of this torture was a Japanese named Anthony Ixida, who was once scalded for thirty-three days because of his adherence to Catholicism. He was beatified after his death but never canonized as a saint.

21. **Skinning** This involved slowly stripping thick layers of skin

off the victim's body while they remained conscious. Sometimes salt was poured onto the raw exposed flesh.

22. **The Spanish Water Torture** This was a particularly horrifying torture mainly used to extract confessions from suspected criminals. Also known as The Toca, this insidious procedure was used during the Spanish Inquisition and was as feared as foot roasting. A suspect was tied to a rack that swiveled in the middle so that his head could be positioned lower than his feet. The man's head was strapped in place with an iron band and his nose was sealed shut. A thick piece of cloth was then stuffed into his mouth and a slow, steady stream of water was poured into the cloth. The effect combined drowning and suffocation, all while the victim remained completely conscious. This torture was one of anti-Semite Tomás de Torquemada's inventions.

23. **The Stocks** The stocks were a wooden device that had holes in it for the offender's legs. The criminal was locked in the stocks for many hours at a stretch, outdoors, and often had to submit to verbal humiliation as well as confinement. "Bathroom breaks" were not allowed, and after a couple of hours there would be considerable back and leg pain and stiffness.

24. **Teeth Pulling** The torturer would take an iron pincers and, one by one, wrench the victim's teeth out of their mouth. One of the most notable historical personages to undergo this particularly nasty form of persuasion was St. Apollonia, who died in the year 249. Her teeth were yanked for her refusal to renounce her Christianity. She is now the patron saint of dentists. (I'm not kidding.)

25. **Whipping** Flogging was a very popular form of punishment in Olde England, and the scourge of the lash was meted out to both men and women in equal measure. There were two ways a whipping sentence was carried out. One was on a whipping cart, which was wheeled about the town to the sites where a flogging was needed. The guilty party was stripped naked in the street, tied to the back of the cart, and then whipped publicly until his or her body was bloody. The nudity of both men and women alike was a favorite attraction of flogging. The second type of whipping was done at a whipping post, a sturdy piece of pole in the center of a town that the offender was tied to naked and, as on the cart, whipped until bloody. Eventually the nudity requirement

was modified for convicted women: they were only undressed to the waist, much to the dismay of the sadist voy-
eurs who attended all public floggings. A particularly nasty
English judge named Jeffreys is on record as once saying,
"Hangman, I charge you to pay particular attention to this
lady. Scourge her soundly, man; scourge her till her blood
runs down! It is Christmas, a cold time for a madam to strip.
See that you warm her shoulders thoroughly!" On many oc-
casions, a person was whipped until they died.

Department of Peculiar Parlance:
53 Euphemisms for Testicles

Testicle is such a harsh, clinical word, don't you think? The word
even *sounds* like something that would hurt if it was banged or otherwise maltreated. Perhaps that's why society (mainly men, I'll wa-
ger) has concocted so many alternative ways of euphemistically
describing our ridiculously sensitive little friends. Here are 53 ways
of describing a male's *true* Achilles' Heel.

1. Allsbay
2. Apples
3. Bangers
4. Baubles
5. Beecham's Pills
6. Berries
7. Birds' Eggs
8. Booboos
9. Bullets
10. Bum Balls
11. Buttons
12. Cannon Balls
13. Charlies
14. Chestnuts
15. Clangers
16. Clappers
17. Clock Weights
18. Coffee Stalls
19. Cojones
20. Crystals
21. Cubes
22. Danglers
23. Diamonds
24. Dodads
25. Dohickeys
26. Family Jewels
27. Frick and Frack
28. Gooseberries
29. Jingleberries
30. Knockers
31. Love Apples
32. Male Mules

33. Marbles
34. Marshmallows
35. Mountain Oysters
36. Niagara Falls
37. Nicknacks
38. Nutmegs
39. Nuts
40. Orchestra Stalls
41. Oysters
42. Pebbles
43. Plums

44. Rocks
45. Seeds
46. Spunk Holders
47. Stones
48. Swingers
49. Tallywags
50. Testimonials
51. The Twins
52. Vitals
53. Whirlygigs

46 Incredible Religious Phenomena, Including Weeping and Bleeding Statues and Sightings of the Virgin Mary, All of Which Have Taken Place in the Past 25 Years

Atheists don't believe that there is anything other than this world. Their ideology states that there is no God, that miracles are impossible, and that the purpose of organized religions is to keep the masses intellectually and emotionally sedated.

They dismiss religious experiences such as Virgin Mary sightings or other unexplainable spiritual phenomena as mass hallucinations. They believe that by turning to, or depending on, an outside force for help, judgment, and forgiveness, we deny our essential humanity and refuse to accept reality.

The bottom line of their philosophy is that belief in God is a crutch, and that until mankind as a species outgrows the need to depend on such fairy tales we will never solve the very real problems of real people in our very real world.

Atheists are entitled to believe what they wish. But what about the *real* miracles? What about the documented cases of seemingly impossible events? What about the following 46 cases—all of which have occurred since 1969—of incredible religious phenomena?

The atheists will dismiss these events as hallucinations or natural phenomena that we cannot yet understand. The faithful will look to them as a sign that there is indeed a supernatural power and that life does indeed go on after our brief stint here on earth. The specific meanings, or lack thereof, of these 46 apparent paranormal occurrences is in the eyes, heart, and soul of the beholder.

Date	Place	Religious Phenomena
December 1969	*Tarpon Springs, Florida, USA*	An icon of St. Nicholas weeps.
1970	*Lanciano, Italy*	Bread and wine that miraculously turned to real flesh and blood in the eighth century are examined scientifically and determined to still be human flesh and blood twelve centuries later.
May 1970	*Chicago, Illinois, USA*	Blood oozes from the 1,700-year-old remains of St. Maximina.
The 1970s	*Havana, Cuba*	The Virgin Mary appears several times, standing on the water of Havana Bay.
January 3, 1971	*Maropati, Italy*	A painting of the Virgin Mary weeps real blood.
1972	*Madrid, Spain*	A statue of the Virgin Mary weeps blood from the eyes and heart a total of eleven times.
1972	*Syracuse, Sicily, Italy*	A limestone crucifix bleeds.
December 19, 1972	*Ravenna, Italy*	A Fatima statue of the Virgin Mary weeps.
January 1973	*Monterrey, Mexico*	A statue of the Infant Jesus breathes, sweats, and weeps every day for 15,000 people.
1973	*Akita City, Japan*	A statue of the Virgin Mary weeps from its right hand.
August 1973	*Naples, Italy*	A picture of Jesus bleeds.
December 1973	*Tarpon Springs, Florida, USA*	An icon of St. Nicholas weeps.

Date	Place	Religious Phenomena
January 1974	*Pescara, Italy*	A plate with an image of Pope John XXIII (and JFK) weeps blood.
1975	*Akita City, Japan*	The statue from 1973 now weeps and sweats.
1975–Present	*Queens, New York, USA*	The Virgin Mary regularly appears and speaks through a Long Island grandmother.
April 1975	*Boothwyn, Pennsylvania, USA*	A statue of Christ bleeds at the hands.
May 26, 1976	*Port-au-Prince, Haiti*	A statue of the Virgin Mary weeps.
1977	*Damascus, Syria*	A statue of the Virgin Mary weeps.
May 25–26, 1979	*Roswell, New Mexico, USA*	A portrait of Christ bleeds.
1980–1983	*Grauhlet, Tarn, France*	In a cemetery chapel, burning napkins appear at the foot of a statue of the Virgin Mary sixteen times in three years.
August 30, 1980	*Niscima, Sicily, Italy*	A statue of the Virgin Mary weeps blood.
1981	*Thornton, California, USA*	A statue of the Virgin Mary weeps oil and moves 30 feet.
1981–1986	*Madrid, Spain*	The Virgin Mary appears in a tree and gives messages.
June 24, 1981	*Medjugorje, Yugoslavia*	The Virgin Mary appears regularly to teenagers. Apparitions continue today.
February 1983	*Baguio City, Philippines*	A statue of the Virgin Mary with her heart exposed visibly bleeds from the heart.

Date	Place	Religious Phenomena
August 15, 1983	*Beit Sahour, Jordan*	The Virgin Mary appears at the Lady's Well grotto.
November 18, 1983	*Rmaïch, Lebanon*	A statue of the Virgin Mary flows blood and olive oil.
May 1984	*Chicago, Illinois, USA*	A statue of the Virgin Mary weeps.
September 1984	*Montpinchon, Manche, France*	The Virgin Mary appears to townsfolk.
December 24, 1984	*Bakersfield, California, USA*	Our Lady of Guadalupe appears in a La Loma barrio.
February 14, 1985	*Asdee, County Kerry, Ireland*	Statues of Jesus and Mary move.
March 15, 1985	*Concord, Sydney, Australia*	A statue of the Lebanese St. Charbal oozes oil that causes a crucifix to drip blood when touched by it.
July 1985	*Ballinspittle, County Cork, Ireland*	A statue of the Virgin Mary moves.
August 16, 1985	*Melleray, Cappoquin, County Waterford, Ireland*	A statue of the Virgin Mary comes to life and gives the faithful messages.
March 1986	*Shoubra, Cairo, Egypt*	The Virgin Mary appears on the roof of the church of St. Damiana in Papadoplo and the apparitions are witnessed by thousands of people.
December 6, 1986	*Chicago, Illinois, USA*	A painting of the Virgin Mary weeps.
1987	*Bessbrook, County Antrim, Northern Ireland*	The Virgin Mary appears regularly to two people in a church.
April 26, 1987	*Grushevo/Hrushiv, Ukraine*	The Virgin Mary appears to an 11-year-old girl.

Date	Place	Religious Phenomena
July 1987	*Mutwal, Sri Lanka*	A statue of the Virgin Mary moves.
October 1987	*Ramallah, Jordan*	A plastic statue of the Virgin Mary oozes olive oil.
October 17, 1987	*Wynne, Arkansas, USA*	A cross appears on a glass door after a woman prays for her dead husband.
1988	*Manila, Philippines*	The Virgin Mary appears to crowds of people.
August 1988	*Lubbock, Texas, USA*	The Virgin Mary appears in the sky above a church.
Good Friday, 1989	*Ambridge, Pennsylvania, USA*	A statue of Jesus closes its eyes.
1992	*New Haven, Connecticut, USA*	A figure of the crucified Christ appears in the limbs of a tree in the Wooster Square park. The apparition becomes known locally as the Jesus Tree. (I have personally seen this one.)
1992	*Marlboro Township, New Jersey, USA*	The Virgin Mary appears to Joseph Januskiewicz in his backyard on the first Sunday of every month.

Postscript: The Vatican has steadfastly refused to sanction the vast majority of religious manifestations and alleged miracles. To date, they have only vouched for seven Virgin Mary apparitions, including Fatima and Lourdes.

7 Items of Information Noted on a Death Certificate

A death certificate must be filed whenever someone dies. Either the attending physician or the coroner fills it out and signs it, after which it is filed in the county where the death occurred.

Death certificates are public records and anyone can look at a filed death certificate at any time. A death certificate *must* be filed before the body is disposed of.

As you can imagine, most death certificates are fairly routine legal documents, but there are a few questions on them that are intriguing and revealing. For instance, one death certificate I saw had a separate block for the question, "Was Decedent of Hispanic Origin?" and if so, it required specifying Mexican, Puerto Rican, Cuban, and so on. There was only one block, however, for every other race, including American Indian, Black, White, and so forth.

This feature abstracts some of the more interesting questions on a typical death certificate, and discusses some of the possible reasons for the particular inquiries.

1. **Age:** This is to be expected, right? Of course, but within the "Age" section are two poignant sections: "Under 1 Year," which requests the number of months and days the child lived, and even more heartbreaking, "Under 1 Day," which requests the number of hours and minutes the newborn survived.

2. **Decedent's Education:** What does this have to do with a person's death and disposition? It must be important to *someone,* I guess.

3. **Method of Disposition:** This section offers five choices: Burial, Donation, Cremation, Removed from State, and Other. I assume the "Other" category would include Burial

at Sea and, I suppose, Being Picked Clean by Birds, a body disposal custom favored by the Parsis of India.

4. **Immediate Cause of Death:** This section is part of the overall "Cause of Death" section and this question acknowledges that there is an immediate cause of death, but that often the underlying cause of death is more important. For instance, a young person could be found dead of cardiac arrest. This is the *immediate* cause of his demise. But it might then be determined that the cardiac arrest was caused by an overdose of crack; thus the *underlying* cause. This reminds me of a line from Jimmy Breslin's hilarious book about the Mafia, *The Gang That Couldn't Shoot Straight.* In it, one of the wiseguys is explaining the death of a rival organized crime soldier. He tells his colleagues that the guy died of "natural causes": "His heart stopped when I put a knife into it."

5. **Underlying Cause of Death:** This information has become even more important in the past decade because of the AIDS crisis. Very often, AIDS victims will die of some form of cancer or pneumonia that they developed because of the devastating effect on the immune system by the AIDS virus. Thus the "Immediate Cause of Death" will necessarily state "Pneumonia" or "Kaposi's Sarcoma," but the "Underlying Cause of Death" will denote AIDS.

6. **Was an Autopsy Performed?** The State wants to know if one was, and if so, what was determined.

7. **Were Autopsy Findings Available Prior to Completion of Cause of Death?** If they weren't, I guess the message is that the "Cause" of death had sure as hell better jibe with the actuality. If it doesn't, there had better be a damn good reason why.

15 Last Meals

More are men's ends mark'd than their lives before:
The setting sun, and music at the close,
As the last taste of sweets, is sweetest last,
Writ in remembrance more than things long past.
—William Shakespeare, *Richard II*, II, i

What would you choose if you had one meal left to eat in this life? That is the question death row occupants must answer.

If I could even *eat* the day of my pending execution, I'd probably want a white pizza (no tomato sauce), with broccoli and extra garlic. (Bad breath would no longer be a concern, eh?) Or then again, I might order a hamburger or a pork chop because as a vegetarian these are foods I never, ever touch.

This feature looks at the last meal requests made by 15 executed prisoners. In the majority of cases, their requests were filled. When they were not, or when the offered meals were refused, it is so noted.

1. **Unnamed Jewish Convict**
   Prison: Sing Sing
   Last Meal: This guy decided to use the opportunity of his final meal to challenge ancient Jewish rules against the eating of pork. He ordered a full-course kosher dinner *and* a ham sandwich.

2. **Prisoner Number 77681**
   Prison: Sing Sing
   Last Meal: His pending death certainly did not affect this prisoner's appetite. For his last meal, 77681 ate a stew made of Long Island duck, peas, and olives. He ate the stew with dumplings, four slices of bread, and boiled white rice on the side. He also had a tomato salad, and for dessert he enjoyed

a nice piece of strawberry shortcake and a pint of vanilla ice cream. He topped all this off with a good cigar.

3. Joshua Jones
Prison: Coudersport, Pennsylvania, Prison
Date: 1839
Last Meal: Joshua Jones selected a symbolic last meal. On the day of his hanging, he found that he had exactly one dollar left to his name. He ate the bill between two slices of bread.
Method of Execution: Hanging

4. Chauncey W. Millard
Prison: Utah State Prison
Date: 1869
Last Meal: Millard apparently wanted to be sailing on a sugar rush when he confronted the business end of his executioners' rifles. Millard's last meal consisted of nothing but candy.
Method of Execution: Firing squad

5. William Rose
Prison: Minnesota State Prison
Date: 1891
Last Meal: Rose ordered a rather elegant last meal of oysters and eggs.
Method of Execution: Hanging

6. Gee Jon
Prison: Carson City State Prison
Date: February 8, 1924
Last Meal: Old habits die hard. Gee Jon's execution was scheduled for early morning and, thus, John ordered a typical breakfast as his last meal. He ate ham and eggs, toast, and coffee.
Method of Execution: Gas chamber

7. Isidore Zimmerman
Prison: Sing Sing
Date: January 26, 1939
Last Meal: Isidore was another big eater. His last meal consisted of a large steak, a salad, and potato pancakes. Zimmerman had originally requested cheese blintzes, but that was one specialty the Sing Sing kitchen could not provide without longer notice. The pancakes were substituted

instead. For dessert, Izzy ate two orders of Jell-O with ice cream. He finished everything off by smoking cigarettes *and* cigars.
Method of Execution: Electrocution

8. Leslie B. Gireth
Prison: San Quentin
Date: 1943
Last Meal: Gireth chose drive-in food as his last meal. He ordered two hamburgers and two Cokes.
Method of Execution: Gas chamber

9. Barbara Graham
Prison: San Quentin
Date: June 3, 1955
Last Meal: Graham forsook her last meal and instead decided on a "last dessert." She ordered and ate a hot fudge sundae.
Method of Execution: Gas chamber

10. Eugene Hickock and Perry Smith (The *In Cold Blood* murderers)
Prison: Kansas State Penitentiary
Date: April 14, 1965
Last Meal: The *In Cold Blood* murderers' eyes were apparently bigger than their stomachs. As their last meal they ordered shrimp, french fries, garlic bread, and for dessert, ice cream and strawberries with whipped cream. They didn't touch a bite of it.
Method of Execution: Hanging

11. Gary Gilmore
Prison: Utah State Prison
Date: December 17, 1976
Last Meal: Gary Gilmore's trial and execution was a media event. His name became a household word and his sordid story was immortalized by Norman Mailer in the best-selling book *The Executioner's Song,* which was later made into a movie. Gilmore's last meal (which was eaten the night before his sunrise execution) was rather pedestrian for such a celebrity, however. He ate a hamburger, potatoes, and eggs.
Method of Execution: Firing squad

12. Stephen T. Judy
Prison: Indiana State Prison
Date: 1981
Last Meal: Stephen Judy skipped the food completely for his last "meal" and instead decided on a "last round." He ordered and drank four bottles of cold beer.
Method of Execution: Electrocution

13. Charlie Brooks
Prison: Texas State Prison in Huntsville
Date: December 7, 1982
Last Meal: Brooks was obviously a "meat and potatoes" kind of guy. His last meal consisted of a steak, french fries, and for dessert, peach cobbler.
Method of Execution: Lethal injection

14. Margie Velma Barfield
Prison: Central Prison in Raleigh, North Carolina
Date: November 2, 1984
Last Meal: Barfield chose a "last snack" over a "last meal," selecting junk food as the last thing she would ever eat in this life. She enjoyed a last repast of Cheez Doodles and Coca-Cola.
Method of Execution: Lethal injection

15. Ted Bundy
Prison: Florida State Penitentiary
Date: January 24, 1989
Last Meal: Bundy refused to order a last meal, so the prison brought him the standard meal of steak and eggs. He refused to eat it, and they sent him to death on an empty stomach.
Method of Execution: Electrocution

Department of Peculiar Parlance:
46 Euphemisms for Dying

No one wants to play in the last scene of this weird stage play called life, and yet, along with taxes, it is the *only* thing in our lives we can be absolutely, positively, bet-the-house sure will happen.

Here are 46 ways to leave your liver—and your heart, and your ankles, and all of your 2,000 other body parts (as a sexy commercial has been known to proclaim)—behind. (With apologies to Paul Simon and Lever soap.)

1. Answer the Last Call
2. Beam Up
3. Bite the Big One
4. Bite the Dust
5. Breathe Your Last
6. Buy Your Lunch
7. Buy the Farm
8. Cash In Your Chips
9. Climb the Golden Staircase
10. Cock Up Your Toes
11. Coil Up Your Ropes
12. Come Over
13. Croak
14. Cross the Great Divide
15. Drop Off the Hooks
16. Fade Away
17. Give Up the Ghost
18. Go Home
19. Go On to a Better World
20. Go the Way of All Flesh
21. Go Tits Up
22. Go to Heaven
23. Go to Meet Your Maker
24. Go to Sleep
25. Go West
26. Hand In Your Chips
27. Join the Angels
28. Join the Great Majority
29. Kick the Bucket
30. Kiss the Dust
31. Lay Down the Knife and Fork
32. Pass In Your Chips
33. Pop Off the Hooks
34. Pull a Cluck
35. Raise the Wind
36. Shit the Bed
37. Snuff It
38. Squiff It
39. Step Into Your Last Bus
40. Step Off
41. Stick Your Spoon in the Wall
42. Sun Your Moccasins
43. Take an Earth Bath
44. Take the Long Count
45. Tip Over
46. Yield Up the Ghost

The 8 Levels of IQ Evaluation, from "Idiot" to "Genius"

IQ is an acronym for Intelligence Quotient. This number (and its associated "grading") is arrived at by the following formula:

$$IQ = \frac{Mental\ Age \times 100}{Chronological\ Age}$$

Do you know *your* IQ? (I know mine, but modesty, ahem, prevents me from revealing it.)

1. **Idiot** = An IQ of 0–25.
2. **Imbecile** = An IQ of 26–50.
3. **Moron** = An IQ of 51–70.
4. **Borderline** = An IQ of 71–80.
5. **Dull** = An IQ of 81–90.
6. **Normal** = An IQ of 91–110.
7. **Superior** = An IQ of 111–140.
8. **Genius** = An IQ of 141 and higher.

16 of the Oddest Side Effects of 5 of the Most Frequently Prescribed Drugs in the United States

The number one prescribed drug in 1977 was Valium. Today, in the 1990's, the number one spot is held by an antibiotic.

Hmmmm.

This list is intended to emphasize the fact that prescription medication is very powerful in the impact it can have on your system, and it's also meant to illustrate just how weird—how *odd* some of your system's reactions can be. It is sometimes said that the cure is worse than the disease. Reading through this list of possible peculiar side effects is a powerful validation of that adage.

1. **Amoxil**

   Type of Drug: Antibiotic.

   Possible Peculiar Side Effects: Blood vessel collapse, skin peeling, oral fungal disease, rectal fungal disease, body warmth.

2. **Premarin**

   Type of Drug: Estrogen supplement.

   Possible Side Effects: Enlargement of the breasts, loss of scalp hair, new hair growth, contact-lens intolerance, increased sex drive, decreased sex drive.

3. **Lanoxin**

   Type of Drug: Prescribed for congestive heart failure and other heart problems.

   Possible Side Effects: Breast enlargement.

4. **Xanax**

   Type of Drug: Tranquilizer.

   Possible Side Effects: Inability to fall asleep.

5. Synthroid

Type of Drug: Thryoid replacement.

Possible Side Effects: Shaking of the hands, sweating, intolerance to heat.

Department of Peculiar Parlance:
25 Euphemisms for Alcohol

A man who exposes himself when he is intoxicated, has not the art of getting drunk.—Samuel Johnson

Alcohol is one of the world's few legal drugs and, as you know, it is *quite* popular. We have many ways of describing that certain chemical compound that makes us slur our words, lose our inhibitions, and try to take our pants off over our head. Here are 25 of the oddest and/or funniest.

1. Bitch's Wine
2. Bug Juice
3. Coffin Varnish
4. Cold Coffee
5. Colorado Coolaid
6. Dutch Courage
7. Embalming Fluid
8. Jungle Juice
9. Mexican Milk
10. Nanny Goat Sweat
11. Panther Piss
12. Pig Sweat
13. Piss Maker
14. Potato Soup
15. Prairie Dew
16. Prune Juice
17. Shampoo
18. Snake Juice
19. Snake Poison
20. Squaw Piss
21. Strip Me Naked
22. Tarantula Juice
23. Tiger Sweat
24. Tonsil Bath
25. Witch Piss

14 Methods of Execution Through the Ages

I hate victims who respect their executioners.
                                                —Jean-Paul Sartre

Society has had to deal with its bad guys for centuries. Sometimes they're fined, sometimes they're locked up, and sometimes they're killed.

Finding new and improved ways to do away with the condemned has occupied great (and not-so-great) minds since before the time of Christ, and as is common with human endeavors, the many and devious ways of ending someone's life have been inventive, to say the least.

This feature looks at 14 of man's favorite ways of saying, "Here's your hat, what's your hurry?" and *really* meaning it.

1. **Beheading** Beheading was a popular form of execution in Greece and Rome before Christ. An ax or sword were the tools of the trade. In the eleventh century, beheading as a form of execution came to England and quickly replaced hanging as the favored method of doing away with a condemned criminal. (The *well-placed* condemned criminal, that is. The poor were still hanged for quite some time.) Beheading was clean and quick, and most believed that it was painless.

   In 1792, beheading became modernized: On April 25, the first beheading by the guillotine took place. The guillotine was invented by Dr. Antoine Louis and Tobias Schmidt, and popularized by Dr. Joseph Guillotin. The condemned's head was placed at the bottom of a grooved channel and a sharpened, extremely heavy blade was dropped onto his neck.

Gravity added urgency to the speed of the blade's descent and, voila, head in a basket.

The guillotine prompted bizarre experiments to ascertain whether or not the decapitated head retained any sensory awareness at all. For a while, French doctors were grabbing the disembodied heads and sticking pins in them and burning their eyeballs to see if there was any response. One doctor reported that "The face bore a look of astonishment." (I'll bet.)

2. **Boiling to Death** The condemned would be placed in a giant pot filled with boiling water and hung over a fire. He would remain there until he was dead.

3. **Broiling to Death** This involved tying the victim to a red-hot griddle and broiling him or her until they died. One notable broilee was St. Lawrence, who was subjected to this because he wouldn't turn over the Church's treasures to Rome. (He showed up with the poor, the sick, and the retarded when ordered to bring to Rome the Church's fortune and told the Emperor that these poor souls *were* the Church's treasures.) After a time tied to the griddle (during which he bore the agony with incredible stoicism), Lawrence asked to be flipped over, as he was cooked enough on one side. His executioners were not amused.

4. **Burning to Death** Burning to death was used as a method of execution for centuries throughout Europe and in America. The condemned was tied to a stake. Wood and kindling were placed around his or her feet and ignited. This form of execution was agonizing, and yet there are many reports of Christian martyrs "staked" who bore their pain with stoic silence, and with their eyes fixed on heaven.

Probably the most well-known victim of burning to death was Joan of Arc, who was burned at the stake in France in 1431 for heresy.

5. **Crucifixion** The Romans are commonly thought to have invented crucifixion as a form of execution. In their quest for homicidal excellence, they came up with not one or two, but *four* ways to crucify someone. The four ways were all variations of the shape of the cross on which the person was hung. These were the Y, the X, the T, and the H. (With the H, the person was hung by one arm and one leg.) Usually the victim was either hung with ropes to the cross or nailed

through the hands and feet, as was Jesus Christ. (Jesus is most often shown crucified on a T cross, but I have also seen paintings that show him on a Y, with the legs bent at the knee. Both were in common use during Christ's life, and it is possible that he may have died by one of the other forms.)

Crucifixion was a slow form of death. Usually the person died from suffocation and/or exposure, but occasionally the executioners would break the crucified's legs and/or stick a sword in their side to hasten the process. The Romans often included the added attraction of a pre-crucifixion scourging, and in some cases they would take the time to insert sharp little pieces of bone under the victim's skin before they raised him on the cross. (Christ's crown of thorns would seem to have been a torture designed specifically for him as a way of mocking his claim of being the king of the Jews.)

In feudal Japan, crucifixion was also used as a means of execution, but they *really* expedited the process: they would tie the condemned man to a cross and then shoot arrows into him until he was dead.

6. **Drawing and Quartering** There were two types of drawing and quartering: the Russian version and the English version. Both were used in the twelfth century and later.

The Russian version (the more well-known) involved tying the condemned's arms and legs to four horses. The horses were then whipped and forced to flee in four different directions. The victim's arms and legs were summarily ripped from their sockets. Since this did not immediately kill the condemned, his torso was then decapitated to finish him off.

The other type of drawing and quartering—also incredibly vicious—was developed in England. In this version, the condemned was dragged behind a horse to the site of his execution. There he was hanged, but not to the death. He was simply strung up by the neck and allowed to slowly suffocate. This was the "drawing" part. While he was hanging and still conscious, though, he was also disemboweled and his intestines were burned in a fire while he watched. This was the "quartering" part. After his guts were ashes, he was decapitated and his corpse cut into pieces.

Notable drawn and quartered historical figures include Thomas Abel, in 1540 (for denying ecclesiastical supremacy of the King of England); Henry Walpole, in 1595 (for being a Catholic priest); Thomas Garret, in 1608 (for refusing to take the Oath of Supremacy); Ambrose Barlow, in 1641 (for refusing to renounce his priesthood); and John Kemble, in 1679 (for being a Catholic priest).

7. **Electrocution** In a typical execution by electrocution, the prisoner is strapped into the electric chair with eight heavy leather straps: on the two ankles, the chest, the upper and lower arms, and the waist. In most cases, a leather mask is placed over the face and secured to the back of the electric chair. Electrodes are attached to the prisoner's head and leg. The amount of voltage and length of the charges differ from state to state, although most executioners will start with a minimum charge of 2,000 volts for up to ten seconds, drop down to 500 volts or so for upwards of thirty seconds, and then finish things off with another 2,000 volts. Death is fairly speedy with this amount of voltage sailing through the condemned's veins. Death occurs within three seconds or so, and the condemned is usually unconscious in less than 1/240 of a second. Electrocution is the favored form of execution in dozens of U.S. states.

8. **The Firing Squad** Today, a firing squad usually consists of five men, all of whom are expert marksmen. Four of their rifles are loaded with live shells; one is loaded with a blank round. This allows each executioner to never be completely sure that he killed a man. (According to many sources, however, experienced riflemen can *always* tell which gun had the blank in it: it's inevitably cooler than the others.) The prisoner is strapped into a chair and blindfolded. The prison physician listens for his heart and places a paper target over it. Upon the warden's signal, the shooters shoot at the heart. The five executioners are concealed behind a wall that has an opening for the rifle barrels. Death is usually immediate.

In the United States, the firing squad is currently a form of execution only in Utah and Idaho. A recent notorious execution by firing squad in the U.S. was that of Gary Gilmore in 1977.

9. **Hanging** Hanging, a form of execution still used today, orig-
inated when someone threw a rope over a tree limb and
slowly pulled the condemned (or the lynched) up by his
neck until he died. Later, the doomed were placed on a ladder and stood upright in a cart, both of which were quickly
pulled away so that the body could be allowed to swing.

According to the National Coalition to Abolish the Death
Penalty and Amnesty International, there are four stages to
a death by hanging. (1) At the moment of the drop, the
body's weight violently tears the neck muscles, the skin, and
blood vessels. If the length of the drop has been calculated
correctly and the knot placed properly, the person's neck
should break. (2) Because of the constriction of the noose,
the veins that move blood to the heart are closed off. (3) Arteries that send blood to the head and brain, however,
remain open, and the condemned experiences an excruciating headache. (4) Eventually, breathing and heart rate slow,
and within ten to twenty minutes after the drop, the person
is usually pronounced dead.

People urinate and defecate when they are hanged and, in
the case of males, will often get an erection and actually ejac-
ulate at the moment of impact. These aspects of hangings
were quite stimulating to sixteenth- and seventeenth-century
public hanging groupies.

Today, hanging is legal in four states: Washington, Montana, Delaware, and New Hampshire. It is a common form
of execution in 73 countries around the world.

10. **Impalement** The executioner would seat the condemned on
a stake—a thick, sharp, long stake. The point of the stake
would be inserted into the rectum and the victim would be
"assisted" in pushing himself down until the stake punctured his intestines and ultimately killed him. This was slow,
torturous, and excruciatingly painful.

11. **Lethal Gas** Lethal gas has been used in the United States as
a method of execution since the 1920s. It is a gruesome
mode of death, and many people who have witnessed a
death by "the big sleep" never want to see another.

The condemned, wearing a stethoscope tube taped to his
chest, is strapped into a chair in the gas chamber. Beneath
the seat of the chair hangs a bag filled with one pound of cyanide pellets. In the floor beneath the chair is a well that

has a pipe feeding it from outside the death chamber. After the prisoner is strapped into the chair and the room is ascertained to be airtight, a liquid mixture of distilled water and sulfuric acid is piped into the well beneath his chair. When the warden signals the executioner, the bag of cyanide pellets is lowered into the acid. The cyanide instantly dissolves and the death vapors begin filling the execution chamber.

Death from lethal gas is not immediate. It could take up to fifteen minutes for the heart to stop beating, and the prisoner is conscious for much of that time.

San Quentin Prison physician Dr. Stanley, quoted in *Until You Are Dead . . .* by Frederick Drimmer, once remarked, "The idea that cyanide kills immediately is hooey. These men suffered as their lungs no longer absorbed oxygen and they struggled to breathe. They died of an internal suffocation against which they had to fight and from which they must have suffered."

Death row prisoners sentenced to die in the gas chamber are usually not given any drugs or sedatives before being executed, although in some prisons the condemned man is allowed a shot of whiskey before taking that long walk.

After the prison physician pronounces the man dead and the gas is drawn out of the death chamber, the prisoner's body, as a precaution for prison personnel, is sometimes sprayed with liquid ammonia to neutralize any gas on the clothing.

12. **Lethal Injection** Lethal injection has of late been looked to as the ultimate humane method of execution. You lay the condemned prisoner on a gurney, inject him with a smorgasbord of deadly chemicals, he goes to sleep, and fifteen or twenty minutes later, he's on his way to the morgue for his autopsy. Basically, that *is* pretty much the way it works in modern Western society, but in the Middle East, the term *lethal injection* takes on a whole new meaning. There, a particularly vile form of lethal injection is neither painless nor humane. A common form of execution for perjurors in the Middle East is intravenous embalming while still alive.

13. **Pressing to Death** Pressing to death, a common form of execution during the Middle Ages, involved tying the condemned to four stakes, spread-eagle on the floor. A large board was then placed on the person's body and heavier

and heavier weights were placed on top of the board until the life was literally crushed out of the person. As you can well imagine, this was an extremely slow process, quite torturous, and could last for several days before the condemned gladly expired.

One famous "pressee" was Margaret Clitherow, who was pressed to death at York, England, on March 25, 1586. Her executioners used an eight-hundred-pound weight to slowly crush the life out of her.

14. **Stoning to Death** The condemned would be brought to an open area and stood in the center of a circle formed by his "executioners." They would then hurl heavy stones and rocks at his body, consciously avoiding throwing stones at his head, so that he would remain conscious.

54 of the Most Bizarre "News" Stories in 2 Issues of the *Weekly World News*

The existence of the *Weekly World News* is a testament to the First Amendment. Why? Because the *Weekly World News* is a weekly tabloid "newspaper" that *makes stuff up* and publishes it!

Okay, I'll be fair. The majority of the articles in the *News* are wire stories with an offbeat angle that the *News* just spices up with a sensationalistic headline and reprints.

But *some* of its "news" stories—particularly the cover stories—give new meaning to the word "story," especially when it's used in the context of a newspaper article. Some of the cover stories it has run in the past include the following:

"Alien Backs Clinton!"
"Bat Child Found in Cave!"
"Half-Human Half-Fish Found in Florida!"
"Bug-Size UFO Found on Playground!"
"Dead Captain Steers Old Ghost Ship into Port!"
"Bat with a Human Face!"
"Hillary Clinton Adopts Alien Baby!"
"Elvis Dead at 58!"
"*Titanic* Baby Found Alive!"
"Clinton Meets with JFK!"

And so on. (One of my recent favorites was a cover headline that claimed that Jesus' cross had been found in the Holy Land. The headline was accompanied by a photo of some guy dragging a huge cross across the sand.)

Admittedly, this is great fun, and thus for those of you who may never have seen an issue of the *Weekly World News* this feature is a sampling of all the stories—complete with the trademark ubiquitous exclamation points!!!!—in a couple of the newspaper's issues.

Who reads the *Weekly World News?* You might think it would be the stereotypical overweight housewife who picks it up every Thursday (coupon day) while waiting in line at the Stop & Shop or the Piggly Wiggly. But there's one consistent feature of the *News* that makes that assumption questionable: every week the tabloid runs several "cheesecake"-type photos of scantily clad *female* models and actresses, complete with "naughty" captions. (Such as, "This dazzling European model shows off her bod and gets our nod in this peekaboo leather dress . . . wow!") This would make one assume that the *News* also has a large male audience, right? Another cliché shot down. (Just for the heck of it, I ran a randomly selected 150-word excerpt from one of the *News*'s articles through my computer grammar checker and the program rated the text as having a reading grade level of 8.1.)

I know a New York mail carrier who tells me that the *Weekly World News* is the most eagerly awaited periodical in the post office each week. (You did know that postal employees read your magazines and newspapers before they deliver them to you, didn't you?)

After reading through this list of *WWN* articles, you'll understand just why this wacky tabloid makes the rounds of the P.O. before it hits your mailbox. (Note: The punctuation for this list is as close as possible to the way the headlines ran in the paper.)

Issue Date: May 18, 1993
Cover:

"FACE OF SATAN APPEARS OVER WACO!"
"Doomsday image rises from flaming compound in Texas!"
"Extra: FBI issues worldwide alert!"
"CULT MADMAN IS ALIVE!"
"WORLD EXCLUSIVE: The most horrifying photo ever published!"

[The *Weekly World News* is available on newsstands everywhere, but if you want to subscribe, write to them at P.O. Box 1286, Des Moines, Iowa 50340–1286. To inquire about back issues, write to their editorial offices at 600 S. East Coast Ave., Lantana, Florida 33462.]

Inside Stories:

1. "REFRIGERATOR FUNGUS KILLS HOUSEWIFE! Slime ate her brains, eyes, liver & kidneys"
2. "TOWN ELECTS MIDGET POLICE CHIEF"
3. "I CAN TAKE YOU TO THE AFTERLIFE! . . . says super psychic who sends men and women beyond the grave to visit their dead relatives"
4. "11-YEAR-OLD BOY RAPED—BY SEX-CRAVED MAID WITH AIDS!"
5. "Unicorn research team lost in Austrian Alps!"
6. RUSSIAN COSMONAUTS MYSTERIOUSLY AGING! They're going blind, losing their teeth and look like they're 100 years old!"
7. "Bank president has $8,000 surgery—so he won't be ticklish!"
8. "Man spends 3 years in his bathroom—TO AVOID GOING TO JAIL!"
9. "Mice commit suicide by eating electrical cables!"
10. "X RAYS REVEAL BABY'S HEAD ON BACKWARD! Doctors will operate to set boy's head straight!"
11. "Man finds whopping 7-ft. worm!"
12. "Why won't my dead sister leave me alone?"
13. "Handgun horror: BABY CATCHES BULLET WITH HIS GUMS!"
14. " 'A CROCODILE TORE MY ARM OFF—and almost ate me alive!' She's going back to Africa to visit grave of severed limb!"
15. "Baby born on Texas soil—in New York City!"
16. "DIRTY HARRY JR. Kindergarten cop, 5, kills drug pushers in playground shoot-out"
17. "SOME PEOPLE TREAT GHOSTS LIKE MEMBERS OF THEIR OWN FAMILY!"
18. "KID WITH 3 ARMS IS BASEBALL SENSATION! Miracle teen turns birth defect into fortune!"
19. "Face of the Devil appears on woman's X ray!"
20. "FACE OF SATAN PHOTOGRAPHED OVER WACO FIRE! Incredible 300-ft. image appears in smoke from blazing compound"
21. WACO MADMAN IS STILL ALIVE! David Koresh escapes

inferno—disguised as an FBI agent! Cult leader vows revenge in taped message to followers"
22. "Man sues over faulty flying carpet!"

Issue Date: May 25, 1993
Cover:

"GOLIATH'S SKULL FOUND IN HOLY LAND!"
"Stone from David's slingshot still stuck in giant's forehead!"
"Dramatic discovery proves Bible story is true!"

Inside Stories:

1. " 'I MADE MYSELF PREGNANT WITH A TURKEY BASTER!' Surrogate mom-to-be stood on her head to make her sister a baby!"
2. "GOLIATH'S SKULL FOUND IN HOLY LAND! Proof that Bible story of 10-foot-tall Philistine is true! The stone from David's slingshot is still stuck in giant's forehead!"
3. "Man jailed for painting zoo animals orange"
4. "NEIGHBORHOOD GARAGE DOORS COME TO LIFE! They're opening and closing by themselves, say shocked residents. Are space aliens zeroing in on Earth's radio frequencies?"
5. "Whale eaters unite"
6. "HUMAN JELLYFISH SAYS . . . RUB MY BELLY FOR GOOD LUCK! GET RICHES, ROMANCE AND HEALTH—INSTANTLY!"
7. "BEAUTY SHOPS FOR CAMELS MAKE BIG $$$!"
8. "ANT ARMY EATS 935 PEOPLE! Millions of killer insects turn city into a sea of skeletons—overnight!"
9. "American jumpers foil Chinese plot to knock Earth out of orbit!"
10. "Man killed by falling Bible!"
11. " 'MY WIFE'S GHOST STILL COOKS, CLEANS & IRONS MY SHIRTS . . . but her constant nagging is driving me bonkers!' "
12. "KILLER BREAKS OUT OF PRISON IN 18-TON ARMY TANK!"

13. "Patient on oxygen lights up—& blows himself to kingdom come!"
14. "New research proves . . . JUNK FOOD CAUSES TEENS TO WORSHIP THE DEVIL!"
15. "Hail the size of bowling balls flattens town!"
16. "Stadium has special area for nudists!"
17. "Angry card player stuffs poker chips down winner's throat!"
18. "Beautiful serial killer murdered 100 men! Female Ted Bundy chopped boyfriends up with an ax!"
19. "Man gives girlfriend perfume made from his own sweat! Eau de B.O."
20. "Chicken farmer finds $20,000 worth of diamonds inside hens' eggs!"
21. "Mailman found stuck in letter slot!"
22. "Sword swallower laughed so hard—he slit his throat!"
23. "WACKY LAW HELPS RATS!"
24. "Burglar busted in bubble bath!"
25. "A message from Heaven!"
26. "Russian town cancels annual Buddy Holly Day!"
27. "Secret ingredient in new skin cream—GLOBS OF HUMAN FAT! Pounds of flab are purchased from liposuction clinics!"
28. "MAYOR OUSTED FOR MAKING JOURNALIST GO TOPLESS!"
29. "Shocking diary of Vatican's top exorcist! 'My most terrifying battles with the Devil!' "
30. "6th graders drug teacher so they can party in school!"
31. "LOST BABY CRAWLS 5 MILES TO GET HOME! 8-month-old survives trek through bear-infested forest—on his hands and knees!"
32. "Church communion can spread AIDS!"

The 22 Most Popular Fantasy Sex Partners in 1993

In the June 1993 issues of *Details* and *Mademoiselle* magazines, the results of a sex survey were published. Part of the survey looked at the celebrities people fantasized about while masturbating, which is now, in the age of AIDS, being touted as the safest sex of all. One conclusion regarding the respondents of this survey is immediately evident: they have excellent taste in fantasy sex partners. (*Note:* Fantasy partners for gay women are not included in this list. An editor at *Details* told me they did not receive enough survey responses from gay women to compile a list.)

Straight Men

1. Cindy Crawford
2. Madonna
3. Sharon Stone
4. Demi Moore
5. Winona Ryder
6. Michelle Pfeiffer
7. En Vogue

Straight Women

8. Luke Perry
9. Andre Agassi
10. Mel Gibson
11. Keanu Reeves
12. Bill Clinton

Gay Men

13. Jean-Claude Van Damme
14. Marky Mark
15. Dolph Lundgren
16. Jason Priestly
17. Chris Isaak
18. Jeff Stryker
19. Mel Gibson
20. Brad Pitt
21. Al Gore
22. Tom Cruise

No-Holds-Barred Descriptions of 43 of the Oddest and Raunchiest Photos in Madonna's 1992 Book, *Sex*

Admit it: it is not likely that you would go out and buy a copy of Madonna's notorious fifty-dollar book, *Sex,* nor would you look through it in mixed company, but you're *dying* to know what's in it, right?

Well, I've gone ahead and done the dirty work for you. This feature offers a detailed, sexually explicit, and *very* graphic description of 43 of the oddest, steamiest, and most controversial photographs in *Sex.*

It is said that satisfying curiosity is healthy.

Here's to your health.

Page 7.

A full-page photo of Madonna sitting on a stool and wearing a black mask, an open-nippled, studded leather bra, a studded leather bikini bottom, and studded leather wrist straps. She has her left middle finger in her mouth and her right middle finger in her vagina. Her right breast is exposed; her left is covered by her left arm.

Page 8.

A full-page photo of Madonna and two women. Madonna is tied to a chair and is wearing a leotard that has been ripped open, exposing her breasts. The two women are naked and have shaved heads with long tufts remaining at the front of their heads. One woman is in front of the chair kissing Madonna's left nipple. The other woman is standing and kissing Madonna's open mouth. Madonna has her tongue out. The woman standing is holding a knife to Madonna's throat.

Page 9.

A full-page photo of Madonna and one woman. Madonna is wearing a leather bra, panties, and boots. She is standing with her legs spread above a water fountain with her back against the wall. The other woman is in front of the water fountain, wearing a similar outfit. The woman has the water turned on and is taking a drink from the stream, which is inches away from Madonna's crotch. Madonna is holding the woman's head close to her groin. The effect is that of a Mapplethorpe-like photo of urination and sex.

Page 12.

Fourteen smaller photos surrounding a larger photo in the center of the page. The photos are of Madonna and the two female skinheads. The two women are topless. Madonna is in a black see-through body suit. In the center photo, Madonna's hands are tied above her head, and one of the women is holding a knife to Madonna's crotch. The other fourteen smaller photos are of Madonna and the two women in the same garb as in the large photo in a variety of bondage poses that take place on a mattress.

Page 13.

Fourteen smaller photos surrounding a larger photo in the center of the page. The photos are of Madonna and the two female skinheads taken at the same time as those on page twelve. In the center photo, Madonna is tied up and gagged. One of the women is grabbing Madonna's hair, and there is a look of fear on Madonna's face. Eight of the other fourteen smaller photos are of Madonna tied to a chair and being kissed and fondled by the two women. Two photos are of Madonna alone in the chair, holding her own breasts. The remaining four smaller photos are of the two skinheads posing topless and kissing.

Page 26.

A photo of Madonna in a leather bra, miniskirt, and boots. She is tied by the wrists and ankles to a low table. Her body is surrounded by burning candles, and there is a huge cross behind the table, which might be an altar of some sort. On the floor in front of the table lies a facedown man in leather pants with his arms extended as in a crucifixion. His body is also surrounded by burning candles. The man balances a burning candle between the two heels of his shoes.

Page 27.

Nine photos surrounded by text at top and bottom. In the typed text, Madonna waxes philosophical about abusive relationships, asserting that she believes that many women who stay in abusive relationships do so because they're getting off on the S&M dynamic. The center photo is of the leg of the guy from page twenty-six. He's wearing shredded jeans and spiked boots. The other photos, which border the page, show a topless Madonna in a "love chair," with the same guy's face in her lap, simulating (?) cunnilingus.

Page 31.

A full-page photo of a bald guy on the floor wearing a dog collar and licking the ankle of a woman wearing fishnet stockings and a high leather boot. The woman, whose face is not seen, has the man on a leather leash.

Page 32.

A full-page photo of Madonna and two men in a school gymnasium immediately prior to what looks like Madonna being raped. The "students" (who are really two of the bald guys from previous photos) are dressed (as is Madonna) to look like high schoolers, and there are books tossed on the floor. One guy is at Madonna's head and is holding her arms back while the other guy is on his knees at her crotch.

Madonna's blouse and skirt have both been pulled up and her panties have been pulled down to her knees. Her white bra and her pubic hair are visible. The two men are smiling, and the guy at Madonna's knees has his hand on her crotch. Madonna is *also* smiling, and that fact makes this one of the most notorious and talked-about photos in the book. This picture appears to depict a rape in progress, and it's clear that the intention is to bring one to the conclusion that the victim seems to be enjoying it. Interestingly, the word *NO* appears (almost subliminally) in big letters on the gymnasium wall next to the basketball backboard above Madonna's head.

Page 34.

A full-page negative photo of a shirtless bald guy with a skull tattoo on his right arm. He has his head back and his mouth open. A thick stream of some liquid is flowing into his mouth.

Page 37.

A full-page photo of Madonna in a black dress, garter belt, stockings, and high heels. She is lying on her back on a round dining room table, with a shirtless guy standing between her upraised legs. Madonna's dress is pulled down, exposing her breasts, and her legs are up in the air and spread. A long-haired blond guy wearing a crucifix is standing between her legs. At first glance it would appear they are having sex, but on closer examination one can see that the man is wearing pants. This does not rule out the possibility that the man simply took out his penis and entered Madonna without pulling down his trousers. The theme of the photo seems to be spontaneous, passionate sex, so that is perhaps why the man is still in pants.

Page 40.

A photo showing Madonna wearing only a pair of panties, lying on her back between the legs of a nude man standing in front of her. She is staring up at his penis, and the man's testicles are visible between his legs.

Page 41.

A full-page photo of Madonna, topless, biting the ass of a man clad only in a jock strap, bending over in front of her. Madonna's nose appears to be between the cheeks of the man's ass.

Page 48.

A full-page, green-tinted photo of Madonna shaving a naked guy's pubic hair.

Page 49.

A full-page, pink-tinted photo of two bald guys and two bald women all urinating at public bathroom wall urinals. A profile of Madonna is superimposed on the wall above the urinals.

Page 51.

A photo of Madonna topless and sucking on a woman's big toe.

Page 54.

A full-page, yellow-tinted photo of a naked woman's butt. A man is kneeling between the woman's legs and sprinkling talcum powder on her tush. His fingers are hidden somewhere between the cracks of her ass. No faces are visible, but it certainly *looks* like Madonna's butt. (By now, we've seen enough of it to recognize it on sight!)

Page 55.

A color photo of Madonna looking at herself in the mirror. She is naked except for a blue T-shirt, which she has pulled up over her breasts. She is cupping her breasts in both hands and staring lustfully at herself. Her pubic hair is visible. This is one of the more genuinely erotic shots in the book.

Page 57.

Another extremely notorious photo: this is the picture that critics of *Sex* claim shows Madonna engaging in bestiality. A dog (it looks like a golden retriever) is lying on its back. Madonna is kneeling over the dog, wearing only the bunny tail thong panty, with her crotch in the approximate vicinity of the dog's head. If you really examine the photo, you'll see that Madonna's legs are closed tight, and that from her position, there's no way the dog's head could be high enough to reach her vagina. But there's no getting around the fact that it definitely *looks like* she's having sex with the dog, and it's obvious that that's exactly what she wanted people to think. That Madonna! She's such a caution, t'ain't she?

Page 58.

Text that looks like the newspaper cut-out ransom notes kidnappers like to use stripped on top of five black-and-white photos. Homoerotic photos showing two nude men kissing and fondling each other, but no penises or testicles.

Page 59.

A black-and-white photo of Madonna sitting in a theater, looking at the camera and embracing a black-clad man. In front of Madonna and the man are seven naked or g-string clad dancers. One naked man is bending over to the camera and his scrotum is completely visible. A naked muscular dancer in black boots is standing to the side, and his uncircumcised, semi-erect penis is visible.

Page 64.

A full-page, black-and-white photo of Madonna running a whip down the thigh of a naked man. His buttocks are visible. Madonna is wearing an evening gown.

Page 66.

Madonna, two guys in tuxes, and a naked man in a group embrace at a stage-side table. Madonna is wearing an evening gown and has her hand on the crotch of one of the tuxedo-clad men.

(Although it should be acknowledged that the man Madonna is groping has very feminine features. Even if he is *not* a woman in drag, it seems that the photo's intention is to suggest that possibility. At the very least, the gropee is androgynous.)

Page 67.

A photo of Madonna lying on top of a guy as their image is reflected in two full-length mirrors. Two naked men are watching them have sex, and one appears to be masturbating. A tuxedo-clad guy smoking a cigarette in a holder and drinking a beer also watches.

Page 69.

A black-and-white photo of Madonna naked, spread-legged, straddling, and reclining (face up) on a huge fish fountain that is shooting a stream of water into a pool. The immediate effect—and obvious intention—of this photo is for it to look like Madonna is urinating. Madonna's hair is wet, her nipples are erect, and her toenails are painted.

Page 70.

A color photo of Madonna wearing only sunglasses, a towel as a turban, and what looks like men's briefs. She has her tongue out and her left hand is pulling down her pants. She may be using her thumb to masturbate. Her nipples are erect, and overlayed on the photo is a letter from Dita to Johnny.

Page 77.

A full-page, black-and-white photo of Madonna wearing only panties and straddling a full-length mirror on the floor. Her panties are pulled down and she is masturbating while staring at her reflection. The bottoms of her feet are a little dirty.

Page 80.

An interesting full-page, black-and-white photo of a dark-haired guy lying in bed and smoking a cigarette. He has his hands behind his head and Madonna is sitting next to him holding a hand mirror up to her own breast. Her left breast is reflected in the mirror and she is holding the mirror so that it is positioned exactly where the guy's left breast is, making it look like he has a female breast.

Page 81.

A full-page, black-and-white photo of Madonna standing in front of a wall mirror and wearing an old-fashioned white bra. Her blouse is pulled down around her waist. An old man is standing behind her with his hand on her shoulder, watching them in the mirror. He looks ready to kiss her neck.

Page 83.

Madonna sitting in an armchair on an old guy's lap. She is topless and smoking a cigarette. He is holding her left breast in his left hand.

Page 86.

A full-page, orange-tinted photo of Madonna kneeling nude on the beach. She is wearing a very long blond hair fall. This is a very erotic photo with a very low sleaze quotient.

Page 87.

A full-page, black-and-white photo of Isabella Rossellini, dressed in a man's suit, with her hands on the chin and top of the head of a bare-breasted woman.

Page 88.

Seventeen black-and-white photos of Madonna and Isabella Rossellini frolicking in a pool in various stages of full and partial nudity.

Page 89.

Sixteen black-and-white photos of Madonna, Ingrid, and Isabella in various stages of embrace and undress. Ingrid and Isabella are dressed as men.

Page 91.

A full-page, black-and-white photo of Isabella Rossellini enclosing Madonna inside the man's sport coat she is wearing. Only Madonna's eyes are visible.

Page 96.

Thirty black-and-white photos of Madonna and Vanilla Ice in various stages of embrace and undress. Included are four photos in which Madonna straddles him as he's sitting on the toilet.

Page 103.

Thirty-one photos of Madonna and Big Daddy Kane, who is wearing patterned swim trunks. Madonna is behind Kane in all of the photos.

Page 105.

A full-page, green-tinted photo of Madonna in a three-way embrace. Madonna is nude, and behind her is model Naomi Campbell, who is also nude. Madonna is French-kissing Campbell. In front of Madonna is Big Daddy Kane, who is wearing bikini briefs. He has his hand on her crotch.

Page 107.

A full-page, purple-tinted photo of Naomi Campbell and Madonna. Campbell is nude and lying on her back on the tile parquet next to a beach. She is covering her breasts with her own hands. Madonna, also nude except for those leopard pumps, is standing over Campbell, straddling her, and holding a bottle of lotion at crotch level. She is squeezing the lotion onto Campbell's belly. The pose is blatantly meant to suggest a man ejaculating semen onto a nude woman. In fact, there are already gobs of white lotion on Campbell's body.

Pages 108–109.

A two-page, black-and-white photo of Madonna lying on the side of a pool, topless, and wearing only the bottom of a polka-dot bikini. Her legs are spread and in the air. Naomi Campbell is in the pool on her stomach on a raft and is completely nude. Campbell is floating between Madonna's legs and has her hands on Madonna's legs. Lesbian cunnilingus is the visual theme of this photo. Big Daddy Kane is standing in the water next to Campbell and has his hand on her ass.

Page 115.

A full-page, black-and-white, full-length photo of Madonna hitchhiking naked. She is wearing leopard pumps, smoking a cigarette, and carrying a black handbag. *Entertainment Weekly* ran this photo (censored, of course) on the cover of their magazine and caught holy hell for it from many of their readers.

Page 116.

Five black-and-white photos of Madonna pumping gas with her halter top pulled down so that her breasts are exposed. In one particularly artistic shot (I'm being sarcastic), she is holding the gas hose nozzle between her legs from behind.

Page 117.

A full-page, black-and-white, full-length photo of Madonna eating pizza naked. The shot was taken without warning the pizzeria owners. When Madonna stripped down, they called the cops.

And that, my curious friends, is the end of *Sex*. Was it good for you?

97 Notable and/or Notorious Nude Scenes by 56 Renowned Celebrities, Actors, and Actresses

The Naked Truth

I kept a couple of criteria for inclusion in mind when compiling this feature. The actor, actress, or celebrity had to be either a mega-star, a former TV star, or someone you would not expect to have done nudity, and/or the nude scene(s) had to be notable or notorious for some reason (for instance, scenes that are quite raw, extremely sexy or erotic, or surprisingly graphic). Some stars were also included because they happen to be personal favorites of mine.

My sources for this feature include Craig Hosoda's incredible compilation *The Bare Facts* (more about this volume later); various issues of the major movie magazines, including *Premiere* and *Movieline;* the celebrity nudie-watcher mag *Celebrity Sleuth* (various issues); most of the major film directories, including *Leonard Maltin's Movie Video Guide* (various years) and Mick Martin and Marsha Porter's *Video Movie Guide* (various years); Danny Peary's terrific compendium *Cult Movie Stars;* and *The Phantom's Ultimate Video Guide* by the always-outlandish Phantom of the Movies.

Regarding *The Bare Facts:* This wondrous tome has a cover blurb by none other than drive-in film critic Joe Bob Briggs, who gushes, "[*The Bare Facts* is] the most useful film book of the last ten years."

What elicited such praise from Mr. Briggs is the fact that *The Bare Facts* catalogs the nude scenes of thousands of actors and actresses and, most amazingly, provides the *exact spot* (in time) on the video-

tape where the scene can be found. And if that type of completeness isn't enough (You say you're not happy? You want more for
your money?), Craig Hosoda also tells you exactly what body parts
are exposed and considerately rates the scenes by their heat/
visibility factors.

The *Bare Facts* rating system consists of the following:

· = "Yawn. Usually too brief or hard to see for some reason."
·· = "Okay. Check it out if you are interested in the person."
··· = "Wow! Don't miss it. The scene usually lasts for a while."

Check out this sample entry (abridged) for Sharon Stone.

- *Irreconcilable Differences*
  ·· 0:56—Topless lowering her blouse in front of Ryan O'Neal
  during film test.
- *Action Jackson*
  ·· 0:34—Topless in a steam room. Hard to see because of all
  the steam.
  · 0:56—Brief right breast, dead, on the bed when police view
  her body.
- *Total Recall*
  ·· 0:04—Brief right breast in gaping lingerie when leaning
  over Arnold Schwarzenegger in bed.

If you're even remotely interested in celebrity nudity, *The Bare
Facts* is a must. You will find yourself referring to it often to look
up an actor or actress you might come across on a TV show or in
a magazine.

Several of my own books have been compulsively researched and
extremely detailed popular culture reference books, so I am all too
familiar with the effort and tedious attention to detail it took for
Craig to compile the information he needed to put *The Bare Facts*
together. Sure, it's fun, but it's also a ton of work. But as is usual
when someone really puts the effort into a labor of love, the quality shows in the finished product. *The Bare Facts* is available in bookstores everywhere, and I wholeheartedly recommend it.

The Stars Revealed

1. **Maud Adams** Maud Adams has not done any film work that received the attention and notoriety that her appearance in *Tattoo* did. Why? Because there were rumors that during her love scene with co-star Bruce Dern, the two of them actually did the nasty for real. Hype? Perhaps, but Adams's nude and sex scenes in this 1981 film *are* some of the hottest committed to celluloid. Her other films include *Rollerball, Laura,* and the James Bond film *Octopussy.*
   - *Tattoo* (1981)

2. **Kirstie Alley** *Cheers*'s repressed Rebecca in a nude scene? In the 1984 film *Blind Date,* Alley is topless, but it's difficult to really see anything because the scene is shot dimly.
   - *Blind Date* (1984)

3. **Julie Andrews** Mary Poppins's mammaries: That's what Julie Andrews proudly showed off in her now-notorious topless scene in the 1981 film *S.O.B.* She later did another nude scene (in which she showed her tush as well) in the 1987 film *Duet for One.*
   - *S.O.B.* (1981)
   - *Duet for One* (1987)

4. **Rosanna Arquette** Remember the Toto song "Rosanna"? That song was about none other than Rosanna Arquette, a woman whom some consider not to be beautiful in a classic or traditional sense, but whom many (including this writer) find incredibly attractive, appealing, and erotic. Arquette did a topless scene in *S.O.B.*, a film notable for another notorious nude scene (see Julie Andrews). Arquette's most erotic nude scenes, though, occur in the 1982 film about killer Gary Gilmore, *The Executioner's Song.*
   - *S.O.B.* (1981)
   - *The Executioner's Song* (1982)

5. **Priscilla Barnes** Barnes is included here because of her TV work. Often, fans are surprised to learn that some of their favorite sitcom stars have done nudity and sex scenes in feature films. Barnes replaced Suzanne Somers in *Three's Company* from 1981 to 1984, and it's obvious from her casting that the producers of the show wanted to continue the titillation (sorry) factor for as long as they could. In addition to

the film listed, Barnes also appeared in *Penthouse* magazine under the name Joann Witty.
- *Texas Detour* (1977)
- *Penthouse* (March 1976)

6. **Kim Basinger** Real estate magnate and trouble magnet. The sultry Kim Basinger has lately been somewhat reluctant to bare it all, but who can forget her sizzling performance in that ode to a well-stocked refrigerator, *Nine ½ Weeks?* Her early *Playboy* appearance is also worth checking out. To this day Basinger acknowledges her *Playboy* pictorial as a major contributing factor to her success in the movie industry. I recently read an interview with the blond beauty in which she revealed how surprised she was by the response to her nude spread. She said the magazine appeared and her phone started ringing. That isn't always the case with a *Playboy* appearance, but in Kim's case it seems to have worked.
- *Nine½ Weeks* (1986)
- *Playboy* (February 1983)

7. **Kathy Bates** This one's a real surprise, isn't it? In 1990, Kathy Bates won an Academy Award for Best Actress for her portrayal of the psychotic nurse Annie Wilkes in the film version of Stephen King's chiller *Misery*. Prior to that performance, Bates had appeared in several respected films, the most notable being *Straight Time; Come Back to the Five and Dime, Jimmy Dean, Jimmy Dean; Men Don't Leave;* and *Dick Tracy*. She was also in the acclaimed romantic drama *White Palace*. In 1991—before *Fried Green Tomatoes*—she appeared nude in a film that also bared some other famous bods, including Tom Berenger and Daryl Hannah (see their listings). Guess it must have been some kind of rain forest thing, eh?
- *At Play in the Fields of the Lord* (1991)

8. **Warren Beatty** Mr. Annette Bening. Renowned actor, director, stud, and newly tamed family man Beatty has kept his pants on since 1975, but his derriere display in *Shampoo* is included for its collectibility factor.
- *Shampoo* (1975)

9. **Annette Bening** Mrs. Warren Beatty. It'll be interesting to see if Bening takes on any more roles as steamy (and naked!) as that of Myra in *The Grifters* now that she's all married and everything (See Warren Beatty.)

* *The Grifters* (1990)

10. **Tom Berenger** Berenger is included here because of his huge female following and because of his willingness to walk around almost completely naked in two of his films. In both of the listed films, not only is his butt beheld, but his manly parts are manifested as well. (Berenger made his first-ever TV sitcom appearance on the final episode of *Cheers*, broadcast on May 20, 1993.)
   * *In Praise of Older Women* (1978)
   * *At Play in the Fields of the Lord* (1991)

11. **Candice Bergen** Before she moved to TV and became anchorwoman Murphy Brown (much to the consternation of Dan Quayle), Bergen had a busy movie career. In 1979, she starred with Burt Reynolds in *Starting Over*, in which she had a very brief topless scene. She also sang (quite badly, if the truth be told) in the film, and her attempted musical seduction of Reynolds is classic.
   * *Starting Over* (1979)

12. **Corbin Bernsen** Attorney Arnie Becker in TV's *L.A. Law*. Bernsen's buns were bare in the entertaining 1989 baseball movie *Major League*.
   * *Major League* (1989)

13. **Valerie Bertinelli** Bertinelli is best known for her role as younger sister Barbara in the long-running sitcom *One Day at a Time*, but in 1986, two years after the series ended, she appeared topless in the film *Ordinary Heroes*. Bertinelli is ("Right Now") married to rocker Eddie Van Halen.
   * *Ordinary Heroes* (1986)

14. **Jacqueline Bisset** Bisset, a respected and talented actress, rocketed into celebrity notoriety with her see-through wet T-shirt scenes in the 1977 film version of Peter *"Jaws"* Benchley's novel *The Deep*. Prior to that film, she had also appeared nude in a little-known 1971 film called *Secrets*, which has now attained cult status because of Bisset's bod-baring.
   * *Secrets* (1971)
   * *The Deep* (1977)

15. **Linda Blair** Puking pea soup and masturbating with a crucifix are two of the notorious things Linda Blair did in the legendary 1973 horror film *The Exorcist*. Even though it was thought that the role of Reagan in *The Exorcist* would estab-

lish her career as a major actress, she has never been able to snare high-profile roles, instead taking on numerous "bimbo/sex kitten" roles in low-budget action films (often with the word *Savage* or *Heat* in the title). She has often discussed her breasts in public: "I am a well-developed person, and I photograph very womanly, very . . . um . . . *healthy*. I am very 'full,' so to speak. Someone told me very recently that I have very heavy breasts. 'No wonder you weigh so much,' he told me, 'your tits must weigh ten pounds each!' " Blair's most notorious role after *The Exorcist* (other than her role as rocker Rick James's squeeze) would have to be that of the inmate raped by her fellow cons in 1974's *Born Innocent.*

- *Born Innocent* (1974)
- *Chained Heat* (1983)
- *Red Heat* (1987)

16. **Marlon Brando** Marlon Brando in the buff: now that's a scary thought. But Marl didn't always shop in the "Portly" section of the local Gap, and in 1972, in the notorious *Last Tango in Paris,* he bared his buns mooning a woman.
- *Last Tango in Paris* (1972)

17. **Danielle Brisebois** Little Stephanie in *All in the Family* showed her stuff in *Big Bad Mama II,* four years after she stopped working on *All in the Family.* Because many people are greatly interested in TV people's "not for prime time" movie work, a couple of little Danielle's topless scenes are offered. Brisebois has not done much film work of note lately and seems to be remembered mainly for her years with Archie Bunker, and for the couple of seasons she did on *Knots Landing* as Mary-Frances Sumner.
- *Big Bad Mama II* (1987)
- *Kill Crazy* (1989)

18. **Glenn Close** It's always a bit of a surprise when this respected actress does nudity in films, and until *Fatal Attraction,* her only notable nude scene had been the moment in *The Big Chill* when she sat naked and cried in the shower. But then she really raised eyebrows (and also started the Psycho Killer Other Woman trend in movies) with the aforementioned *Fatal Attraction* when she and Michael Douglas (he really does get all the fun parts, doesn't he?) did it

everywhere—including in an elevator and on the kitchen sink.
- *The Big Chill* (1983)
- *Fatal Attraction* (1987)

19. **Joan Collins** Collins is included here because of the cult interest in her pre-*Dynasty* nude movie work. Collins played mega-bitch Alexis in *Dynasty* from 1981 through 1989, and she abandoned working nude as soon as her name became a household word. (TV has a way of doing that with names.) But before her stardom, Collins bared her boobs in several films, mostly of British origin, and mostly in the seventies. *The Stud* and *The Bitch* are the ones seen most often on cable and are the more readily available to rent, although *Oh, Alfie!* should be checked out for her sex scene with Michael Caine–wannabe Alan Price.
- *Oh, Alfie!* (1975)
- *The Stud* (1978)
- *The Bitch* (1979)

20. **Rita Coolidge** I have a friend who is terminally hot for both Rita Coolidge and Bonnie Raitt. As far as I know, Bonnie has never done a nude scene in a movie (I don't think she's ever even *acted,* come to think of it, although she did appear as a performer in *No Nukes*) but Coolidge did have a brief nude scene in the otherwise forgettable *Pat Garrett and Billy the Kid.* I wonder if my friend knows?
- *Pat Garrett and Billy the Kid* (1973)

21. **Kevin Costner** Megastar Costner has bared his extremely expensive buns in a couple of films, but *Dances with Wolves* is probably the most accessible.
- *Dances with Wolves* (1990)
- *Revenge* (1990)

22. **Cindy Crawford** Supermodel and Mrs. Richard Gere. Raunchy (and hilarious) comedian Denis Leary once did a routine for MTV built around one of his "Cindy Crawford" fantasies. He liked to imagine Ms. C. stark naked on top of the Empire State Building, eating a Mallomar. Hmmm. He also hungrily pined for an "all Cindy, all the time" cable station. Crawford appeared nude in the July 1988 issue of *Playboy.* I wonder if *Denis* knows?
- *Playboy (July 1988)*

23. **Tom Cruise** In his early years, this now "buns only" mega-

bucks superstar once did a nude scene in which he was frontally nude, hanging out there for all to see. Cruise (formerly married to actress Mimi Rogers) is currently married to actress (and his *Far and Away* co-star) Nicole Kidman, who is not included in this list but is in *The Bare Facts.*

- *All the Right Moves* (1983)

24. **Jamie Lee Curtis** Jamie Lee has always been beloved by horror movie fans because of her appearance in *Halloween,* the film that many look to as the granddaddy of the contemporary "impossible-to-kill-killers" horror film. (You know, the *Friday-the-13th-Nightmare-on-Elm-Street* et al. genre.) But just plain old Jamie Lee Curtis fans delight in her drop-dead gorgeousity on display in a few of her early eighties non-horror films.

- *Trading Places* (1983)
- *Grandview, U.S.A.* (1984)
- *Love Letters* (1984)

25. **Tyne Daly** In 1993, on the occasion of their fortieth anniversary, the editors of *TV Guide* voted Tyne Daly the best television dramatic actress of all time. They were clearly focusing on her Emmy Award-winning work from 1982 through 1988 on the memorable series *Cagney and Lacey,* since Daly's made-for-TV movies have been essentially forgettable, and her feature film work (such as it has been) didn't qualify for consideration. But almost ten years before her breakthrough role as Mary Beth Lacey, Daley appeared in a little known turkey about an impotent husband who hires a gigolo to keep his young, voluptuous wife satisfied sexually. (I have not found one critic who did not rate this film a bomb.) This has to be one of those roles Daly is sorry she accepted, but for her fans, it is notable because she is topless several times in the film, and thus it must be considered a camp collectible.

- *The Adulteress* (1973)

26. **Rebecca De Mornay** The hand that rocked the cradle. In that now-notorious (and culturally significant—see Zoë Baird) 1992 film, De Mornay played Peyton, a nanny with vengeance on her mind who turned her "host family" 's home into "Peyton's Place." Prior to that film, De Mornay did a couple of films with some steamy nude/sex scenes, including the 1983 smash *Risky Business.*

- *Risky Business* (1983)
- *And God Created Woman* (1988)

27. **Robert De Niro** Is there a better all-around actor working today? Many say no, and I happen to agree. De Niro *never* works nude, but he did make one exception, and that is the film you should rent if you'd like to see a bare Bobby. Also, let me take this opportunity to recommend a few De Niro films that are particular favorites of mine, but are movies that some of his fans might not have seen. They're all Martin Scorsese works and I think they must be considered some of De Niro's best flicks: *Mean Streets* (1973); *Taxi Driver* (1976); *New York, New York* (1977); and *King of Comedy* (1983). [Also check out *Brazil* (1985) for something *completely* different.) And don't forget *Midnight Run* (1988).]

- *The Deer Hunter* (1978)

28. **Susan Dey** Susan Dey once figured prominently in a very funny Top Ten list one night on *Late Night with David Letterman.* I don't remember what the topic was, but one of the list items was "From *First Love* to *Looker:* The Movies in Which Susan Dey Appears Nude," or something along those lines. It got a big laugh because at that time Dey had only made one or two movies and she was nude in both. Back then, people were still refusing to let her forget her "Laurie Partridge" character from *The Partridge Family,* and thus the nudity struck a lot of people as funny. David Letterman's writers were right, though, and to this day, if you want to rise to a nude Dey, those are the two movies you should rent.

- *First Love* (1977)
- *Looker* (1981)

29. **Angie Dickinson** Everyone thought Dickinson's nude shower scene in *Dressed to Kill* was the hottest thing she'd ever done until it was revealed that the shape in the shower was actually the bod of body double Victoria Lynn Johnson. For genuine de-clothed Dickinson, you have to go back a few years. Check out *Big Bad Mama* for a *truly* outrageous cult moment in film history: Angie "Police Woman" Dickinson and William "Captain James T. Kirk" Shatner in a steamy nude sex scene. Does Spock know?

- *Big Bad Mama* (1974)

30. **Patty Duke** Many actors and actresses have a nude scene from their past that they'd like to forget. In most cases these

scenes fall into one of two categories: the "I Was Young and Needed the Money" category, or the "My Career Desperately Needs a Jumpstart and Maybe a Nude Scene Will Do the Trick" category. In Patty Duke's case, I have a feeling that category number 2 applied, in that the only nudity she's ever done occurred at a time when she was not what you'd call busy in the film biz. And she did it in a Canadian film, which is usually a sign that an actor or actress is looking for some of that nice long video green. In any case, her role as the lesbian fashion designer Helen, who decides she wants to have a baby, in the 1981 film *By Design* is unanimously considered to be one of her worst performances. But for her fans, she does appear topless and thus it is a collectible.

- *By Design* (1981)

31. **Mia Farrow** Mia has had her problems of late, hasn't she? In 1992 and 1993, the ethereal waif-like actress was embroiled for several months in a vicious and embarrassing child custody battle with former paramour and employer Woody Allen. Since 1982 and *A Midsummer Night's Sex Comedy*, through 1992 and *Shadows and Fog*, Mia did not appear in any films other than those directed by Woody Allen. In 1992, she signed a $3 million deal to write her autobiography, and shortly thereafter she dropped out of the first film she got an offer for after splitting with Woody: Mike Nichols's *Wolf* (with Jack Nicholson). Prior to her "Woody" career, Mia appeared in ten mostly forgettable (other than the 1968 shocker *Rosemary's Baby*, of course) movies, a couple of which are notable for her topless scenes. If you're a fan of the young Mia Farrow (as was Frank Sinatra), rent these two early Farrow flicks.

- *Rosemary's Baby* (1968)
- *A Wedding* (1978)

32. **Farrah Fawcett** Remember that poster? At the height of *Charlie's Angels* mania, it seemed as though Farrah's infamous bathing suit poster was on the bedroom wall of every young male in America. There was really nothing notably different or scandalous about the poster. It was a basic, cheesecake-type photo. There was Farrah, with her wall-to-wall big hair, in a relatively modest, blue, one-piece bathing suit. So what was the big deal? Farrah's nipples were erect in

the poster, that's what, and they not only drew the eye to them like a magnet, but truly seemed to want to pop through the front of her bathing suit. It has long been my theory that if FF's erect nipples had been airbrushed out of the final version of the picture, the poster would not have sold a thousand copies. There was something undeniably erotic about her visible nipples, and when that eroticism bonded with the untouchability of her TV persona, you had a lusty phenomena that catapulted the sexy poster to record sales in no time at all. Shrewdly cognizant of the allure of the forbidden, Fawcett did not capitalize on the universal horniness for her that that poster generated by posing nude for a magazine or immediately doing nudity in films. But there have been a couple of times over the past decade or so when it has been possible to catch a brief glimpse of what that forbidding bathing suit concealed.

- *Saturn 3* (1980)
- *Extremities* (1986)

33. **Sally Field** The former Flying Nun is one of those actresses that must be considered a member of the Hollywood elite. She is a name brand actress, like Goldie Hawn, Meryl Streep, Glenn Close, Susan Sarandon, Geena Davis, Whoopi Goldberg, Demi Moore, and others of their ilk. Thus, nudity is not typically required of these performers, and if the script *absolutely* calls for it, a body double is usually used. As far as we know, Sally Field has only showed genuine skin once in her career, and that was way back in 1976. *Stay Hungry* offered a tantalizingly brief glimpse of Fields's backside and bosom, but it is difficult to see. The film is included here for those fans for whom anything is better than nothing.

- *Stay Hungry* (1976)

34. **Teri Garr** Teri Garr has appeared on David Letterman's show so often that his staff is frequently asked if the two are married. They are not, but they are good friends, even if their banter on the show seems occasionally (genuinely) nasty and argumentative. Garr has been in a lot of movies since the sixties, but she is probably best known for her role opposite Michael "Batman" Keaton in the 1983 blockbuster *Mr. Mom.* It seems as though Garr has only done nudity once, and a good guess as to why would be because of the

director. Garr appeared as Frannie in Francis Ford Coppola's 1982 bomb *One from the Heart*. In that film, she appeared topless a few times. If you're a Teri Garr fanatic, then *One from the Heart* is a must-see. The film is visually stunning, albeit emotionally unsatisfying, yet definitely worth a viewing, as are all of Coppola's films.

- *One from the Heart* (1982)

35. **Richard Gere** Mr. Cindy Crawford. My wife has been a serious Richard Gere fan since the mid-seventies, and yet even she did not know about Gere's full frontal nude scene in the 1983 remake *Breathless*. Gere's butt has been bared many times in many films throughout his career, but like his colleague Tom Cruise, he has only done frontal nudity once or twice. Gere is a brilliant actor who has a phenomenal screen presence. He is an avowed Buddhist and starred with Jodie Foster in the Civil War drama *Sommersby*. He can be difficult, though. I read an interview with his wife, model Cindy Crawford, that overlapped into an interview with Gere because he came home while the reporter was there. After a couple of tag team questions, Gere declared the interview over and told the writer to leave because he had to "knock up [his] wife." To her credit, Crawford was nonplussed. I guess Buddhism doesn't teach manners, eh?

- *American Gigolo* (1980)
- *Breathless* (1983)
- *Final Analysis* (1992)

36. **Mel Gibson** Women love Mel. What amazes *me* about him is his ability to turn his Australian accent on and off. It is quite something to hear him speak with a perfect American accent as his *Lethal Weapon* character Riggs, and then watch him effortlessly drop the accent and revert to his "down under" patois for an interview. From all accounts, he is a genuine nice guy. For the purposes of this list, there is really only one movie, and one scene, that qualifies as a truly notable Mel Gibson nude scene. I have a lesbian friend who told me that the scene in *Lethal Weapon* where Gibson gets out of bed in his trailer and walks to the refrigerator totally nude even turned *her* on. And this is a woman who is not inclined toward male eroticism. A must-own collectible for Gibson fans.

- *Lethal Weapon* (1987)

37. **Melanie Griffith** Mrs. Don Johnson. There is a hint of "Dr. Jekyll/Mr. Hyde" to Melanie Griffith's career path in the movie biz. On the one hand she has worked diligently to perfect the nubile sex kitten persona that her looks and voice are so suited for, and yet on the other she has tried to take on roles that are more than the "sum of her parts" so to speak. Most of the time it doesn't work and there are moments, as in *Shining Through,* when she is *savaged* by the critics. Nonetheless she does have a sexy screen presence. For her fans, there are several films in which Melanie appears nude. Also, for a look at a very young Griffith (romping naked with her future husband, Don Johnson), there is an issue of *Playboy* worth checking out.

   - *Body Double* (1984)
   - *Fear City* (1984)
   - *Something Wild* (1986)
   - *Shining Through* (1992)
   - *Playboy* (January 1986)

38. **Daryl Hannah** I once wrote a song called "All I Really Want" that had as its chorus the deathless lines, "All I really want out of life/Is a kiss from Daryl Hannah." As you can probably surmise, I have been a major Daryl Hannah fan for most of her career. I have followed her from her early years as a replicant and a mermaid (in, respectively, Ridley Scott's incredible *Blade Runner* and Ron Howard's charming *Splash*), suffered through her *Clan of the Cave Bear–High Spirits–Crazy People* missteps; and reveled in her *Legal Eagles–Roxanne–Wall Street–Steel Magnolias* home runs. For those of you interested in Daryl doffed, check out the following three must-see films.

   - *Reckless* (1984)
   - *Splash* (1984)
   - *At Play in the Fields of the Lord* (1991)

39. **Mariel Hemingway** Ernest's granddaughter and Margaux's sister is included here for the sheer novelty of being able to see Mariel both pre- *and* post-breast enlargement. Hemingway did nudity in 1982 in *Personal Best* before she had her implant surgery. A year later, in *Star 80,* she was topless for a great deal of the picture.

   - *Personal Best* (1982)
   - *Star 80* (1983)

40. **Marilu Henner** Henner has become quite popular since she took on the role of Burt Reynolds' wife, Ava, on the CBS sitcom *Evening Shade.* It is a classic bit of showbiz irony that ten years earlier Henner was topless in bed with Reynolds in the 1983 remake *The Man Who Loved Women.*
    - *The Man Who Loved Women* (1983)

41. **Mick Jagger** Mega-lipped Jagger bares the seat of a Stone in the hard-to-find 1986 film *Running Out of Luck.* Rae Dawn Chong also stars.
    - *Running Out of Luck* (1986)

42. **Don Johnson** Mr. Melanie Griffith. Don Johnson became a movie star thanks to the TV series *Miami Vice.* Prior to that huge hit, he hadn't really done much that he'd probably want to remember. Including the movie that qualifies him for listing here, *The Harrad Experiment.* In that 1973 film, Don's Johnson is briefly on display, and thus, for his legions of fans, at least one rental is mandatory.
    - *The Harrad Experiment* (1973)

43. **Marta Kristen** Remember the lovely Judy Robinson in the much-revered cult TV series *Lost in Space?* (All through high school, I was in love with Judy's "kid sister," played by the lovely and talented Angela Cartwright. She even sent me a picture once.) Well, that was Marta Kristen, and in 1974, four years after the end of the series, Kristen did a steamy nude lesbian love scene in *Gemini Affair,* a film that *is* available on video but is difficult to find. (It isn't even listed or reviewed in most of the standard video guides, so if you're a "Judy Robinson" fanatic, you'll have to do some hunting.)
    - *Gemini Affair* (1974)

44. **John Lennon** In *Imagine: John Lennon,* the masterful 1988 biographical documentary about John, there is a scene during the bed-in for peace segment where self-described "Neanderthal Fascist" cartoonist Al Capp vitriolically and cruelly confronts John and Yoko about their notorious *Two Virgins* nude album cover. Capp unfairly describes the cover as "filth" and the first time I saw the documentary, I was praying for John to fire back the inevitable question: "Exactly what is so filthy about the nude human body?" But he didn't. Capp was so mean and insulting that I'm sure John didn't have the presence of mind to logically attempt to counter Capp's right-wing thinking. Be that as it may, the

Two Virgins album cover did cause an unbelievable commotion when it was first released (which happened to be exactly two weeks before the release of the Beatles' incredible double "White Album"). The front of the *Two Virgins* album features John and Yoko standing naked together, facing the camera. The back of the album shows them (of course) from the rear.

- *Unfinished Music No. 1—Two Virgins* (1968)
- *Imagine: John Lennon* (1988)

45. **Traci Lords** Interestingly, the September 1984 issue of *Penthouse* is collectible for another, even *more* notorious, reason than the fact that it featured raunchy photos of Miss America Vanessa Williams in the buff. The September '84 issue contained a multipage nude photo spread of X-rated-now-gone-straight actress Traci Lords. The text that accompanied the explicit photos said that Traci was a *twenty-two*-year-old model and actress. At the time, Traci was actually *fifteen* years old and not only posing nude for magazines but making hardcore, X-rated films. Those seventy films are now off the market [they're illegal and are considered child pornography because of Traci's age at the time] but Lords has apparently been one of the few sex stars to have successfully crossed over from porn to mainstream films. (Marilyn Chambers is also trying but hasn't had any luck yet.) Lords talked about her infamous past in a January 1993 interview with *USA Today*: "I'm shocked when people *don't* ask me about it. It would be nice if you could let the past be, but I don't look for that. People still ask me; they will always ask me. It'll be on my tombstone." In May 1993, Lords starred in the ABC miniseries adaptation of Stephen King's novel *The Tommyknockers.*

- *Penthouse* (September 1984)

46. **Lisa Loring** She was little Wednesday Thursday on *The Addams Family* in the mid-sixties. Twenty-five years later she was married to a porn star (Jerry Butler), a star on a daytime soap (Cricket on *As the World Turns*), and stark naked in a forgettable (and thus, hard-to-find) thriller. Crazy business, no?

- *Iced* (1988)

47. **Rob Lowe** Did you know that you can actually buy a copy of the notorious home video that got Rob Lowe into so much

trouble? It's available from Midnight Blue (c/o Media Ranch, Inc., P.O. Box 432, Old Chelsea Station, New York, NY 10013). It shows Mr. Lowe engaging in activities you're surely not gonna see in *Wayne's World II*. This one video is a textbook example of what is meant by the word "notorious."

- *Rob Lowe's Home Video* (1989)

48. Madonna The siren of scandal. A story is told of a woman critic attending a screening of Sigourney Weaver's film *Half Moon Street*. After witnessing several topless scenes by Weaver, the woman is reported to have said out loud (to much laughter and applause), "God, I am *so* sick and tired of her tits!" It may not be long before that sentiment is expressed regarding Madonna's glorious delight in public exhibitionism. For those who *would* like to eyeball the blond one's bodacious bod, though, opportunities abound. *Playboy* and *Penthouse* have both published extensive raunchy pictorials of Madonna in the nude, and Madonna herself has made the anatomy quest even easier with the 1992 publication of her notorious picture book *Sex*. The most notable Madonna *film* nudity occurs in her "pre-fame" film, (the putrid) *A Certain Sacrifice,* and in her own concert rockumentary *Truth or Dare*. (See the feature on *Sex* and *A Certain Sacrifice*.)

- *A Certain Sacrifice* (1981)
- *Truth or Dare* (1991)
- *Playboy* (1985)
- *Penthouse* (1985)
- *Sex* (1992)

49. Rob Morrow Morrow plays Dr. Joel Fleischman on TV's brilliant hit series *Northern Exposure,* in which, because it is set in Alaska, it is apparently much too cold to take off his clothes. In fact, when he and Maggie finally did the four-legged frolic (actually flopping in *real* hay), it appeared that not too many articles of clothing were truly removed. But it was different in 1985 when Morrow exposed his southern exposure in a mindless comedy (that also starred the later-to-be-hot Johnny Depp) called *Private Resort*.

- *Private Resort* (1985)

50. Suzanne Somers Every warm-blooded American male was in love with blond airhead Chrissy (short for Christmas) Snow, one of the two female roommates on the hit seventies TV series *Three's Company*. One can only imagine the testosterone-inspired fantasies. And then in 1980, *Playboy* made those fantasies a reality. The magazine published a long-forgotten Playmate photo test shoot that Somers had posed for and suddenly there she was: Chrissy Snow wearing *nothing* but a thin gold waist chain. Adolescent America was never quite the same.

- *Playboy* (February 1980)
- *Playboy* (December 1984)

51. **Sissy Spacek** Sissy Spacek played Carrie White in the film version of Stephen King's novel *Carrie*, and it was that role that made moviegoers and Hollywood honchos sit up and take notice of this major talent. Even though Spacek had done a topless nude scene in the 1972 crime drama *Prime Cut*, what made her nude scene in *Carrie* a textbook example of a notorious moment in cinematic history is that not only is she completely nude in the opening shower scene, but the character of Carrie White actually has her first menstrual period during the scene, *on camera*, while her classmates watch and taunt her. If that wasn't sufficiently over-the-top cinematically, Carrie then runs frantically from the shower to her laughing classmates for help, still nude, only now with the menstrual blood all over her hands. Instead of comforting her, though, her vicious classmates pelt her with sanitary napkins until the gym teacher breaks it up. Classic. Spacek has since kept her clothes on for the past decade (is it any surprise?), appearing in such superb films as *Missing, The River, Marie, The Long Walk Home* (one of my favorites), and *JFK.*

- *Prime Cut* (1972)
- *Carrie* (1976)

52. **Sylvester Stallone** Sly will probably never live down his appearance in the 1970 porno film *A Party at Kitty and Studs,* in which he is totally nude throughout the film. (We know, we know: You were young. You needed the money.) After his breakthrough into the big time in 1975 with *Rocky,* the owners of *Party* retitled it *The Italian Stallion* and re-released it to capitalize on Stallone's new fame. It is still available for rental and has achieved cult status.

- *A Party at Kitty and Studs* (1970)

53. **Sharon Stone** As a *major* Woody Allen fan (I wrote the 1992 book *The Woody Allen Companion*), it has always been a real

kick for me to casually drop into a conversation the factoid that sex queen mega-star Sharon Stone got her movie start in a Woody Allen movie. Stone was the enticing yet unreachable blonde on the train across from Woody's in the opening moments of *Stardust Memories*. I admire Stone, and not simply because she is gorgeous and brilliant. (She supposedly has a genius-level 148 IQ.) I admire her because she is honest and forthright about her beliefs, about her willingness to do nudity, and about the absurdity of a woman in her mid-thirties becoming a major sex goddess in the perversely youth-fixated Hollywood motion picture establishment. In the June 1993 issue of *Movieline* magazine, Stone is quoted as saying, "I find that since becoming famous, I get to torture a higher class of men than I used to." I like that attitude, don't you? (And I believe her as well.) Stone has done nudity in many of her films. The most notable and/or notorious are listed.

- *Irreconcilable Differences* (1984)
- *Blood and Sand* (1989)
- *Scissors* (1990)
- *Basic Instinct* (1992)
- *Sliver* (1993)

54. **Vanessa Williams** Here she is, Miss America. Williams had to give back her 1984 Miss America crown when steamy, explicit, and quite erotic lesbian/S&M-themed photos appeared in two issues of *Penthouse* magazine. (We know, we know: You were young. You needed the money.) Ironically, the scandal that dethroned her also gave her a singing career. Williams is also famous (infamous?) as one of the handful of Miss Americas who is actually *remembered*.

- *Penthouse* (September 1984)
- *Penthouse* (November 1984)

55. **Debra Winger** Winger is included for her nude sex scenes with Richard Gere in *An Officer and a Gentleman*. What makes the scenes notable and somewhat notorious is that we now know that Winger was so distraught about doing the intimate and explicit scenes that she was actually crying *on camera* during the action. If you didn't know how upset she was, you'd think it was passion. She revealed the truth later in interviews, and knowing how she felt puts a whole different spin on those scenes when viewed now.

     • *An Officer and a Gentleman* (1982)

56. **Sean Young** Unconventional (some would call bizarre) actress Sean Young did a surprisingly revealing nude scene in the 1991 thriller *Love Crimes,* which co-starred Julia Roberts's nasty *Sleeping with the Enemy* husband, Patrick Bergin. In *Love Crimes,* Young stands up in a bathtub completely naked while Bergin watches. Young was also topless in *No Way Out,* which achieved some notoriety for its limo coupling scene, which is far less revealing than its reputation would have you believe. Eccentric as she might be, Young still possesses classic beauty and manifests extraordinary screen presence.

     • *No Way Out* (1987)
     • *Love Crimes* (1991)

Department of Peculiar Parlance:
45 Euphemisms for an Erection

This list consists of other names for what many men consider to be their best friend. (*Note:* This list does *not* duplicate the "Euphemisms for the Penis" list.)

1. The Bazooka
2. A Bit of Hard
3. A Bit of Stiff
4. The Bone
5. A Boner
6. Captain Standish
7. The Cockstand
8. Colleen Bawn
9. Crack a Fat
10. The Cunt Stretcher
11. Fixed Bayonets
12. A Full
13. The Golden Rivet
14. A Hard-on
15. The Horn
16. In One's Best Clothes
17. In One's Sunday Best
18. An Irish Toothache
19. Jack
20. A Lance at Rest
21. The Marquess of Lorn
22. Morning Pride
23. Old Hornington
24. Old Horny
25. Be on the Stand
26. Be Piss Proud
27. Be Proud Below the Navel
28. The Rail
29. The Ramrod
30. The Reamer
31. To Rise in One's Levi's
32. The Roaring Horn
33. Roaring Jack
34. The Rock Python
35. The Spike
36. The Stalk
37. The Standard
38. The Standing Member
39. Standingware
40. Stiff and Stout
41. A Stiff One
42. Stiffy
43. A Toothache
44. A Wood
45. A Woody

The Numerological Meaning of the Numbers 1 Through 9

Numerology is a form of divination in which numbers are said to possess prognosticative powers. Numerology zealots (who embrace as their "hero" the Greek philosopher and mathematician Pythagoras) point to the universal notion held by many that particular numbers are "lucky" as evidence of the assumed mystical power of numbers. They assert that our leaning toward (and away, in the case of "unlucky" numbers) a particular number is a subconscious acknowledgment of their sway over our life paths.

Bernard Gittelson, in his informative 1987 overview of psychic phenomena *Intangible Evidence,* defined the subtext of numerology:

> Numbers are the tool of choice for the numerologist. Much as an astrologer uses the position of the planets at the time of your birth as the basis for analysis of character and to forecast your future, numerologists use calculations based on the numerological values of your name and birth date. How can numbers have any predictive value? How can they reveal character? Numbers, say the adepts, have accumulated meanings in the collective unconscious to which we unknowingly respond. Our name, our birth date, is an intrinsic part of our makeup; we are under its influence. We also build personal associations to numbers throughout our lives, which add to the universal associations another layer of significance.
>
> Many adepts claim that numerology is not actually the study of numbers so much as it is the study of the symbols for the numbers and their cultural and psychological significance, both conscious and unconscious, symbolic and literal. [pp. 385–86]

Numerologists differ on assigning "carved in stone" meanings to specific numbers, but generally, the following traits and characteristics apply to the numbers 1 through 9.

1. Strength of will and individualism.
2. Reason and docility.
3. Happiness and energy.
4. Stability and organization.
5. Self-confidence and impatience.
6. Art and balance.
7. Thought and introspection.
8. Leadership and materialism.
9. Mental and spiritual wisdom.

There are several ways to determine your personal number and thus your personal numerological "reading." The most important personal number is your *birth force* number. This is arrived at by adding up the digits in the numbers of your birthday.

At the risk of revealing the unvarnished truth about myself, I will now use my own birthday as an example to illustrate the calculation of my own personal birth force number.

I was born on July 16, 1953, which is written numerically as 7-16-1953. Step one is to add up the digits of my date of birth:

$$7 + 1 + 6 + 1 + 9 + 5 + 3 = 31$$

Step two is to add up the resulting digits:

$$3 + 1 = 4$$

Thus, my birth force number is 31/4. The most important reading is generated by the 4, but supposedly you're supposed to also look at the 3 and the 1 to see where the 4 came from.

Therefore, according to my birth force number, stability and a sense of organization are my motivating characteristics, and those specific personality traits are manifested due to an inner happiness and sense of energy (the 3) and a strength of will (the 1).

Now you know everything there is to know about me, right?

Nope! Now we move on to my *name* number.

There are several ways to determine your *name* number using the letters in your name, but one popular system (an ancient method still used) is based on the Hebrew alphabet that uses the digits 1 through 8.

The alphabet is laid out according to the following chart:

1	2	3	4	5	6	7	8
A	B	C	D	E	U	O	F
I	K	G	M	H	V	Z	P
Q	R	L	T	N	W		
J	S	X					
Y							

You spell out your complete name and put the appropriate number beneath the letters.

S	T	E	P	H	E	N	J	S	P	I	G	N	E	S	I
3	4	5	8	5	5	5	1	3	8	1	3	5	5	3	1

You then add them up:

$$3 + 4 + 5 + 8 + 5 + 5 + 5 + 1 + 3 + 8 + 1 + 3 + 5 + 5 + 3 + 1 = 65$$

Reduce the sum down:

$$6 + 5 = 11$$

And then again:

$$1 + 1 = 2$$

My *name* number is 2, which indicates that I have a reserve of reason, but that I can occasionally be too docile and unassertive. (Don't you feel that you *really* know me now?)

Other important numbers include the *soul* number, which is the numerical total of all vowels in your name, and the *personality* number, which is the total of all consonants in your name.

A professional numerologist will take many different calculations to arrive at a series of numbers that he will then interpret for a full-fledged reading.

Another much-used system utilizes the following chart:

1	2	3	4	5	6	7	8	9
A	B	C	D	E	F	G	H	I
J	K	L	M	N	O	P	Q	R
S	T	U	V	W	X	Y	Z	

You might also try calculating your numbers using this method to see if the results change.

Other important numbers in the annals of numerology include the following:

- 11: This was the number of Christ's faithful disciples and thus stands for revelation and truth.
- 12: This is a very significant number and some of its associations include the 12 signs of the zodiac, the 12 hours in the day and night, the 12 gods of Olympus, the 12 tribes of Israel, the 12 apostles, and the 12 days of Christmas. The number 12 thus stands for completeness.
- 13: Traditionally considered an unlucky number that signifies doom and bad luck, 13's bad reputation is said to stem from the fact that Jesus and his 12 apostles totaled 13 men, and the 13th (Judas) was a traitor.
- 22: This number is said to be important because there are 22 letters in the Hebrew alphabet and because there are 22 cards in the "major arcana" of the Tarot deck. The number 22 also signifies completeness.
- 40: This number, like the number 12, has many associations in history and religion, including the 40 days and nights of the Great Flood, the 40 days Moses spent on Mt. Sinai, and the 40 days Jesus spent fasting in the desert. Once again, we have a number signifying completeness.

Numerology does have its followers, although it is always included in the basket of pseudosciences (some would call "phony" sciences) that contains astrology, palmistry, and the reading of tea leaves. Regardless of the veracity of its claims, though, if numerology is looked upon as a psychological tool that can possibly reveal truths about oneself, it must be considered useful. For instance, if during a numerology reading a person is told that his or her number indicates stability and organization and yet he or she knows *the opposite* to be true, the person might then make a conscious effort to change negative traits into positive ones.

Hey, it's cheaper than ten years of psychotherapy, right?

99 Odd Books Sold by Loompanics

entropy . . . 3. The degradation of the matter and energy in the universe to an ultimate state of inert uniformity.—*Webster's New Collegiate Dictionary*

The entropy of the universe tends to a maximum.—The Second Law of Thermodynamics

Loompanics is a mail-order company that sells books and videos.

That sounds relatively benign, right?

Wrong.

Loompanics sells what they describe as "unusual" products.

They understate.

Their slogans are "You Are What You Know, You Are What You Do, Help Yourself" and "No More Secrets, No More Excuses, No More Limits."

They are not kidding.

This feature lists 99 of the more intriguing titles offered in Loompanics 1993, 280-page catalog. The catalog, dedicated to the second law of thermodynamics, contains a disclaimer that states, "Certain of the books and papers in this catalog deal with activities and devices which would be in violation of various Federal, state and local laws if actually carried out or constructed. Loompanics Unlimited does not advocate the breaking of any law. Our books are sold for informational purposes only."

They also include a "Special Notification Regarding Books Seized by Authorities," which states that Loompanics cannot be responsible for any shipment of books seized by government bodies. They make note that this especially applies to shipments made to Canada and to prisoners.

In the introduction to the catalog, President Michael Hoy describes Loompanics as a source for "anarchists, survivalists, icon-
oclasts, self-liberators, mercenaries, investigators, dropouts,
researchers, and just about anyone interested in the strange, the
useful, the arcane, the oddball, the unusual, the unique and the di-
abolical."

He continues: "So controversial are the books we offer that most
magazines will not allow us to advertise. That's OK with us. We
know where we belong: *we are the lunatic fringe of the libertarian movement.* Because we do not believe in limits. We do not believe in
laws, rules and regulations. We have contempt for censorship, secrecy and dogmatism. We don't give a damn about being 'respectable,' or Politically Correct. We don't care about anything except
having fun and your right to find out anything you want to know.
Nothing is sacred to us, not even skepticism and self-reliance."

Whew.

The Loompanics catalog has 35 provocative sections:

- The Underground Economy
- Big Brother Is Watching You
- Tax Avoision
- Conducting Investigations
- Money-Making Opportunities
- Crime and Police Science
- Privacy and Hiding Things
- Locks and Locksmithing
- Fake I.D.
- Self Defense
- Revenge
- Drugs
- Guns
- Rock 'N' Roll
- Weapons
- Intelligence Increase
- Bombs and Explosives
- Science and Technology
- Guerrilla Warfare
- Heresy/Weird Ideas
- Murder and Torture
- Anarchism and Egoism
- Survival

- Work
- Self-Sufficiency
- Mass Media
- Head for the Hills
- Censorship
- Gimme Shelter
- Reality Creation
- Health and Life Extension
- Self-Publishing
- Paralegal Skills
- Miscellaneous
- Sex

Mike concludes his introductory remarks with, "This catalog is for knowledge. It is for joy and pleasure. It is for the unlimited potential of each individual—for the undying spirit of human freedom and resistance to tyranny. Do not let *anyone* tell you what to think or feel—*decide for yourself.*"

Interested yet?

The following 99 books are all listed in Loompanics' current catalog, which offers over 800 similarly exotic titles. Loompanics does not have a retail store, they do not publish their phone number, and they can only be reached by mail. Their address is: Loompanics Unlimited, P.O. Box 1197, Port Townsend, Washington, 98368 USA.

Their huge and informative catalog (which is really a trade paperback book loaded with book and video reviews, photos, articles, and fascinating features) is $5.00, which includes shipping. If one of the following titles sounds like something you'd like to read, you'll be happy to know that the Loompanics catalog has a complete, alphabetical index of every unique book and video they sell. For your entertainment and enlightenment, a few excerpts from the catalog descriptions and from selected titles are included here.

Tell 'em Steve sent ya.

1. *Advanced Lock Picking*
2. *The Art & Science of Dumpster Diving*
3. *The Art of the Bullwhip* [VHS video]
4. *The B&E Book: Burglary Techniques and Investigation*
5. *Basement Nukes*

6. *Be Your Own Undertaker*
7. *The Best Cat Houses in Nevada*
   "PEARL NECKLACE: Sexual activity involving the man plac-
   ing his tumescent love club between a woman's breasts, then
   rocking gently back and forth culminating in ejaculation of
   his pearl drops love beads around her neck from his wank-
   wank sack bag." [From the "Sex Glossary," p. 165.]
8. *Birth Certificate Fraud*
9. *The Bouncer's Guide to Barroom Brawling*
10. *The Church of Satan*
11. *The CIA Catalog of Clandestine Weapons, Tools and Gadgets*
12. *CIA Improvised Sabotage Devices*
13. *Confessions of a Holocaust Revisionist*
14. *Conquering the Urine Tests*
15. *Construction and Operation of Clandestine Drug Laboratories*
16. *Counterfeit Currency*
17. *Counterfeit I.D. Made Easy*
18. *Covert Surveillance & Electronic Penetration*
19. *Credit Card Fraud*
20. *Crimes Involving Poisons*
21. *DEA Classified Intelligence Reports*
22. *Disguise Techniques*
23. *Disruptive Terrorism*
24. *Divorce Dirty Tricks*
25. *Drug Enforcement Administration Narcotics' Investigators Manual*
26. *Drug Smuggling*
27. *Electronic Funds Transfer Systems Fraud*
28. *Electronic Spying*
29. *Electronic Surveillance and Civil Liberties*
30. *The Encyclopedia of Unusual Sex Practices*
    "FELLCHING: Fellching (fellare: to suck, fell: animal hide)
    refers either to stuffing animals into the vagina or anus, or
    to a partner sucking semen out of one of these orifices (See
    ANAL SEX, OPHIDICISM, SAFE SEX, STUFFING and ZO-
    OPHILIA)"
31. *Exotic Weapons: An Access Book*
32. *Fingerprint Identification System*
33. *Freaks*
34. *Genitology*
35. *Get the Facts on Anyone*
36. *Getting Started in the Underground Economy*

"Complete step-by-step instructions are given for making gelatin explosives, powdered explosives, liquid explosives, slurry explosives, prilled explosives, and cast explosives.

"Among the everyday materials used in the manufacture are such things as: fertilizer, fuel oil, diesel oil, gasoline, wax, aluminum powder, water, charcoal, antifreeze, magnesium powder, sulfur, motor oil, alcohol, moth balls, soybean oil, coffee, sawdust, and many other commonly available and easily found materials.

"*Kitchen Improvised Fertilizer Explosives* belongs in everyone's explosives library. Because of the nature of this material, *we must warn that this book is sold for informational purposes only.*"

72. *The Magic of Female Ejaculation* [VHS video with books]

"The medical term for female ejaculation is Prostatic fluid. It does not look or smell like urine in any way. Most studies conclude that the fluid is produced by the paraurethral gland, which is surrounded by the urethral sponge. (An interesting note is that during fetal development, the urethral sponge in women becomes the prostrate in men.)

"This short video covers references to female ejaculation in literature and history, where exactly the fluid comes from, and what it is. Then, an attractive and comely young lady of the female sex masturbates on camera, climaxing with ejaculation. Fascinating!"

73. *Manual of the Mercenary Soldier*
74. *Nuclear War Survival*
75. *100 Deadliest Karate Moves*
76. *Physical Interrogation Techniques*

"*Amputation:* An 'eye for an eye' may be a great punishment technique, but amputation is of less use as an interrogation technique. Interrogation techniques must proceed slowly by small increments. Gouging an eye, cutting off a limb, removing the sex organs, usually proceed too quickly to be of much use. But if major mutilation seems to be the correct technique for your situation, they can be drawn out.

"Don't just cut off his ear, slice away little bits at a time. You can do the same with his nose, his eyelids, his lips. Facial mutilation can be very psychologically devastating.

"Instead of chopping off his hand, nail it down, questioning as each nail goes in. For variety pull off his fingernails then start slicing off bits of skin and muscle. Finally chop away the bone. Make him watch you do this to just one of his fingers and he'll probably be talking before you have to do it to any of the remaining nine.

"If you are going to gouge an eye, do it slowly, taking care not to damage the optic nerve. Then you can leave the eyeball hanging on his cheek still functioning. His brain will still receive the visual information but will be unable to turn away or close eyelids as, for example, you mutilate his genitals."

77. *Portfolio of Schematic Diagrams for Electronic Surveillance Devices*
78. *Ragnar's Guide to Home and Recreational Use of High Explosives*
79. *Secrets of International Identity Change*
80. *Secrets of Methamphetamine Manufacture*
81. *Sell Yourself to Science*

"Part One of this book deals with how you can legally profit by renting out your body for experimentation. Being a professional test subject or 'human guinea pig,' is one of the easiest and most rewarding ways to make a living off your body. You can earn up to $100 a day, plus benefits, helping pharmaceutical companies test drugs. Though not always pleasant, the work is safe, requires no skill, and has the side benefit of helping bring comfort to the ill.

"Part Two deals with actually selling your body parts or products. Some of this is legal in the United States, some of it's not. But all of it is legal somewhere in the world. This section also gives you the current market prices for most of your bodily goods. Of course, prices are subject to change without notice.

"Lots of body parts and products can be sold while you're alive: bone marrow, blood, sperm, hair, etc. Others, like your heart and brain, are best not sold until you don't need your body anymore.

"This book rests on the idea that your body, including anything it produces, belongs to you and you alone. It was given to you by God to do with it what you will, for whatever purpose you choose. There is nothing immoral about renting or selling your body. The fact that you can do a lot of good for yourself and others by renting and selling your body only reaffirms this truth. One good thing you can do with your body is make a living off it, thus providing a nice vehicle for your soul." [From the author's Introduction]

82. *Silencing Sentries*
83. *Subterranean Worlds*
84. *Subway Survival*

85. *Surreptitious Entry*
86. *Survival Poaching*
87. *Surviving Major Chemical Accidents*
88. *S.W.A.T. Team Operations*
89. *Techniques of Burglar Alarm Bypassing*
90. *Techniques of Revenge*
91. *Techniques of Safecracking*
92. *Techniques of the Professional Pickpocket*
93. *"Top Secret" Registry of U.S. Government Radio Frequencies*
94. *Tune In on Telephone Calls*
95. *21 Techniques of Silent Killing*
96. *The Vigilante Handbook*
97. *War Tax Resistance*
98. *Where There Is No Dentist*
99. *The X-Rated Bible*

30 Odd Films About 6 Historical Figures

Hollywood has a tendency to grab hold of something and refuse to let go.

When a western such as *Unforgiven* wins a few Academy Awards, it doesn't take long for a slew of cowboy flicks to appear in your local cineplex.

It's the same with historical figures. There have been figures throughout the ages who have been so colorful, so intriguing, so *larger-than-life*, that they have proved irresistible to the Hollywood hotshots who green light film projects. Here is a look at 30 of the most peculiar films made about 6 legendary historical figures.

1. Billy the Kid

1. *Billy the Kid vs. Dracula* (1966)
2. *Bill & Ted's Excellent Adventure* (1989)

2. Count Dracula (Vlad the Impaler)

1. *Dracula's Daughter* (1936)
2. *Son of Dracula* (1943)
3. *Abbott and Costello Meet Frankenstein* (1948)
4. *The Magic Christian* (1970)
5. *Dracula vs. Frankenstein* (1971)
6. *Dracula A.D. 1972* (1972)
7. *Legend of the Seven Golden Vampires* (1972)
8. *Count Dracula and His Vampire Bride* (1973)
9. *Andy Warhol's Dracula* (1974)
10. *Son of Dracula* (1974)
11. *Dracula's Dog* (1978)

12. *Dracula and Son* (1979)
13. *Love at First Bite* (1979)
14. *The Monster Club* (1980)
15. *Dracula's Widow* (1989)

3. Adolf Hitler

1. *Hitler's Children* (1943)
2. *Which Way to the Front?* (1970)
3. *Zelig* (1983)
4. *Hitler's Daughter* (1990)

4. Jesus Christ

1. *Jesus Christ Superstar* (1973)
2. *The History of the World, Part I* (1981)
3. *Hail Mary* (1985)
4. *The Last Temptation of Christ* (1988)
5. *Jesus of Montreal* (1989)

5. Abraham Lincoln

1. *Bill & Ted's Excellent Adventure* (1989)

6. Napoleon

1. *Love and Death* (1975)
2. *Time Bandits* (1981)
3. *Bill & Ted's Excellent Adventure* (1989)

14 Odd Foot-, Panty Hose-, and/or High Heel–Oriented Features in One Issue of *Leg Show* Magazine

Her pretty feet
Like snails did creep
A little out, and then,
As if they started at bo-peep,
Did soon draw in agen.
                    —Robert Herrick, "Upon Her Feet"

Leg Show magazine is one of many mainstream fetish photo magazines. (I'm calling it mainstream because it's sold on newsstands, rather than by ads in the back of men's magazines or in adult theaters and bookstores.)

Leg Show's editorial focus is the erotic display of women's feet and legs. The women are almost always nude and exposing their breasts, buttocks, and genitals, but the visual focus of the photos is always on either the high heels or panty hose the model is wearing, or the model's bare feet.

The culture of foot fetishism is one of the most meticulously structured of all fetishes (with the possible exception of S&M), and *Leg Show* knows the ropes and *all* of the tricks of the trade. (Back issues can sell for $15 each or more.)

Foot freaks have specific fetishistic interests, some of which are incredibly narrow and strictly defined. One cannot help but wonder just what triggered an erotic interest in women's toes, and not their heels or ankles or arches. A strong element of domination and humiliation figures in many foot fetish photo features.

This feature is a rundown of 14 of the oddest and/or most intriguing features in one issue of *Leg Show* (the October 1992 issue), with a look at the thematic focus of each section.

1. **The Cover:** The cover of this issue boasted that *Leg Show* was "Number One in the World!" Feature stories listed on the cover included the following:
   - "Twist and Suck with our Contortionist Covergirl"
   - "Perfect Size Sixes Photos and Video"
   - "Plastered! An Outrageous Footsie"

   The cover photo was of a woman in bra, garter, and nylons with her ankles behind her head and her pantied crotch staring at the camera. It was obvious that she was the "Contortionist Covergirl" so proudly bragged about.

2. **"Just My Opinion":** A one-page essay by the publisher (a woman named Dian) titled "The Most Embarrassing Four Letter Word." (What could it be, we salaciously wonder? *"Feet,"* maybe?) The word, we quickly learn, is *"Love."* The essay's thesis was that even though most men are into porn because they have a "friction addiction" (as Dian put it), lust without love "leaves you feeling alone." The piece actually attempted to encourage better, more open and loving relationships between men and women. Dian posited that men are afraid of love and thus turn to porn as a necessary straight line to sexual release.

3. **"Leg Forum":** A "Letters' section. Letters from readers included the following:
   Pedal Pumping Film Fest: A listing of 50 films and 6 TV series in which there are scenes of women stepping on a car's gas pedal, either while wearing shoes or barefoot. The letter also listed 25 actresses who have been seen "gas-pedal pumping." (See what I mean about specific interests?)

   Spiked Balls: A letter from a guy who approached a gorgeous woman at a party and knelt down at her feet on a dare. He ended up in an erotic S&M relationship with her in which the woman massaging his testicles with spiked heels played a big part in their sex life. The writer enclosed color photos of himself lying on the floor with an erection and a high-heeled woman standing above him.

4. *Leg Show* Life Styles: A color photo feature in which a woman dressed like a nurse "examines" a male patient by

making him kiss her shoes, smell her feet, and submit to a rectal examination.

5. **Elmer Batter's Black Stocking Seduction:** A black-and-white photo spread featuring two women topless and wearing black nylon stockings who fondle each other and suck each other's toes. The feature concluded with an order form for Elmer Batter videotapes. The ad read:

   If the SUCCULENT TOES of a PRETTY GIRL STIMULATE your SEXUAL APPETITE then I have the SEXIEST THING next to the REAL THING when it comes to STIMULATING your SEXUAL APPETITE i.e., VIDEO TAPES in COLOR and SOUND featuring the SUCCULENT TOES of 40 different PRETTY YOUNG GIRLS.

6. **Home Photos:** Photos sent in by readers. Shots included women wearing black panty hose and nothing else, women masturbating their men with their feet, women's bare feet (no other body parts visible), women in high heels, and naked women kneeling on a bed with their butt, vagina, and bare feet facing the camera.

7. **Danielle Ashe, Hollywood Hot Foot:** A photo feature of Danielle Ashe, an actress (*Hollywood Hot Tubs III* seems to be the extent of her resume) who has enormous breasts and who is a favorite of foot fetishists for an erotic act she performs in which she picks things up with her toes.

8. **Calistra, Bendable Babe:** The "Covergirl Contortionist." Calistra is seen in various types of underwear with her feet in her mouth or behind her head.

9. **"The Masturbatrixes":** A short story. ("Submitted by the Ladies Masturbation Society, Greenwich, CT") Two women go on a sexually explicit talk show and masturbate a masked foot fetishist who just so happens to be their husbands' boss. Basically this was written for humiliation foot freaks. The women take great delight in sexually torturing the helpless executive, even to the point of forcing him to take off his mask and reveal who he is and what company he works for.

10. **Jenny, Traditional Values:** A photo feature of a barefoot Oriental girl wearing nothing but a fishnet body stocking that has holes torn in it. The accompanying text describes her humiliation at having her anus stretched for anal sex, "begging him to honor me with the gift of his semen."

11. **"The Pretenders":** A short story subtitled "Their Crutches Supported Their Passions." It tells the story of a woman with

"a great pair of legs" (she even quotes the commercial), who uses crutches to attract men. (There's nothing wrong with her legs.) She meets a female amputee in a bar one night and they go home together and have sex.

12. **Footsie, All-Star Cast:** A photo feature of a man kissing and licking the toes of a woman wearing a cast. Several photos are of her masturbating his erect penis with her foot.

13. **Personal Please,** *Leg Show* **Classified Ads:** Three pages. A sample: "Wife loves jerking me off with her stocking feet. WMC [White Married Couple] wants to trade homemade videos. Your tape must feature panty hose or stockings. Other interests: cumshots, spread pussies, blow jobs, M/F masturbation. We don't sell."

14. **Several Pages of Ads for Escort Services, 900 Numbers, Videos, and Magazines:** Tapes offered include "Close Shave," which shows a woman shaving off her pubic hair, and "Foot Fever," featuring the cult favorite JoAnn.

Department of Peculiar Parlance:
96 Euphemisms for Masturbation

This list consists of euphemisms for that most private of all pursuits: orgasm on demand. Interestingly, the vast majority of these euphemisms refer to male masturbation. (Maybe because we're so good at it?) There *are* a few terms for female masturbation, though, and they should be easily identifiable. (After all, men do not have a clitoris, so it should be fairly obvious that a phrase such as "Strum Your Clitty" refers to women.

1. Ball Off
2. Beat Off
3. Beat Your Hog
4. Beat the Bishop
5. Beat the Dummy
6. Beat the Meat
7. Beat the Pup
8. Belt Your Hog
9. The Blanket Drill
10. Bop the Baloney
11. Box the Jesuit
12. Bring Down by Hand
13. Chicken Milking
14. Choke the Chicken

15. Coax the Cojones
16. Cuff Your Governor
17. Diddle Yourself
18. Do Paw-Paw Tricks
19. Dong Flogging
20. Fight Your Turkey
21. Fist Fuck
22. Five Against One
23. Flog Yourself
24. Flog Your Log
25. Flong Your Dong
26. Fondle Your Fig
27. Frig Yourself
28. Fuck Mary Fist
29. Gallop Your Antelope
30. Get a Hold of Yourself
31. Get Your Nuts Off
32. Gherkin Jerking
33. Grip It
34. Hand Jive
35. A Hand Job
36. Handle Yourself
37. Jack Off
38. Jag Off
39. Jazz Yourself
40. Jerk Off
41. Jerk Your Gherkin
42. Keep the Census Down
43. Lizard Milking
44. Manipulate Your Mango
45. Manual Exercise
46. Manual Pollution
47. Milk the Lizard
48. The One-Legged Race
49. Paddle the Pickle
50. Play with Yourself
51. Plunk Your Twanger
52. The Portuguese Pump
53. Pound Off
54. Pound Your Pomegranate
55. Pound Your Pud
56. Pound the Meat
57. Prod the Peepee
58. Pull Yourself Off
59. Pull Your Pud
60. Pull Your Pudding
61. Pull Your Wire
62. Pump Your Pickle
63. Pump Your Python
64. Rub Off
65. Shag Off
66. She-Bop
67. Shower Spank
68. Simple Infanticide
69. Sling Your Jelly
70. Sling Your Juice
71. Snap the Rubber
72. Snap the Whip
73. A Soldier's Joy
74. The Solitary Sin
75. Spank Yourself
76. Squeeze the Lemon
77. Stroke Yourself
78. Stroke the Lizard
79. Strum Your Clitty
80. Take Yourself in Hand
81. Tickle Your Crack
82. Tickle Your Pickle
83. Toss Off
84. Twang Your Wire
85. Wank Off
86. Whack Off
87. Whack the Bishop
88. Whang Off
89. Whank Off
90. Whip Off
91. Whip the Dummy
92. Whip Your Wire
93. Work Off
94. Yank Off
95. Yank Your Strap
96. Yank Your Yam

20 Odd Names for Groups of Animals

A group of human beings is known simply as a group or occasionally as a crowd (or every so often as a mob, when widespread misbehavior is going on).

Not so in the animal kingdom. The names used to describe a gathering of a certain type of wildlife are strange and perplexing (a *crash* of rhino?).

This list details how to properly address a big bunch of critters.

1. A drove of ass
2. A cete of badgers
3. A sloth of bears
4. A gang of elk
5. A business of ferrets
6. A shoal of fish
7. An earth of fox
8. An army of frogs
9. A tribe of goats
10. A leap of leopards
11. A nest of mice
12. A troop of monkeys
13. A span of mules
14. A crash of rhino
15. A pod of seals
16. A dray of squirrels
17. A knot of toads
18. A bale of turtles
19. A gam of whales
20. A rout of wolves

21 Truly Odd Fan Clubs or Organizations

These are all real fan clubs or organizations and are all listed in Gale Research's *Encyclopedia of Associations*. Their existence illustrates what could happen if someone happened to have just a wee bit too much free time on their hands. (Only kidding, folks. I've always been a big fan of corkscrews. Honest.)

1. The American Guild of English Handbell Ringers
2. Club of the Friends of Ancient Smoothing Irons
3. Committee for Immediate Nuclear War
4. Cookie Cutter Collectors Club
5. Flat Earth Research Society International
6. Flying Funeral Directors of America
7. Friends of the Tango
8. The Institute of Totally Useless Skills
9. The International Association of Sand Castle Builders
10. The International Connoisseurs of Green and Red Chile
11. The International Correspondence of Corkscrew Addicts
12. The International Petula Clark Society
13. The International Society of Animal License Collectors
14. The International Stop Continental Drift Society
15. Mikes of America
16. National Association of Mall Walkers
17. The National Pygmy Goat Association
18. The National Society for Prevention of Cruelty to Mushrooms
19. The Society of Earthbound Extraterrestrials
20. Spark Plug Collectors of America
21. The Witches Anti-Discrimination Lobby

34 Odd Things People Eat, Including Dishes That Use Insects, Sperm, Rats, Shark Fins, Testicles, Faces, and Blood as Their Main Ingredients

> Tell me what you eat and I will tell you what you are.
> —Anthelme Brillat-Savarin, *Physiologie du goût*

These recipes are real, and people around the world do, in fact, eat these dishes. As Americans, we have a narrowly ethnocentric sensibility about what we consider "normal." This mind-set extends to food, lifestyles, attitudes, and even moral codes.

We tend to be a bit intolerant of other cultures and philosophies, believing that ours is the ultimate manifestation of a truly civilized society. Hell, we're so fragmented as a culture that we even consider people from other *states* as "outsiders."

This is foolish and arrogant, to say the least, as well as being genuinely naive. It would do us all a world of good if we became a bit more educated about how other people live—and eat.

This feature is a good place to start.

1. **Baked Armadillo** *(American)* This tank-like mammal is stuffed with potatoes, cabbage, apple slices, carrots, and spices, and then baked until tender.
2. **Baked Bat** *(Samoan)* First the bat is torched to "de-hair" it. Then it is cleaned, and baked or fried with salt, pepper, and onions.
3. **Barbecued Cow Heart** *(Peruvian)* The cow's heart is chopped up, basted with ground chili peppers, and broiled.

4. **Bear's Paw Stew** *(Chinese)* The paw is cut into chunks and simmered in a pot with ham, chicken, and sherry.

5. **Beef Blood Pudding** *(Norwegian)* Beef's blood is mixed with milk, sugar, ginger, and cloves.

6. **Beef Udder Pot Roast** *(French)* The cow's mammaries are simmered with vegetables in beef stock.

7. **Broiled Beetle Grubs** *(Japanese)* The larvae are marinated and then broiled.

8. **Broiled Puppy** *(Hawaiian)* The puppy is broiled flat over hot coals and served with sweet potatoes.

9. **Broiled Sparrows** *(Japanese)* The birds are split, marinated, and then grilled.

10. **Coconut-Cream-Marinated Dog** *(Indonesian)* Pieces of dog are marinated in a coconut cream and then broiled on skewers.

11. **Cow Brain Fritters** *(French)* The cow's brains are mashed up, mixed with spinach, and fried.

12. **Cow Heels** *(English)* The cow's heels are cut up and simmered in a stew with beef stock and spices.

13. **Cow Lung Stew** *(Jewish)* The cow's lung is chopped into pieces and simmered with tomatoes, carrots, and potatoes.

14. **Cow Tongue Salad** *(Danish)* Julienned beef tongue is served with beets, apples, and hard-boiled eggs.

15. **Fish Sperm Crepes** *(French)* Fish sperm is baked in crepes with mushrooms, butter, and cheese.

16. **Fried Calf's Head** *(Hungarian)* The head is sliced, breaded, and fried.

17. **Fried Grasshoppers** *(Chinese)* The bugs are quick-fried in sesame oil and allowed to drain and cool. They crunch.

18. **Fried Turkey Testes** *(American)* The gonads are coated with bread crumbs and then fried in olive oil or butter.

19. **Golden Calf Testicles** *(French)* The testes are sliced and fried and then baked in a casserole.

20. **Grilled Horsemeat** *(Japanese)* The meat is sliced up, marinated, and then broiled on a hibachi.

21. **Grilled Rat** *(French)* Le rodent is brushed with olive oil and shallots and then broiled.

22. **Lamb Brain Tacos** *(Mexican)* The lamb's brain is chopped up, fried with onions, tomatoes, and chilies, and then used as a taco stuffing.

23. **Pig's Face and Cabbage** *(Irish)* The blanched face is baked with seasonings and served with boiled cabbage.
24. **Pig's Feet with Bananas** *(Filipino)* The feet are simmered with bananas in a soup.
25. **Pork Testicles in Cream** *(French)* The testes are fried in butter and cream.
26. **Roasted Caterpillars** *(Laotian)* The insects are salted, roasted, and then eaten with white rice.
27. **Sea Urchin Gonad Sauce** *(French)* Fish testes or ovaries are mashed with olive oil and then mixed with either Hollandaise sauce or mayonnaise.
28. **Shark's Fin Soup** *(Chinese)* Pieces of shark fin are simmered in a chicken stock with flaked crabmeat.
29. **Snake Soup** *(Chinese)* Chunks of snake are simmered in a fish or chicken stock with scallions.
30. **Stewed Cat** *(Ghanaian)* Sliced cat is fried in peanut oil and butter and then simmered in a pot with red peppers.
31. **Stuffed Calf's Eyes** *(French)* The eyes are stuffed with mushrooms (after the corneas, lenses, and irises have been removed) and baked.
32. **Stuffed Cow Spleen** *(Jewish)* The cow's spleen is stuffed with bread crumbs and baked.
33. **Sun-dried Maggots** *(Chinese)* Fly larvae are dried in the sun and then eaten as a snack or as a side dish with a meal.
34. **White Ant Pie** *(Zanzibari)* White termites are mixed with sugar and banana flour and blended into a paste.

6 Odd Ways of Dying Accidentally on a Farm

City-trapped Americans often dream about giving up the rat race and moving out to the country where they will live and work on a farm. They fantasize about the endless acres of rich soil and the beauty of sunrises and sunsets.

They think the peace and contentment they seek will be found there.

Perhaps.

But before you sell the co-op and buy three dozen flannel shirts and a bunch of overalls, read this feature on odd ways you can die on a farm. Okay, you might be killed in a hold-up or by a runaway cab in the big city, but at least you'll never have to worry about getting stuck in a corn picker or being stampeded to death (unless you're at a Metallica concert, that is) in the concrete jungle.

1. KICKED IN YOUR SAC BY THE COW YOU'RE HUMPING

1. **Being Crushed:** A painful way of dying on a farm is to be crushed to death when a tractor or another piece of heavy riding equipment rolls over you.

2. **Being Fumigated:** Inhaling deadly fumes or gases in a silo is a mode of death on a farm.

3. **Being "Picked":** A nasty form of farm death is getting caught in the machine called the corn picker.

4. **Being Stampeded:** Death can occur when a ranch hand is crushed by stampeding cattle. If a cowboy falls down in the midst of a frightened herd of steer, it can be goodbye, Hank.

5. **Buried Alive:** Farm personnel sometimes fall into corn bins, are buried, and then suffocate to death when they can't climb out.

6. **Strangled:** A loose piece of clothing can get caught in a piece of moving farm equipment and strangle or crush the wearer to death.

9 Outlandish Fringe Myths, Beliefs, and "New Age" Philosophies, Including Flat Earth Theory, Channeling, and UFOs

Weird beliefs and interests have been around since the first caveman saw a light in the northern sky and imagined a monster from *out there* coming to get him.

There are people who believe that the earth is flat.

Or hollow.

Or that they can channel spirits from another realm through their own bodies.

Or that they have been abducted by aliens.

Or that a piece of amethyst can heal their inflamed gallbladder.

Or that the world will come to an end on Wednesday, September 13, 1998.

Or that they have lived before as an Assyrian slave concubine named Oha.

And what's especially interesting about these enthusiasts of the odd is that they are as fervent about their convictions as any church-going, communion-taking, genuflecting and confessing Roman Catholic could ever be. It's just that their strange doctrines and dogmas are a little bit more unusual than the strange doctrines and dogmas many people are accustomed to accepting on faith. Their argument is, if you can believe that your God was born of a virgin, rose from the dead, and walked on water, why can't I believe that a million-year-old entity from the planet Venus speaks to me every Thursday morning in my vegetable garden?

This feature looks briefly at nine of the more intriguing fringe interests. This section is not meant to be comprehensive regarding these topics; books are required for that. Rather, let this serve as an introduction to these subjects, as well as an opportunity for me to offer some personal thoughts.

1. **Astral Projection:** Astral projection is also known as an out-of-body experience. It involves leaving the physical body and traveling to a place outside of and away from where the body happens to be at the time. OBEs have been reported throughout history, and they all share similar characteristics. In many cases, stress will trigger one, and occasionally there are reports of people being able to initiate an astral projection at will. Evidence exists that these experiences are real, mainly because the "traveler" can describe a place he or she has never been to, or report on events that occurred at a distant location while they were physically someplace else.

   I have a friend who is convinced he has had at least one out-of-body experience. It took place at night while he was in bed (but he's positive he was not sleeping). He claims he left his physical body and was able to look down on his prone form on the bed below him, in a manner similar to what people who have had near-death experiences report. If you think you have experienced an OBE, there are numerous books available that describe the common experiences of OBE percipients.

2. **Channeling:** Apparently there is a realm where legions of spirits exist, many of whom have a lot to say and really like to talk, and whose preferred mode of communication with our world seems to be to inhabit one of us Earthlings and speak through his or her body.

   I personally find this incredibly farfetched, although there are advocates who are convinced that they have spoken to entities from another plane, channeled through someone they know. Some channelers claim to channel big names such as Jesus Christ, Mark Twain, and Albert Einstein. Others claim their sources are from other planets, including the common ones such as Mars and Venus, as well as planets we allegedly don't know about yet.

   There are numerous channelers who claim many paranormal sources, including Seth, Lazarus, Ramtha, and Ra. Books and tapes on channeling abound, and if you're interested, study up on the subject before you pay someone for supposedly channeled advice.

3. **Crystal Healing:** Crystal healing is a practice that uses the positive "energy" in natural, mined quartz crystals to heal. According to their advocates, crystals are a type of natural therapeutic tool that can be used to cure all manner of ailments, both physical and emotional. Their assertion is that crystals are more than just rocks, and, in fact, their real powers are regrettably mostly unknown and under-utilized. Belief in the healing powers of crystals seems to me to require more than just a simple leap of faith: I would suggest a pole vault.

4. **Doomsday Mythologies:** Doomsdayers look to the Bible, to prophets, and occasionally to science (both mainstream and fringe) to predict with absolute certainty the day the world is going to end. (Or at least until the day they predict as doomsday comes and goes with nary a peep.) The Book of Revelation in the Bible is a big favorite for doomsdayers, as are the writings of Nostradamus.

It has always amused me no end to watch these so-called "prophets" tap dance around their failed predictions. It is not so funny, however, when gullible and naive people put their faith in these phonies. *Far Out* magazine recently detailed one such travesty:

Doomsday predictions are generally harmless, usually resulting in nothing worse than Christian best-sellers and bad television miniseries. But sometimes the consequences can be deadly. The most recent example is the Dami Mission, a Korean Christian sect that believed the world was coming to an end on October 28, 1992. Four of the mission's followers committed suicide in anticipation shortly before midnight of that day. Others sold their houses, had abortions and bequeathed their life savings to less fortunate pilgrims. Now they have nothing.

Currently, armageddon advocates believe that we are in the first year of the Rapture, the seven-year period prior to the Second Coming of Christ that will cleanse the world of sinners and take the righteous bodily into heaven. This is scheduled for the year 2,000, as are many other millennium-based doomsday events.

Apocalyptic religious beliefs are one thing, but I don't think it's a good idea to sign your pension fund over to the homeless guy who lives on the heating duct outside your apartment building because you'll be in heaven pretty soon and you won't need it. Give him a couple of bucks if you want, but leave the IRAs alone.

5. **Flat Earth Theory:** The people who propound the Flat Earth theory (their motto is "Restoring the World to Sanity") reject the notion that our planet is round, satellite photos notwithstanding. (They believe that NASA imagery is nothing more than "entertainment for the masses.") The Flat Earth people believe that Gaia is an enormous flat disk floating in space. According to Flat Earthers, we are all in constant danger of falling off the edge into the great void. The father of the Flat Earth movement is a retired aircraft mechanic named Charles K. Johnson, who operates the Flat Earth Society and publishes the *Flat Earth News* for his 3,500 subscribers out of his desert home in Lancaster, California. In a 1993 interview with *Far Out* magazine, Johnson explained that he believes that most of the world is water and that the fact that oceans and rivers are not "humped" in the middle proves that the planet is a flat plane. As he put it, "Water seeks its own level and lies flat." He also explained that the known world is actually surrounded by a giant frozen ring of ice that measures about 64,000 miles in length.

The Flat Earth Society publishes a map of what they call the "real world" that posits that "This Flat Earth Does Not Spin or Whirl" and lays claim to the Earth as the "Center of the Universe." In one of their newsletters they proudly include George Washington and Christopher Columbus in the ranks of Flat Earthers. If this intrigues you and you want to know more, write to the Flat Earth Society at P.O. Box 2533, Lancaster, California 93539.

6. **Hollow Earth Theory:** Hollow Earthers believe that the world is a hollow sphere, entered by large holes at either pole, or by secret entrances scattered around the globe. Inside the Earth is a small sun, as well as a race of advanced beings who are responsible for the UFO sightings throughout history. Photos exist that purport to show the polar entrances (I have seen them—the photos, that is). Current believers look to a woman named Ruth Leedy for guidance.

Leedy publishes a newsletter called *The Abyss*, which explains the complex Hollow Earth theories and conspiracies. If you're interested in learning more, send $3 for postage and handling for an information packet to Ruth Leedy, RD#3, Box 240-B, Dover, Delaware, 19901.

7. **Past Lives and Reincarnation:** Reincarnation zealots believe that this life is just one of many that our eternal soul will live. They believe that we have all lived before and that our past lives are stored somewhere within us, deeply buried in our unconscious/subconscious, ready to be accessed by the proper technique.

Many believers look to the concept of karma as the determining factor as to whether we move forward or backward on our eternal, celestial journey. The theory goes that our soul is like an empty bank account when we are born into a certain life. The good we do during our life adds to the account; the bad we do deducts from our account. If there's a positive balance in the account at the time of our death, we move forward; if we're in the red, we move backward. When we have developed our spiritual self to its highest level, we reach nirvana and enter into a oneness with the universe. Nirvana releases us from the cycle of reincarnations and completely extinguishes the self, thereby allowing us to become part of the all. Most religions have a similar philosophy, although the language is different. Entering heaven, becoming one with God, knowing God, and other phrases are all used to describe this state of absolute blessedness.

A current New Age craze is to consult with a "past lives counselor," a person who can supposedly allow you to tap into your past lives at will and learn from what you were in the past. How much of these regression sessions are pure imagination is difficult to say, although advocates claim to recall people and events they could not be aware of unless they had lived during another period. (See Albert Brooks's film *Defending Your Life* for one particularly clever approach to the theory of reincarnation.)

8. **Spontaneous Human Combustion:** In 1853, Charles Dickens killed off his character Krook in *Bleak House* by spontaneous combustion. According to an 1859 newspaper report, at the time, people cringed and doctors smiled: such a ridiculous death could never occur in the real world. Now, almost 150

years after Dickens's bitter tale, incidences of spontaneous human combustion are still being reported worldwide.

Spontaneous human combustion is the term used to describe a person burning up from within. There is usually no external source of fire, and the fire is often contained to the immediate surroundings of the person, such as the chair or bed. Oftentimes, the person's clothing does not completely burn up, but the body does, although sometimes the extremities are left intact. I have seen one photo of a person who spontaneously combusted, and all that was left of him was his right calf and foot.

Medical science has no definitive explanation for SHC, although some have tried to find a link between excessive alcohol ingestion and bursting into flames. Students of the supernatural look to poltergeists and "fire spooks" as the cause, but the truth is that SHC is one of the genuinely unexplainable phenomena on the paranormal landscape.

9. **Unidentified Flying Objects and Alien Abductions:** UFO sightings are a ubiquitous element of human experience and a phenomenon that has been reported since Biblical times. What are UFOs? Where do they come from? The speculative answers to these questions have filled volumes of books. Carl Jung posited that UFOs might be some type of subconscious hallucinatory manifestation of our collective unconscious. But then there are those clearly rational people (military people, law enforcement people, doctors, and lawyers, among others) who have seen UFOs and who purport to have real evidence of their experiences, such as photos, objects from alien crafts, and physical wounds from close encounters.

There are many people who claim to have been abducted by aliens and taken aboard extraterrestrial spacecraft, where they have been examined and/or assaulted. Most of these abductees cannot be shaken in their belief that they were kidnapped by aliens.

Most UFO sightings can be attributed to natural phenomena such as ball lightning, clouds, planets, and weird geographical anomalies. But no matter how many sightings are "written off," so to speak, there will always be that small percentage of encounters that are genuinely unexplainable and that could possibly be of extraterrestrial origin.

19 "Paul Is Dead" Clues

In September, October, and November of 1969, a horrible rumor swept the world.

The rumor was that Paul McCartney was dead.

And not only was he dead, but he had been dead for three years.

The story, which began in Ann Arbor, Michigan, in the fall of 1969, was that Paul had been killed in a dreadful car accident in England in November of 1966. The surviving Beatles decided that they would not reveal this tragedy to their fans but instead replace Paul with a double, a musical doppelgänger.

Paul's "replacement" was a guy by the name of William Campbell, who just so happened to be the winner of a Paul McCartney look-alike contest. Not only was Campbell the spitting image of the "cute" Beatle, he was also musically and vocally gifted enough to be able to duplicate Paul's writing, playing, and singing abilities. After a period of "training" by John, George, and Ringo, Campbell took Paul's place in the Beatles.

The story continues that even though the Beatles did not want to shock the world by revealing the truth about Paul's violent death, they had too much respect for their fans not to let them somehow know of his demise. Thus, they began planting "clues" on Beatles albums that would alert the attentive fan to the terrible reality.

It was all a hoax, of course, and there are many theories as to who started it, and why. (One critic claims it was a deliberate prank by the Beatles themselves.) Paul is assuredly alive and well. I recently saw him perform in Charlotte, North Carolina. It was his last appearance on his U.S. *Off the Ground* tour and he never sounded better.

Nevertheless, the rumors surrounding Paul's alleged death grew into a cottage industry. Special edition magazines and TV shows were devoted to the rumors, and countless newspaper articles fueled the fervor. (I can remember trading clues with fellow

Beatlefans when I was in my teens, aghast at the thought that rumors might actually prove to be true. They weren't, as we now know, and it would be another decade before we actually would have to go through the *real* death of a Beatle.)

This feature collects (in no particular chronological or discographic order) 19 of the most pervasive—and seductive—"Paul is Dead" rumors. If these intrigue you, pull out your old Beatles albums and check them out yourself. You'll find that they are most certainly there.

Or are they?

1. **"Lovely Rita"** (*Sgt. Pepper's Lonely Hearts Club Band*): There's a line in "Lovely Rita" that reads, "I took her home, I nearly made it." This is supposed to refer to the woman passenger named Rita that Paul had with him in the car when he was in the accident that killed him.

2. *Magical Mystery Tour:* In the centerfold photo of the *Magical Mystery Tour* album, Ringo is playing a drum kit that has "Love 3 Beatles" written on it. This is supposed to indicate that there were only three surviving Beatles.

3. **"Revolution 9"** [*The Beatles* ("The White Album")]: If "Revolution 9" is played backward, "Turn me on dead man" and "Let me out" can be heard. The "dead man" was supposed to be Paul, and "Let me out" is what he was supposed to have screamed when his car overturned and caught fire. (See the feature "20 Rumored Secret Subliminal Messages on Records and the Truth About What Is Really There" in this volume.)

4. *Sgt. Pepper's Lonely Hearts Club Band:* On the album's inside photo spread, Paul is seen wearing a sleeve patch that reads "O.P.D." This was supposed to be telling us that Paul was "Officially Pronounced Dead." (It actually reads "O.P.P.," which stands for Ontario Provincial Police.)

5. *Sgt. Pepper's Lonely Hearts Club Band:* In the front cover photo, a white hand is seen above Paul's head, an alleged religious symbol that is supposed to signify that he's passed on.

6. **"I'm So Tired"** [*The Beatles* ("The White Album")] John can be heard mumbling at the end of "I'm So Tired." If the mumbling is played backward, "Paul is dead, miss him, miss him" can be heard. (See the feature "20 Rumored Secret

Subliminal Messages on Records and the Truth About What Is Really There" in this volume.)

7. *Abbey Road:* The front jacket photo of *Abbey Road* is supposed to be a symbolic representation of Paul's death and burial. The four Beatles are seen walking across Abbey Road. John is in the lead, dressed all in white, followed by Ringo in formal black tails, then Paul in black and white and barefoot, and finally, George, in denim. John was supposed to be the preacher, Ringo the undertaker, Paul the corpse, and George the gravedigger.

8. *Abbey Road:* In the front jacket photo, Paul is carrying an unlit cigarette, which is supposed to symbolize death.

9. *Abbey Road:* In the background of the front jacket photo, a parked Volkswagen can be seen with the license plate 28IF, which is supposed to mean that Paul would have been 28 years old *if* he had lived.

10. *Abbey Road:* Some people claim that they can see a skull, symbolizing death, on the wall in the back jacket photo.

11. *Abbey Road:* In the back jacket photo, the word *Beatles* has a crack in it, symbolizing the fragmenting of the group after Paul's death.

12. *Sgt. Pepper's Lonely Hearts Club Band:* The words "Bet at Leso" are alleged to be written in the hyacinths in the front jacket photo. Leso is supposed to have been an underwater island the Beatles owned and where a horribly disfigured Paul was hiding.

13. **"Strawberry Fields Forever"** (*Magical Mystery Tour*): At the end of "Strawberry Fields Forever," John can be heard saying, "I buried Paul." (See the feature "20 Rumored Secret Subliminal Messages on Records and the Truth About What Is Really There" in this volume.)

14. **"A Day in the Life"** (*Sgt. Pepper's Lonely Hearts Club Band*): The line "He blew his mind out in a car" is supposed to be describing Paul's car accident.

15. **"Revolution 9"** [*The Beatles* (**"The White Album"**)]: The sounds of Paul's fatal car crash are supposed to be audible in this sound montage.

16. *Magical Mystery Tour:* In the *Magical Mystery Tour* film and in the album photo, Paul can be seen as the only Beatle wearing a black carnation, which was supposed to symbolize that he was the dead one.

17. *Abbey Road:* Paul is seen barefoot on the front of the album. Did you know that corpses are buried barefoot?

18. **"Glass Onion"** [*The Beatles* **("The White Album")**]: John tells us that "The walrus was Paul" (referring to "I Am the Walrus" in which *John* sang, "I am the walrus"). Supposedly, the word *walrus* means "corpse" in Greek. (It doesn't.)

19. **"Come Together"** (*Abbey Road*): John tells us that "1 and 1 and 1 is 3," which was supposed to indicate that there were only three surviving Beatles.

7 Peculiar Sexual Phobias

Brenda Love, in her superb *Encyclopedia of Unusual Sex Practices* had this to say about sex phobias:

> A sex oriented phobia may be caused by societal guilt, a negative experience with intimacy, a lack of experience in coping with fear, temporary stress, or by separation, overprotection, or rejection by parents when young.

Phobias come in many shapes and forms: Most of us are familiar with "dirt" phobias, often manifested by compulsive hand washing and other "cleanliness" behavior, and with agoraphobia, the fear of open space. This is the phobia that keeps people confined to their houses for years at a time.

But sexual phobias aren't often talked about. And yet they can be as equally crippling as any of the other more "social" terrors.

This list offers a few sex phobias. A phobia becomes a problem when it becomes all-consuming. A fear of pregnancy is a good thing when you're a single teenager. But when you're a married woman and you're so terrified of pregnancy that you steadfastly avoid sex with your husband—even when you're using birth control pills, a condom, and a diaphragm—you're into the realm of phobic behavior. The following list is just a sampling of some of the things many people fear.

1. **Coitophobia:** This is a repugnance for and fear of sexual intercourse.
2. **Gamophobia:** This is a complete obsessive aversion to marriage. I can now hear my reading audience writing their own joke: We all know an awful lot of people with this phobia, right? A simple unwillingness to give up a carefree bachelor/bachelorette life is a lifestyle choice. When the single person

does find Mr. or Ms. Right, though, and even then is terrified of wedding this person, *then* it's a phobia.

3. **Gymnophobia:** No, this is not an aversion to taking gym class. Gymnophobia is a problem with being naked. (Come to think of it, maybe this *is* a gym class phobia after all.) Gymnophobes are afraid to be unclothed in front of someone else, and as you can imagine, this type of phobia can have a somewhat dampening effect on a lover's libido. (We've all heard of people who get undressed in the closet year after year and who will only have sex with the lights off.)

4. **Harmataphobia:** This is a paralyzing fear of sexual inadequacy, either in the size department (penis length for men, breast size/butt size/and so on for women) or in the performance department. There are some who contend that the recent prevalence of X-rated videos has contributed to a flare-up of this particular phobia. In porno films, the men all have huge penises, some over ten inches when erect, and the women are all sexual dynamos, always ready and willing for a romp. There are some people, the argument goes, who cannot help comparing themselves and their own performance to these sexual superstars, and because such an assessment is clearly a no-win situation, phobic fears can easily rear their incapacitating heads.

5. **Pathophobia:** A fear of sexually transmitted diseases. Wait a minute: Did AIDS suddenly disappear? No? Then why, I'd like to know, is this a *phobia?* Just sounds like good thinking to me.

6. **Scopophobia:** This is an obsessive fear of being looked at, but only when it comes to a sexual situation. Most people with this phobia have no problem getting through their day and having people look at them. It's when it comes to sex that they have a problem. This would seem to be an offshoot of gymnophobia, although I suppose there are instances when people with this fear even have a problem with being looked at during necking and clothed foreplay.

7. **Spermatophobia:** This is a crippling fear of semen loss. In some eastern religions, semen loss is considered deadly—a serious drain of the man's vital life force. To circumvent this and yet still be able to enjoy orgasm, some men have developed a technique whereby they press on their "jen mo" spot at the moment of orgasm. This spot is between the scrotum

and the anus and it apparently re-routes the ejaculation into the bladder. This supposedly preserves the life-giving properties of the sperm for the *man's* body and does not deplete the life force.

A friend of mine got into the sexology of Tao philosophy for a while and actually attempted to detour his ejaculation by pressing on his jen mo spot during intercourse. He encountered the exact problem that I imagined would crop up when I first heard about this technique: How does one reach beneath one's scrotum, *during intercourse,* to apply pressure to one's "spot" at the precise moment of orgasm without causing your partner to wonder just what the hell you're doing down there, and without interrupting the moment? Last time I spoke with him about this, he was attempting to re-route his ejaculation during masturbation. He thought it might be easier to learn it that way first. After a few weeks of trying, though, he had carpal tunnel syndrome in his left wrist from bending it repeatedly into a somewhat "unusual" position; he had somehow made his hemorrhoids bleed, and he was still ejaculating out of the head of his penis and "wasting" all his life essence. Thanks, but no thanks.

31 Peculiar Tourist Attractions

There's a very funny moment in the Chevy Chase film *National Lampoon's Vacation* that perfectly encapsulates America's fascination with peculiar tourist attractions. In one scene, Chevy's character, the astonishingly inept Clark Griswold, tells his family to hurry up so that they can get the Family Truckster back on the road. If they wait much longer, he frets, they won't have enough time to visit the world's largest house of mud on their way to Wally World.

America has some very strange tourist attractions.

One of the best guidebooks to the "weird and the wacky" is *The New Roadside America,* by Mike Williams, Ken Smith, and Doug Kirby. These guys actually *visited* hundreds and hundreds of these odd tourist sites. They wallowed in the kitsch and the camp, but they also took the whole thing quite seriously in an attempt to document this offbeat and quintessentially American road-trip art form.

They succeeded.

They catalog hundreds of places that are so strange one's first reaction is, "Aw, you're makin' that up." But, no, Virginia, there actually is a Bra Museum (see No. 6) and a Pet Casket Company that offers guided tours (No. 10). Not to mention the World's Largest Anything-You-Can-Imagine, and the annual Clinton, Montana, Testicle Festival.

Here is a sampling of 31 of America's most peculiar roadside "attractions."

1. **The Atomic Bomb Crater** *(Mars Bluff, South Carolina):* This one serves as a metaphor for all that is wonderful about tourist sites. In 1958, a B-47 pilot accidentally dropped a bomb on a guy's farm. It exploded, and the result was a huge hole that is now a tourist attraction.
2. **The Dan Blocker Memorial Head** *(O'Donnell, Texas):* It's

a big granite head of Hoss in the O'Donnell (his home-town) town square.

3. **The Donner Party Museum** *(Truckee, California):* It's a mu-seum commemorating the mountain excursion that culmi-nated in members of the Donner Party eating other (dead) party members in order to survive. Bring the kids.

4. **The Five-Story-Tall Chicken** *(Marietta, Georgia):* It's made of sheet metal and is 55 feet tall. Not much else to say, is there?

5. **Flintstone Bedrock City** *(Vail, Arizona):* Visit a replica of the town the modern Stone Age family calls home.

6. **Frederick's Bra Museum** *(Hollywood, California):* Bras, bras, and more bras!

7. **The Hair Museum** *(Independence, Missouri):* Weird things made out of human hair. A haircut is actually included in the admission price.

8. **The Hall of Mosses** *(Port Angeles, Washington):* Admit it: You've always dreamed that one day all the myriad forms of mosses would be gathered in one place. Well, dream no more.

9. **Hobbiton, USA** *(Phillipsville, California):* It's a life-size rep-lica of Bilbo Baggins's hometown (from J.R.R. Tolkien's *The Lord of the Rings* trilogy).

10. **The Hoegh Pet Casket Company** *(Gladstone, Michigan):* The tour includes the casket showroom and factory, as well as a look at a prototype pet cemetery.

11. **Holy Land, U.S.A.** *(Waterbury, Connecticut):* Religious shrines, dioramas, and statues galore, all done in a manner that brings to mind a religious Disneyland.

12. **The House of Telephones** *(Coffeyville, Kansas):* It's a house that has 1,000 phones in it.

13. **Jimi Hendrix Viewpoint** *(Seattle, Washington):* It overlooks a zoo and is surrounded by purple bushes.

14. **The Liberace Museum** *(Las Vegas, Nevada):* It's in a shop-ping center and serves as the ultimate tribute to the Key-board King of Kitsch.

15. **The Museum of Questionable Medical Devices** *(Minneapolis, Minnesota):* It's in a mall. One of the items on display is a prostate warmer.

16. **The Nut Museum** *(Old Lyme, Connecticut):* It's run by Eliza-beth Tashjian, who has been on *Late Night with David Letter-*

man. Twice. Elizabeth loves nuts and has even composed a "Nut Anthem."

17. **Philip Morris Cigarette Tours** *(Richmond, Virginia):* They show you how cigarettes are made and brag about their factory's ventilation system. Hmmm.

18. **The Soup Tureen Museum** *(Camden, New Jersey):* Near Campbell's headquarters, it's a museum dedicated to the noble soup tureen. I'm serious.

19. **The Spam Museum** *(Austin, Minnesota):* Everything you've always wanted to know about Spam, including things you probably wish you never asked.

20. **Spongeorama** *(Tarpon Springs, Florida):* Sponges, sponges, and more sponges!

21. **The Testicle Festival** *(Clinton, Montana):* No, it's not a gathering of male porno stars. It's a banquet. That's all I have to say.

22. **Toilet Rock** *(City of Rocks, New Mexico):* It's a giant rock formation that looks like a flush toilet. People come from miles.

23. **The Tupperware Awareness Center** *(Kissimmee, Florida):* Better ways to burp the tops of Tupperware containers so as to get all of the air out, plus a wondrous display of *all* the Tupperware products known to man.

24. **The Urinal Used by JFK** *(Salem, Ohio):* It's in the men's room in Reilly Stadium. "C'mon in and take my picture standing next to it, honey. The guys won't mind."

25. **The Wonderful World of Tiny Horses** *(Eureka Springs, Arkansas):* The title pretty much says it all. (They boast the world's smallest horse, a little stallion measuring all of 20 inches in height.)

26. **The World's Largest Artichoke** *(Castroville, California):* A commonly heard comment at this attraction is, "That's a big artichoke."

27. **The World's Largest Chest of Drawers** *(High Point, North Carolina):* It has four drawers and sleeps six.

28. **The World's Largest Crucifix** *(Bardstown, Kentucky):* A 60-foot-high reminder of one of mankind's more vicious forms of execution. Let's pack a picnic lunch!

29. **The World's Largest Office Chair** *(Anniston, Alabama):* It's 33 feet tall. If you want to put your feet up while sitting in it, use the apartment building across the street.

30. **The World's Largest Stump** *(Kokomo, Indiana):* It's 57 feet around and 12 feet high. The tree didn't mind being cut down: It *wanted* to be a dead landmark.

31. **The World's Largest Twine Ball** *(Darwin, Minnesota):* It is 12 feet around and weighs 21,140 pounds. Do you think the guy who "built" it had just a *wee* bit too much time on his hands?

Personality Characteristics of the 12 Astrological Signs

The stars do not compel; but rather impel.—John White

I'll bet you read your horoscope in the paper at least once a week. Am I right?

Astrology continues to be an interest for many Americans, and you won't come across too many people who do not know their astrological sign. What is astrology and how did it get this stranglehold on our culture's consciousness?

A few years back, while researching one of my books about writer Stephen King, I had the opportunity to work with the New York Astrological Society, an organization that has taken astrology into the next century by developing highly sophisticated and complex astrological computer programs. My friends at the Society provided me with comprehensive readings of King, readings I was told were more complete and probing than any individual astrologer could provide.

I read them carefully, and frankly, I was amazed. I had originally ordered the reports without telling them who I was investigating, and so they generated the readings based only on King's birthdate, time, and location.

There was much in the reports that could apply to anyone, but there was also much that could only apply to King, including specific years in which milestone events in King's life occurred, and very specific personality traits that King has manifested in interviews and in his work.

The Society also sent me *my* report, and once again there was an awful lot in the reading that was true about me, including the month and year of the publication of my first book. (Apparently I had something transiting something or some "aspect" aspecting. It's all Greek to me.)

My personal feeling about astrology is actually more of an agnostic, questioning attitude. Here's my question: If the pull of the moon can affect not only the tides but even menstrual blood flow, then isn't it remotely possible that there are some type of waves or vibrations or forces emanating from the planets (still beyond our understanding) that can have an impact on people's enzymes or genes or chromosones or whatever and thus influence their personality and ultimately their actions? Just because something is unproven does not mean it cannot be proved.

This feature offers a rundown of the twelve astrological signs, the calendar periods they span, and the positive and negative personality characteristics traditionally associated with them. The signs of the zodiac are traditionally listed in the following order: Aries, Taurus, Gemini, Cancer, Leo, Virgo, Libra, Scorpio, Sagittarius, Capricorn, Aquarius, and Pisces. I have rearranged the signs of the zodiac in calendar order so as to make it easier to locate your own month and day.

1. **Capricorn (The Goat)**; *December 22–January 19*
   Positive Trait: Ambition.
   Negative Trait: Rigidity.

2. **Aquarius (The Water Bearer)**; *January 20–February 18*
   Positive Trait: Wisdom.
   Negative Trait: Perversity.

3. **Pisces (The Fishes)**; *February 19–March 20*
   Positive Trait: Compassion.
   Negative Trait: Weakness.

4. **Aries (The Ram)**; *March 21–April 19*
   Positive Trait: Leadership.
   Negative Trait: Selfishness.

5. **Taurus (The Bull)**; *April 20–May 20*
   Positive Trait: Stability.
   Negative Trait: Stubbornness.

6. **Gemini (The Twins)**; *May 21–June 21*
   Positive Trait: Intelligence.
   Negative Trait: Stodginess.

7. **Cancer (The Crab)**; *June 22–July 22*
   Positive Trait: Creativity.
   Negative Trait: Self-Pity.

8. Leo (The Lion); *July 23–August 22*
Positive Trait: Generosity.
Negative Trait: Intolerance.

9. Virgo (The Virgin); *August 23–September 22*
Positive Trait: Organization.
Negative Trait: Obsessive/Compulsive Tendencies.

10. Libra (The Balance); *September 23–October 23*
Positive Trait: Judgment.
Negative Trait: Indecisiveness.

11. Scorpio (The Scorpion); *October 24–November 21*
Positive Trait: Passion.
Negative Trait: Secrecy.

12. Sagittarius (The Archer); *November 22–December 21*
Positive Trait: Optimism.
Negative Trait: Irresponsibility.

8 Plagued Places: An Ephemeris of Selected Blizzards, Cyclones, Earthquakes, Epidemics, Famines, Floods, Hailstorms, Hurricanes, Plagues, Tidal Waves, Tornadoes, Typhoons, and Volcanic Eruptions

Do you like where you live?

If you could, would you move somewhere else? Read through this feature and think twice before you answer.

There are places on this planet that have had more than their share of bad luck. The history of certain countries and regions reads like a Baedeker of bad news: famines, earthquakes, epidemics, and typhoons. All manner of dire occurrences seem to plague certain spots with depressing regularity. This feature looks at a selection of the dreadful things that have occurred in 8 places on God's green earth.

1. **China**
   Earthquakes
   - January 23, 1556: Northern China; 830,000 die.
   - November 30, 1731: Peking; 100,000 die.
   - December 16, 1920: Gansu (8.6 on the Richter scale); 180,000 die.
   - July 28, 1976: Tangsham (8.2 on the Richter scale); between 240,000 and 750,000 die.
   Floods
   - 1642: Hunan Province; hundreds of thousands die.

- September 1911: Yangtze River; 200,000 die.
- July 1915: Kwangtung and Kiangsi; over 100,000 die.
- August 1931: Yangtze River; 3,700,000 die.
- November 1939: Northern China; 200,000 die.
- August 1950: Eastern China; 89 die, 10,000,000 homeless.
- July 1954: Central China; 40,000 die.
- May 1991: Southeastern China; 1,700 die

Typhoons
- July 27, 1862: 40,000 die.
- August 2, 1922: 60,000 die.

Famines
- 1876–1879: 13,000,000 die.
- 1928–1929: 3,000,000 die.
- 1936: 5,000,000 die.
- 1939: 200,000 die; 25,000,000 left homeless.

2. England
Epidemics
- 1485: Sweating sickness; thousands die. Writer Raphael Holinshed described the scene in this manner: "Scarce one amongst an hundred that sickened did escape with life, for in all maner as soone as the sweate tooke them . . . yielded up the ghost."
- 1507: Sweating sickness in London; thousands die.
- 1518: Sweating sickness in London; thousands die.
- 1665: Bubonic plague in London; 100,000 die.
- 1684: Smallpox in London; 100,000 die.
- 1851–1855: Tuberculosis; 250,000 die.
- 1853: Cholera epidemic in London; thousands die.

3. India
Cyclones
- October 7–11, 1737: Calcutta; 600,000 die.
- December 1789: Coringa; over 20,000 die.
- June 1822: The Ganges River; 50,000 die.
- May 1833: Calcutta; 50,000 die.
- October 5, 1864: Calcutta; 80,000 die.
- October 31, 1876: Bengal; 100,000 die

Famines
- 1769–1770: Hindustan; millions die.
- 1790–1792: Bombay; unknown millions die. As the famine wore on, cannibalism was rife. This famine was known

as the "Skull Famine" because of the tens of thousands of unburied corpses piled everywhere.

- 1866–1870: The Bengal Region; 1,750,000 die. The total number of dead includes 250,000 who died from a fever epidemic that spread throughout northern India after the famine was over.
- 1876–1878: Southern India; 5,000,000 die.
- 1896–1897: 1,250,000 die.

Plagues
- 1903–1908: 4,000,000 die.
- 1910–1913: The Black Plague; millions die.

Hurricanes, Tidal Waves, Hailstorms, and Floods
- June 5, 1882: Hurricane and tidal waves in Bombay; 100,000 die.
- April 30, 1888: Hailstorm in Moradabad; 250 die.
- October 16, 1942: Hurricane in Bengal; 389 die.
- July 1993: Massive flooding in Calcutta; 4,300 die.

Earthquakes
- May 31, 1935: Quetta (7.5 on the Richter scale); 50,000 die.
- September 30, 1993: Bombay (6.3 on the Richter scale); 25,000+ die.

4. **Iran (Persia)**
Earthquakes
- 1040: Tabriz; 50,000 die.
- 1727: Tabriz; 75,000 die.
- September 1, 1962: 4,500 die.
- August 31, 1968: (7.8 on the Richter scale); 12,000 die.
- September 16, 1978: Northeast Iran (7.7 on the Richter scale); 25,000 die.
- June 21, 1990: Northern Iran (7.7 on the Richter scale); 50,000 die.

5. **Italy**
Volcanic Eruptions
- 79: Mount Vesuvius; Pompeii and Herculaneum; 16,000 die.
- 427: Mount Vesuvius; scores die.
- 1169: Mount Etna; 15,000 die. The deaths occurred from the earthquake and tidal waves that followed the eruption.

- December 16, 1631: Mount Vesuvius; 4,000 die.
- March 11, 1669: Mount Etna; 20,000 die. This was Mount Etna's worst eruption. (So far.)
- April 24, 1872: Mount Vesuvius; close to 30 die.

Earthquakes

- December 5, 1456: Naples; 35,000 die.
- July 30, 1626: Naples; thousands die.
- 1693: Naples; 93,000 die.
- 1693: Catania; 60,000 die.
- February 4, 1783: Southern Italy; 60,000 die.
- July 26, 1805: Naples and Calabria; 26,000 die.
- August 1819: Genoa and Palermo; thousands die.
- December 28, 1908: Messina, Sicily (7.5 on the Richter scale); between 160,000 and 250,000 die.
- November 23, 1980: Southern Italy; 5,000 die.

6. Japan

Earthquakes and Undersea Earthquakes

- December 30, 1703: Tokyo; 37,000 die.
- 1847: Nagano; 34,000 die.
- March 21, 1857: Tokyo; 107,000 die.
- August 31, 1886: Off the Japanese coast (undersea); 28,000 die.
- October 28, 1891: Central Japan; 7,300 die.
- June 15, 1896: Off the Northeast Japanese coast (undersea); 28,000 die.
- September 1, 1923: Tokyo; 140,000 die.
- July 12, 1993: Hokkaido (7.8 on the Richter scale); 12 die.

7. The United States

Epidemics and Plagues

- 1699: Yellow fever epidemic in Charleston, South Carolina, and Philadelphia, Pennsylvania; 370 die.
- 1735–1740: Diphtheria epidemic in New England; 80 percent of the children die.
- 1793: Yellow fever epidemic in Philadelphia, Pennsylvania; 4,044 die.
- 1832: Cholera epidemic in New York City; 4,000 die.
- 1863: Yellow fever epidemic in New Orleans, Louisiana; 7,848 die.

- 1861–1865, The Civil War: Typhoid, dysentery, and other diseases; 187,000 die.
- 1878: Yellow fever epidemic in New Orleans, Louisiana, and Memphis, Tennessee; 14,000 die.
- 1878: Smallpox epidemic in Deadwood, the Dakota Territory. A 26-year-old nurse named Martha Jane Canary nurses the sick, ignoring her own health. Because of her efforts, she becomes known as Calamity Jane.
- 1900: Bubonic plague epidemic in Honolulu, Hawaii (still only a U.S. territory); thousands die.
- 1900: Bubonic plague epidemic in San Francisco, California; 117 die.
- 1903: Typhoid epidemic in New York City.
- 1907: Bubonic plague epidemic in San Francisco, California.
- 1907: Bubonic plague epidemic in Seattle, Washington.
- 1914: Bubonic plague epidemic in New Orleans, Louisiana.
- 1916: Polio epidemic; 6,000 die.
- 1919: Bubonic plague epidemic in New Orleans, Louisiana.
- 1924: Bubonic plague epidemic in Los Angeles, California.
- 1931: Diphtheria epidemic; 17,000 die.
- 1952: Polio epidemic; 50,000 infected, 3,300 die.
- 1980–?: The AIDS epidemic; 175,000 dead, 10,000,000 infected.

Hurricanes
- September 1841: Saint Jo, Florida; 4,000 die.
- August 27, 1881: Southern U.S. Coast; 700 die.
- August 28, 1893: Southern U.S.; 1,000 die.
- October 1, 1893: Gulf of Mexico states; 2,000 die.
- May 8, 1900: Galveston, Texas; 6,000 die.
- September 17, 1926: Florida; 450 die.
- September 10, 1928: West Palm Beach, Florida; 5,000 die.
- September 2, 1935: Florida Keys; 400 die.
- September 21, 1938: New England; 500 die, 14,000 buildings destroyed.
- September 14, 1944: New England; 389 die.
- October 12, 1954: Hazel hits the U.S. East Coast; 411 die, $1 billion in damage.

- June 27, 1957: Audrey hits Texas, Louisiana, Mississippi; 500 die.
- September 6, 1960: Donna hits the U.S. East Coast; 143 die.
- August 17, 1969: Camille hits the Southeastern U.S.; 258 die, $1.5 billion in damage.
- June 21–26, 1972: Agnes hits the U.S. East Coast; 118 die, 116,000 houses destroyed.
- September 7, 1979: David hits the Southeastern U.S.; 2,000 die.
- September 12, 1979: Frederick hits Alabama and the Mississippi Coast; 5 die, $2.3 billion in damage.
- August 24, 1992: Andrew hits Florida, Louisiana, Southern U.S. states; 30 die, 250,000 people homeless, over $20 billion in damage.

Earthquakes
- 1755: Boston, Massachusetts; no deaths.
- December 15, 1811: New Madrid, Missouri; few deaths.
- August 31, 1886: Eastern U.S.; 110 die.
- April 18, 1906: San Francisco, California (8.3 on the Richter scale); 700 dead, 225,000 homeless.
- March 27, 1964: Anchorage, Alaska (8.6 on the Richter scale); 118 die.
- October 17, 1989: San Francisco, California (6.9 on the Richter scale; 60 die.
- August 8, 1993: Guam (8.1 on the Richter scale); millions of dollars in damage.

Tornados and Cyclones
- September 10, 1811: Charleston, South Carolina; over 500 die.
- May 7, 1840: Natchez, Mississippi; 317 die.
- June 16, 1842: Natchez, Mississippi; 500 die.
- February 19, 1884: Southern U.S. (cyclone); 800 die.
- May 27, 1896: St. Louis, Missouri; 306 die.
- May 26, 1917: Southern and Midwestern U.S.; 249 die.
- March 18, 1925: Missouri, Illinois, Indiana; 689 die.
- September 29, 1927: St. Louis, Missouri; 85 die. This tornado lasted five minutes and destroyed 1,800 houses.
- January 9, 1953: Worcester, Massachusetts; 90 die, 4,000 buildings destroyed.
- April 11, 1965: U.S. Midwest (35 at one time); 271 die.

- April 3–4, 1974: South and Midwest (over 148 at one time); 315 die.

Blizzards

- November 17–21, 1789: New England; hundreds die.
- March 12, 1888: Eastern U.S. Coast; 800 die.
- November 26–27, 1898: Northeastern U.S. Coast; 455 die.
- January 27–29, 1922: Eastern U.S. Coast; 120 die.
- March 15, 1941: North Dakota and Michigan; 151 die.
- January 14, 1952: The Sierra Nevadas; 26 die.

Floods

- May 31, 1889: Johnstown, Pennsylvania; 2,200 die.
- April 1927: The Mississippi Valley; 313 die.
- January 1937: The Ohio River Basin; 137 die.
- February 26, 1972: Logan, West Virginia; 107 die.
- July 1993: The Mississippi River and 55 of its tributaries in the upper Midwest (*massive* flooding), including Iowa, Missouri, Minnesota, Wisconsin; 20 die, 33,700 evacuated, 7,500+ homes damaged, 2 million acres under water, $2.4 billion+ in crop losses, 100+ breached levees, $5 billion+ overall damage.

8. **The World**
   Epidemics
   - 1893–1894: Cholera epidemic; millions die.
   - 1918–1919: Spanish flu epidemic, between 22,000,000 and 25,000,000 die.
   - 1957–1958: Asian flu epidemic; millions affected, but few deaths.
   - 1980–?: The AIDS epidemic; unknown number of deaths.

25 Prostitution Services Offered on a Typical "Menu" at Legal Bordellos

I enjoy sex. It's fun. I don't have an orgasm every time, but I do sometimes, and if that's what you want to hear, let me know. If you want me to act like your wife in bed, make a lot of noise, and say that you're the best ever, I'll be happy to do it. Just tell me what you want. I enjoy having a nice time and making the guy feel good.—Cissy, one of the ladies at the New Sagebrush Ranch

Prostitution has been called the oldest profession for a reason. It dates back thousands and thousands of years, and has never been regulated, legislated, taxed, or preached out of existence.

Today (in addition to the regrettable practice of streetwalking), there exists respectable, clean, and unquestionably safe legal brothels where any and all manner of sexual delights can be had for a price.

There are 36 very popular, licensed "cathouses" (as they have come to be known) in Nevada. These include the Calico Club, the Cherry Patch, the Cottontail Ranch, Mabel's Whorehouse, Pussycat, and of course, the world famous Mustang Ranch.

All of these establishments offer one thing: sex.

The ladies at these houses will usually do anything a gentleman wants, including anal sex, oral sex, golden showers, and bondage and discipline.

Two very popular clubs right next door to each other (they're owned by the same couple) are the Calico Club and the Desert Club. (Both are on North 2nd Street in Battle Mountain, Nevada.) These clubs both have bars, and their business is mainly repeat customers.

The two owners of the clubs, Ginger and Chuck Barrett, put together a "Menu" of erotic specialties for their clientele, samples from which are reprinted below. (For your edification, the items with a superscript number refer to explanations of the terminology that follow the menu.)

[My main source for this feature was J. R. Schwartz's book *The Official Guide to the Best Cat Houses in Nevada,* which is available from Loompanics (see their address in this volume) or from Schwartz at Box 1810, Boise, Idaho, 83710-1810.]

Menu
A wide selection of delectable treats for the discriminating gentleman

Appetizers . . .[1]

1. Massage
2. Breast Massage
3. X-Rated Movies
4. Hot Tub Party
5. Champagne Bath
6. Bubble Bath
7. Lingerie Show
8. Body Paint

Entrees . . .

9. Straight Party
10. Half & Half [2]
11. 69 Party
12. 69 Party Lay
13. Double Party Show
14. Double Party French
15. Double Party Lay
16. Drag Party
17. Dominating Woman
18. Vibrator Party
19. Friends & Lovers
20. All Night Date[3]
21. Out Date[4]

Desserts . . .

22. Hot & Cold French[5]
23. Creme De Menthe French[6]
24. Binaca Blast French[7]
25. Flavored Pussy Party[8]

*If you don't see your personal preference
listed, do not hesitate to ask.*

Explanations

1. These are all fairly self-explanatory.
2. Half oral sex, half straight intercourse.
3. From 2:00 A.M. to 7:00 A.M.
4. A house call.
5. Oral sex alternating hot and cold, often using coffee and ice cubes.
6. Oral sex with Creme de Menthe liqueur.
7. Oral sex with Binaca breath freshener.
8. Cunnilingus with various flavorings added to the vagina.

36 Really Long Movies

And you thought *JFK* was long!

This list offers movies that require catering.

For the purposes of this list, I used 5 hours as the minimum length required for inclusion, and this still left out almost three dozen films listed in my sources that were released with running times of 4 hours to 4 hours, 58 minutes.

The list begins with the "shortest" films (relatively speaking, that is) and concludes with the longest films known.

1. 5 hours, 2 minutes: *Winifred Wagner und die Geschichte des Hauses Wahnfried* (1975)
2. 5 hours, 5 minutes: *Les Misérables* (1927)
3. 5 hours, 6 minutes: *Petersburgskije truscoby* (1915)
4. 5 hours, 14 minutes: *Potopi/The Deluge* (1974)
5. 5 hours, 16 minutes: *1900* (1978)
6. 5 hours, 20 minutes: *Vindicta* (1923)
7. 5 hours, 32 minutes: *Les Misérables* (1933)
8. 5 hours, 50 minutes: *Fanny and Alexander* (1983)
9. 5 hours, 54 minutes: *Soldati Svobodi* (1977)
10. 5 hours, 57 minutes: *Little Dorritt* (1988)
11. 6 hours: *Idade de Terra* (1979)
12. 6 hours: *Khan Asparouch* (1982)
13. 6 hours, 10 minutes: *Die Nibelungen* (1924)
14. 6 hours, 24 minutes: *Foolish Wives* (1922)
15. 6 hours, 30 minutes: *Sleep* (1963)
16. 6 hours, 40 minutes: *Hitler: A Film from Germany* (1977)
17. 7 hours: *Der Hund von Baskerville* (1914–1920)
18. 7 hours, 45 minutes: *Francais si vois savez* (1973)
19. 7 hours, 58 minutes: *Iskry Palmja* (1925)
20. 8 hours: *Empire* (1964)
21. 8 hours, 27 minutes: *War and Peace* (1963–1967)
22. 8 hours, 32 minutes: *La Roue* (1921)

23. 9 hours: *Wagner* (1983)
24. 9 hours: *Napoleon* (1927)
25. 9 hours, 21 minutes: *Shoah* (1985)
26. 9 hours, 29 minutes: *The Human Condition* (1958–1960)
27. 12 hours, 40 minutes; *Out 1: Noli me Tangerey* (1971)
28. 12 hours, 43 minutes: *Comment Yukong deplace les montagnes* (1976)
29. 13 hours: *The Old Testament* (1922)
30. 15 hours, 21 minutes: *Berlin Alexanderplatz* (1980)
31. 15 hours, 40 minutes: *Heimat* (1984)
32. 24 hours: **** (1967)
33. 27 hours: *The Burning of the Red Lotus Temple* (1928–1931)
34. 48 hours: *The Longest Most Meaningless Movie in the World* (1970)
35. 50 hours: *Mondo Teeth*
36. 85 hours: *The Cure for Insomnia*

10 Really Tall People

Odd things can go "wrong" with the human body, and excessive height is one of those growth features that is *really* noticeable. A guy 8 feet tall does tend to stand out in a crowd.

Here is a listing of ten of the more notable cases of extreme height in humans, not counting basketball players. (It's your call regarding Goliath.)

1. **Goliath** (Biblical account; unconfirmed)
   Peak Height: 9 feet.

2. **Robert Wadlow** (February 22, 1918–July 15, 1940)
   Peak Height: 8 feet, 11¹⁄₁₀ inches.

3. **Zeng Jinlian** (June 26, 1964–February 13, 1982)
   Peak Height: 8 feet, 1¾ inches.

4. **Adam Ranier** (1899–1950)
   Peak Height: 7 feet, 8 inches.

5. **Ella Ewing** (1875–1913)
   Peak Height: 7 feet, 6 inches.

6. **Sandy Allen** (b. June 18, 1955)
   Peak Height: 7 feet, 7¼ inches.

7. **Anna Hanen Swan** (1846–1888; married Martin Van Buren Bates)
   Peak Height: 7 feet, 5½ inches.

8. **Martin Van Buren Bates** (1845–1919; married Anna Hanen Swan)
   Peak Height: 7 feet, 2½ inches.

9. **Michael Lanier** (b. November 27, 1969; James Lanier's twin)
   Peak Height: 7 feet, 4 inches.

10. **James Lanier** (b. November 27, 1969; Michael Lanier's twin)
    Peak Height: 7 feet, 4 inches.

The Recording Session Dates and Studio Times for 5 Unforgettable Beatles Songs

The Beatles changed history. They were a manifestation of a time and a culture and their influence is still being felt today.

This features looks at the actual recording times for five Beatles songs. The times listed are the periods the Beatles were in the studio working on and recording the specific song noted. (It should be pointed out that sometimes other songs were also recorded during many of these sessions, but the song in question was committed to tape during these periods in the Abbey Road studio). These times are actual Beatles recording times and do not include mixing or editing time, work often exclusively the domain of George Martin and/or the Abbey Road recording engineers. (The five songs are listed in chronological order.)

1. **"Yesterday"** (*"Yesterday" . . . and Today*)

   • Monday, June 14, 1965: 7:00 P.M.–10:00 P.M. (3 hours)
   Total recording time: 3 hours.

2. **"Taxman"** (*Revolver*)

   • Wednesday, April 20, 1966: 2:30 P.M.–2:30 A.M. (12 hours)
   • Thursday, April 21, 1966: 2:30 P.M.–12:50 A.M. (10 hours, 20 minutes)
   • Friday, April 22, 1966: 2:30 P.M.–11:30 P.M. (9 hours)
   • Monday, May 16, 1966: 2:30 P.M.–1:30 A.M. (11 hours)
   Total recording time: 42 hours, 20 minutes.

3. "A Day in the Life" *(Sgt. Pepper's Lonely Hearts Club Band)*

- Thursday, January 19, 1967: 7:30 P.M.–2:30 A.M. (7 hours)
- Friday, January 20, 1967: 7:00 P.M.–1:10 A.M. (6 hours, 10 minutes)
- Friday, February 3, 1967: 7:00 P.M.–1:15 A.M. (6 hours, 15 minutes)
- Friday, February 10, 1967: 8:00 P.M.–1:00 A.M. (5 hours)
- Wednesday, February 22, 1967: 7:00 P.M.–3:45 A.M. (8 hours, 45 minutes)
- Wednesday, March 1, 1967: 7:00 P.M.–2:15 A.M. (7 hours, 15 minutes)

Total recording time: 40 hours, 25 minutes.

4. "I Am the Walrus" *(Magical Mystery Tour)*

- Tuesday, September 5, 1967: 7:00 P.M.–1:00 A.M. (6 hours)
- Wednesday, September 6, 1967: 7:00 P.M.–3:00 A.M. (8 hours)
- Wednesday, September 27, 1967: 2:30 P.M.–5:30 P.M. (3 hours)
- Wednesday, September 27, 1967: 7:00 P.M.–3:30 A.M. (8 hours, 30 minutes)
- Thursday, September 28, 1967: 4:00 P.M.–5:30 P.M. (1 hour, 30 minutes)

Total recording time: 27 hours.

5. "Martha My Dear" [*The Beatles* ("The White Album")]

- Friday, October 4, 1968: 4:00 P.M.–4:30 A.M. (12 hours, 30 minutes)

Total recording time: 12 hours, 30 minutes.

73 Renowned Literary Classics Initially Rejected as Unpublishable by a Publisher

Aspiring but unpublished writers take note: This list will be the most encouraging thing you will ever read. You will suddenly—and with piercing clarity—realize that literary rejection is neither personal *nor* a definitive judgment of your talent. It is simply the nature of the beast. There are far more writers than there are outlets for their work and thus the enormously depressing publisher rejection rate. But take heart: As this list so dramatically illustrates, you are in good company. In fact, you are in *extremely* good company. Just think: You, as a writer, have something in common with Jane Austen, William Faulkner, F. Scott Fitzgerald, D. H. Lawrence, Ernest Hemingway, Gustave Flaubert, and even *James Joyce* and *Walt Whitman*. (Although to be fair, you are *also* in the same company as Jacqueline Susann.)

So stop whining and go write, will ya please?

The Rejects
The 1800s

1818 *Northanger Abbey* by Jane Austen
1819 *The Sketch Book* by Washington Irving
1846 *Typee* by Herman Melville
1851 *Moby Dick* by Herman Melville
1855 *Leaves of Grass* by Walt Whitman
1856 *Madame Bovary* by Gustave Flaubert
1857 *Barchester Towers* by Anthony Trollope
1887 *A Study in Scarlet* by Arthur Conan Doyle
1891 *Tess of the D'Urbervilles* by Thomas Hardy

1891 *The Picture of Dorian Gray* by Oscar Wilde
1895 *Poems* by William Butler Yeats
1895 *The Time Machine* by H. G. Wells
1898 *The War of the Worlds* by H. G. Wells

1900–1910

1900 *Sister Carrie* by Theodore Dreiser
1905 *Man and Superman* by George Bernard Shaw
1906 *The Jungle* by Upton Sinclair
1908 *The Wind in the Willows* by Kenneth Grahame
1909 *Three Lives* by Gertrude Stein

1911–1920

1912 *Riders of the Purple Sage* by Zane Grey
1912 *Under the Moons of Mars* by Edgar Rice Burroughs
1913 *Swann's Way* from *Remembrance of Things Past* by Marcel
Proust
1915 *The Rainbow* by D. H. Lawrence
1916 *A Portrait of the Artist as a Young Man* by James Joyce
1918 *Cornhuskers* by Carl Sandburg
1919 *Winesburg, Ohio* by Sherwood Anderson
1920 *The Mysterious Affair at Styles* by Agatha Christie
1920 *This Side of Paradise* by F. Scott Fitzgerald

1921–1930

1922 *Poems* by George Santayana
1922 *Ulysses* by James Joyce
1925 *Gentlemen Prefer Blondes* by Anita Loos
1926 *The Torrents of Spring* by Ernest Hemingway
1928 *Lady Chatterley's Lover* by D. H. Lawrence
1929 *Look Homeward, Angel* by Thomas Wolfe
1929 *Sartoris* by William Faulkner

1931–1940

1931 *Sanctuary* by William Faulkner
1931 *The Good Earth* by Pearl S. Buck
1934 *Lust for Life* by Irving Stone
1934 *The Postman Always Rings Twice* by James M. Cain
1937 *And to Think That I Saw It on Mulberry Street* by Dr. Seuss

1941–1950

1943 *The Fountainhead* by Ayn Rand
1944 *The Razor's Edge* by W. Somerset Maugham
1945 *Animal Farm* by George Orwell
1947 *Under the Volcano* by Malcolm Lowry
1948 *The Naked and the Dead* by Norman Mailer
1950 *The Book of Merlyn* by T. H. White

1951–1960

1951 *Malone Dies* by Samuel Beckett
1951 *Molloy* by Samuel Beckett
1952 *Kon-Tiki* by Thor Heyerdahl
1952 *The Diary of Anne Frank* by Anne Frank
1954 *Lord of the Flies* by William Golding
1954 *The Bridge Over the River Kwai* by Pierre Boulle
1955 *Lolita* by Vladimir Nabokov
1955 *Peyton Place* by Grace Metalious
1955 *The Deer Park* by Norman Mailer
1955 *The Ginger Man* by J. P. Donleavy
1957 *Atlas Shrugged* by Ayn Rand
1957 *The Assistant* by Bernard Malamud
1958 *A Separate Peace* by John Knowles
1960 *Welcome to Hard Times* by E. L. Doctorow

1961–1970

1961 *Catch-22* by Joseph Heller
1961 *Mastering the Art of French Cooking* by Julia Child et al.
1961 *The Tin Drum* by Günter Grass
1963 *The Ipcress File* by Len Deighton
1963 *The Spy Who Came in from the Cold* by John Le Carré
1966 *Giles Goat-Boy* by John Barth
1966 *In My Father's Court* by Isaac Bashevis Singer
1966 *Valley of the Dolls* by Jacqueline Susann
1967 *The Chosen* by Chaim Potok

1971–1980

1973 *Crash* by J. G. Ballard
1976 *A River Runs Through It* by Norman MacLean
1980 *A Confederacy of Dunces* by John Kennedy Toole
1980 *The Clan of the Cave Bear* by Jean Auel

1981–1990

1983 *Ironweed* by William Kennedy

1990–

1992 *A Time to Kill* by John Grisham
[Fill in Title of Your Book]

24 Representative "Self-Appraisal" Questions Asked on a Typical State Trooper Job Application

Here are a couple of dozen representative questions asked of people who apply for State Trooper jobs. Each state has its own series of questions, of course, but these seem to be common to many applications.

A thought occurs to someone reading through these queries: Who, in their right mind, would answer "incorrectly" the questions, "Can you resist a bribe?" or "Are you afraid of the dark"? But I suppose the application process must start somewhere, and here is where it begins.

I have only listed a sampling of the "self-appraisal" questions found on the applications. Some of the applications I've seen run three, four, or even more times as long as this one, some of them approaching a hundred questions or more.

1. While driving an automobile, can you move your head from side to side *without* moving your body?
2. Are your arms long enough to hold an Ithaca Model 37 pump-action shotgun steady and perfectly level at shoulder height?
3. Can you climb over a four foot high fence?
4. Can you enter a window from the top of a ladder?
5. Can you climb lengthwise over a full-sized, sedan-type automobile?
6. Can you crawl through a three foot by three foot opening?
7. Can you change a car tire?
8. Could you pull a 120 pound object off the highway by yourself?

9. Could you work effectively without regular, structured meal breaks?
10. Are you missing any fingers or toes?
11. Are you missing any arms or legs?
12. If required, could you poke someone with a nightstick?
13. Could you kill a vicious or injured animal at close range with a gun?
14. Would you be able to handle the recoil of a .357 Magnum handgun?
15. Have you ever been fired from a job?
16. Do you have an uncontrollable need for sleep?
17. Do you have any speech defects?
18. Are you a hypochondriac?
19. Are you afraid of the dark?
20. Are you an alcoholic?
21. Can you precisely move both of your eyes in the same direction at the same time?
22. Are you afraid of firearms?
23. Could you resist a bribe?
24. Would you be able to resist free meals?

14 Ridiculous U.S. Sex Laws

Society will legislate against anything, it seems, and nowhere is this more evident than in the battery of laws against any and all types of sexual behavior between people, animals, and objects of all shapes and sizes.

1. **In Harrisburg, Pennsylvania,**
   There's a Law Against: Having sex with a truck driver in a toll booth.

2. **In Nevada,**
   There's a Law Against: Having sex without a condom.

3. **In Willowdale, Oregon,**
   There's a Law Against: A husband talking dirty in his wife's ear during sex.

4. **In Clinton, Oklahoma,**
   There's a Law Against: Masturbating while watching two people have sex in a car.

5. **In the state of Washington,**
   There's a Law Against: Having sex with a virgin under any circumstances (including the wedding night!).

6. **In Tremonton, Utah,**
   There's a Law Against: Having sex in an ambulance.

7. **In Newcastle, Wyoming,**
   There's a Law Against: Having sex in a butcher shop's meat freezer.

8. **In Alexandria, Minnesota,**
   There's a Law Against: A man having sex with his wife with the stink of onions, sardines, or garlic on his breath.

9. **In every state in the union,**
   There's a Law Against: Having sex with a corpse.

10. **In Ames, Iowa,**
    There's a Law Against: Drinking more than three slugs of beer while lying in bed with a woman.

11. **In Fairbanks, Alaska,**
    There's a Law Against: Two moose having sex on the city sidewalks.

12. **In Kingsville, Texas,**
    There's a Law Against: Two pigs having sex on Kingsville airport property.

13. **In Ventura County, California,**
    There's a Law Against: Cats and dogs having sex without a permit.

14. **In Washington, D.C.,**
    There's a Law Against: Having sex in any position other than face-to-face.

20 Rumored Secret Subliminal Messages on Records and the Truth About What Is Really There

I am delighted to be able to reprint this chapter from William Poundstone's wonderful book *Big Secrets*. Anything else I could say beyond that would be superfluous. Ladies and gentleman, William Poundstone.

Secret Messages on Records
by William Poundstone

Two mentalities are at work here: 1960s rock fans and 1980s fundamentalist Christians. The idea of phonographically concealed messages dates from the Paul McCartney death scare of 1969. For hard-core types, the secret-message rumors never really died. Avid rock fans have auditioned every album release since the late 1960s for hidden nuances. Backward messages, barely audible messages, and messages on one stereo track only have been alleged. At the other end of the sociosensual spectrum, fundamentalist Christians have gotten into the act. TV programs such as *Praise the Lord* and *The 700 Club* have propagated rumors of a satanic plot in the recording industry, no less, in which various albums conceal "backward-masked" demonic murmurings. If *that* sounds too spacey to be taken seriously, consider that it was the fundamentalist groups who were behind House Resolution 6363, a bill introduced in the House of Representatives by Robert K. Dornan (R., Calif.) in 1982 to label all suspect records: "WARNING: THIS RECORD CONTAINS BACKWARD MASKING THAT MAKES A VERBAL

STATEMENT WHICH IS AUDIBLE WHEN THIS RECORD IS PLAYED BACKWARD AND WHICH MAY BE PERCEPTIBLE AT A SUBLIMINAL LEVEL WHEN THIS RECORD IS PLAYED FORWARD." In February 1983, the Arkansas State Senate passed a similar record-labeling bill by a vote of 86 to 0.

Contributing to the quasi-occult status of these rumors is the difficulty of checking them out on home audio equipment. You pretty much have to take someone else's word for it, or dismiss the rumors out of hand.

From a technical standpoint, there are four simple ways to conceal a verbal message on a recording. The most obvious is to record the message at a very low volume. The message may then be recovered by turning the volume up while playing the record or tape. If the message is faint enough, though, noise levels of home equipment may garble it. If the accompanying music or lyrics are loud enough, or if the message itself is indistinct or electronically modified, it may be hard to hear on any equipment.

A second gimmick is to record a message on one stereo track only. Records and tapes have two independent recordings, of course, normally played simultaneously for stereo effect. On a record, each stereo track occupies one side of the V-shaped groove for the needle. On a tape, the tracks are recorded in parallel lanes of the magnetic material. The two tracks are called "right" and "left" after the stereo speakers they will play on. Otherwise, the tracks are interchangeable—the sound mixer can put anything he or she wants on each track. (High notes do not have to go on one track and low notes on the other.) A message on one track can be masked by simultaneous loud music or lyrics on the opposite track. With normal stereo balance (or mono equipment) the loud track drowns out the message track. At home, single-track messages can be recovered by adjusting the stereo balance so that only the desired track plays. Sometimes this trick also makes indistinct words clearer. Even if the words are not exclusively on one track, they may happen to be more audible on one track.

A message could be recorded at a speed different from the rest of the record. Then the record would have to be played faster or slower than usual to recover the message. Unless the message was at one of the standard speeds (say, 45 rpm on 33⅓ rpm record), it could not be played normally on home equipment.

The fourth and most commonly alleged trick is to record a verbal message backward. Reversed speech has several unexpected features. One is that syllables are not a constant in the reversal process. A one-syllable word can have two or three syllables when played backward. Thus "number nine" in the Beatles *Revolution 9* reverses to "Turn me on, dead man" (or something like it), a jump from three to five syllables.

There is no simple way to predict what a word or phrase will sound like reversed. Obviously, you can't just reverse the letters. The slightly less naïve approach of reversing phonetic spellings—

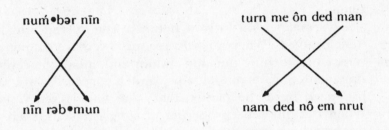

num•bər nīn → nīn rəb•mun

turn me ôn ded man → nam ded nô em nrut

Reversed messages are difficult to recover at home. Record turntables are not built to go backward. Some have a neutral setting, in which the pickup and amplifier remain active and you can turn the record backward by hand. But hardly anyone has a steady enough hand to produce satisfactory results.

With patience, it is possible to reverse a cassette recording. Transfer the music from the original record or tape onto a blank tape cassette. Place the cassette flat on a table. Draw out the part of the tape with the suspected message and snip it off at both ends. Hold the tape segment horizontally. Rotate it 180 degrees, keeping it horizontal at all times. This turns the tape end for end. Splice the reversed tape segment back onto the two loose ends of the cassette with strong adhesive tape. Reel the tape back inside the cassette. The spliced segment will play backward on an ordinary cassette player.

Big Secrets rented a recording studio to test the secret-message rumors. New copies of the records in question were transcribed on quarter-inch master tape. Where rumor alleged that a single stereo track contained a message, right and left stereo tracks were transcribed separately. Records with alleged inaudible messages were treated similarly. To test claims of reversed messages, recordings on the master tape were edited out and spliced in backward. Twenty cuts or portions of cuts from sixteen albums were tested.

1. **"Another One Bites the Dust"**
Queen, *The Game*

Rumor: When played backward, the lyrics say, "It's fun to smoke marijuana."

Findings: There is something that sounds like "It's fun to smoke marijuana" in the reversed music. It is repeated over and over. It might be rendered no less faithfully, however, as "sfun to scout mare wanna." This "message" is the reversal of the song title, which is repeated as a line in the song.

Let's make a distinction between engineered and phonetic reversals. When an artist records a verbal statement, reverses it by turning the tape end for end, mixes the reversed statement onto a master tape, and has records and tapes produced from the master, that is an engineered reversal. When the phonetic properties of song lyrics are such that they can be reversed to sound like something else, that is a phonetic reversal.

"It's fun to smoke marijuana" is clearly a phonetic reversal. The lyrics are perfectly plain played forward ("Another one bites the dust"), not so plain played backward ("sfun to scout mare wanna"). With an engineered reversal, the opposite should hold true: gibberish forward, clear as a bell backward. Some are prepared to believe that phonetic reversals are just as intentional as engineered reversals—that the songwriter painstakingly planned the phonetic *double-entendre*. In the absence of confirming evidence, that just doesn't wash. It's too easy to find coincidences. If, for instance, the letters of the alphabet are recited in conventional fashion (Ay, Bee, Cee, etc.) and reversed, at least five sound like English language words. D reverses to "eden," F becomes "pray," S becomes "say," V becomes "even," and Z becomes "easy." "It's fun to smoke marijuana" is likewise a coincidence.

2. **"A Child Is Coming"**
Jefferson Starship, *Blows Against the Empire*

Rumor: When played backward, "son of Satan."

Findings: Another phonetic coincidence. The repeated "It's getting better" reverses to an iffy "son of Satan," the "of" drawn out and the "Satan" strongly accented on the first syllable.

3. "Eldorado"
Electric Light Orchestra, *Eldorado*
Rumor: When played backward, "He is the nasty one/Christ, you're infernal/It is said we're dead men/Everyone who has the mark will live."
Findings: Coincidence. The supposed message lurks around the line "On a voyage of no return to see." Reversed, this passage becomes the expected syllable salad—no one hearing it cold would describe it as anything but reversed music. Only if you listen while reading along with what you're supposed to hear will you get anything. The rumored version of the message is somewhat fudged. The passage sounds more like "He's to nasty one/Christ you are, Christ, you're fernal/ There wiss suh, we're dead men ..." There is no "in" in what is taken to be "infernal." The line that is supposed to be "Everyone who has the mark will live" isn't even close, though the syllable count is about right.

4. "Shoo Be Doo"
The Cars, *Candy-O*
Rumor: When played backward, the word *Satan* repeated approximately eleven times.
Findings: Coincidence. The rumor refers to the reversal of the "Shoo be doo, shoo be do, shoo be do ..." near the end of the song. Given the mysterious logic of reversed phonemes, these three-syllable units can be heard as a repeated two-syllable word. The word sounds a little like "Satan."

5. "Snowblind"
Styx, *Paradise Theater*
Rumor: According to a mimeographed list of suspect records distributed by Congressman Dornan, the words "Satan move through our voices" when played backward.
Findings: Negative. Despite repeated listenings, it was not even possible to identify the part of the reversed track that Dornan et al. are talking about.

6. "Stairway to Heaven"
Led Zeppelin, untitled, a.k.a. *Stairway to Heaven*
Rumor: In reverse, "I live for Satan ... The Lord turns me off ... There's no escaping it ... Here's to my sweet Satan ... There's power in Satan ... He will give you 666."

Findings: Coincidence. If you listen very carefully to the "and it makes me wonder" lines in reverse, you'll hear something approaching "There's no escaping it." A better description is "There's no escape do." Knock off the last syllable and you have "There's no escape," a complete, intelligible sentence in reverse. It's there, all right, but it's not an unlikely enough coincidence to—well, make you wonder.

The "Satan" in "I live for Satan" is good and clear. The "I live for" part isn't. The other alleged lines are unremarkable. All are phonetic reversals of the entirely lucid forward lyrics and obviously just accidents.

7. "When Electricity Came to Arkansas"
Black Oak Arkansas, *Black Oak Arkansas* and *Ronch and Roll*
Rumor: In reverse, "Satan, Satan, Satan, Satan, Satan. He is God. He is God."
Findings: The *Black Oak Arkansas* cut was reversed. Again, pairs of reversed syllables are being freely interpreted as "Satan." "He is God" was not identifiable.

8. "Rain"
The Beatles, *Hey Jude*
Rumor: The unintelligible lyrics at the end are reversed.
Findings: A true engineered reversal and not really a secret. "Rain" seems to have been the first popular recording to incorporate an obviously reversed lyric. The story is that John Lennon accidentally spliced the last part of the song in backward and liked the effect. When reversed, the strange-sounding vocals at the end become intelligible as a reprise starting with the drawn-out word *sunshine.*

The reversal is less apparent to the casual listener than it might be because the accompanying music is not reversed. The ending fits in smoothly with the rest of the song, the vocals suggesting a foreign language.

9. "Fire on High"
Electric Light Orchestra, *Face the Music*
Rumor: When played backward, "The music is reversible, but time—turn back!"
Findings: "Fire on High" is instrumental. About twenty-six seconds into the music, scrambled speech is heard. It is mostly louder than the accompanying music and begins with

a two-syllable unit repeated several times. The seeming speech lasts for about fourteen seconds.

Reversing the music confirms that there is a true, engineered message. In reverse, a voice (Jeff Lynne's?) says, "The music is reversible, but time—turn back! Turn back! Turn back! Turn back!" All the words are clear and unambiguous. Anyone comparing this to the alleged reversal on ELO's "Eldorado" will have no trouble telling which is genuine.

10. **"Goodbye Blue Sky"**
Pink Floyd, *The Wall*
Rumor: In reverse, "You have just discovered the secret message."
Findings: The "secret message" is at the very end of the instrumental passage following the "Goodbye Blue Sky" vocals. It comes just before the words "What shall we do" at the start of the song that is identified as "Empty Spaces" on the record label and as "What shall we do now?" on the record sleeve. Played forward, the message is less apparent than the "Face the Music" reversal: A reasonably attentive listener might play *The Wall* through and not catch it. It suggests speech not quite close enough to be overheard. In context this is not unusual because the "Goodbye Blue Sky" instrumental passage includes "airport noises" and other sound effects. A loud climax in the music further masks the unintelligible voice.

When played backward, the voice (Roger Waters?) plainly intones, "Congratulations, you have just discovered the secret message. Please send your answer to old Pink, care of the funny farm . . ." As the voice fades out, there may be another word—perhaps "Chalfonte" or "Chelsea"—after "funny farm."

11 **"Heavy Metal Poisoning"**
Styx, *Kilroy Was Here*
Rumor: A red sticker on the *Kilroy Was Here* album cover warns, "By order of the Majority for Musical Morality, this album contains secret backward messages . . ."
Findings: This is a case of second-generation backward-masking. Styx's *Paradise Theater* did not contain a backward message, though a lot of people said it did. So Styx has in-

cluded a sure enough backward message on *Kilroy Was Here*. It is at the very beginning of "Heavy Metal Poisoning." The reversed speech lasts about three seconds. There is no musical background. The words reverse to *"Annuit coeptis. Novus ordo seclorum."* This is the Latin motto encircling the pyramid on the back of a dollar bill. The usual translation: God has favored our undertakings. A new order of the ages."

The cover sticker's "Majority for Musical Morality" is a fictitious Falwellesque group in the *Kilroy Was Here* video. Although the sticker suggests a plurality of "messages," only one was found.

12. "Space Between 'I'm So Tired' and 'Blackbird' "
The Beatles, *The Beatles*, a.k.a. "The White Album"
Rumor: A reversed message. At the time of the Paul-is-dead stories, the segue from "I'm so tired" to "Blackbird" was offered as evidence. It was held to contain John Lennon's voice, reversed, saying, "Paul is dead, miss him, miss him, miss him." The interpretation seems unlikely now, but there is a mysterious low muttering between the songs.
Findings: The mumblings are actually just to the "I'm so tired" side of the shiny "space" between cuts on the record. Each of the stereo tracks was recorded separately, twice, and a copy of each track was reversed. This produced four versions of the two-second passage: right forward, left forward, right reversed, and left reversed. All were equally unintelligible. It was not even apparent whether the voice is forward or reversed. Nor could John Lennon be identified as the speaker. There are nine or ten syllables. The first six (when played forward) are a two-syllable unit repeated three times. There is little or no difference between the stereo tracks. Any claimed interpretation of the sounds seems doubtful.

13. "Strawberry Fields Forever"
The Beatles, *Magical Mystery Tour*
Rumor: It was, of course, claimed that John Lennon says "I buried Paul" at the end. (It's forward, at the very end after the music fades to complete silence, returns, and starts to fade out again.) But Lennon told *Rolling Stone* that the words are "cranberry sauce."
Findings: They are "cranberry sauce." The "sauce"/"Paul"

part is indistinct, but the first syllable sounds a lot more like "cran" than "I."

14. **"Baby You're a Rich Man"**
The Beatles, *Magical Mystery Tour*
Rumor: On one of the tracks the line "Baby you're a rich man too" is sung as "Baby you're a rich fag Jew," a dig at Brian Epstein. Or some think it's "rich fat Jew" and claim it as evidence of Beatle anti-Semitism.
Findings: Negative. The two stereo tracks are nearly identical. It's always possible to hear words as similar-sounding words, but basically the lyrics jibe with the published version.

15. **"Lord Have Mercy on My Soul"**
Black Oak Arkansas, *Black Oak Arkansas*
Rumor: Simulated sex in the background behind Jim Dandy Mangrum's spoken prologue. Also, different voices saying different things on the two stereo tracks.
Findings: The rumors refer not to the song itself but to the prologue and the whispering behind it. The whispering starts after Mangrum's words, "God and the Devil, however you want it." Played in stereo, the whispering seems to be someone saying, "I want it, I need it, I want it, I need it . . ."

When the stereo tracks are split, it is apparent that there are two voices. The right track contains some low breathing or moaning before the whispering starts, and then a male voice repeating "I want it." The "I need it"s begin a moment later, in a female voice on the left track. Another left-track voice repeats "Good" between the "I need it"s in a more or less sexual 1½-second rhythm. The running-water sound at the end of the prologue is on both stereo tracks.

16. **"Wild and Loose"**
The Time, *What Time Is It?*
Rumor: Different voices on the two tracks, in the party conversation in the middle of the song.
Findings: The same assignment of genders to stereo tracks as above: male voices on the right track and female voices on the left. The main female voice switches over to the right stereo track when she talks to lead singer Morris Day.

17. "I Am the Walrus"
The Beatles, *Magical Mystery Tour*

Rumor: The fadeout contains several lines from *King Lear.*
According to *The Beatles A to Z* by Goldie Friede, Robin
Titone, and Sue Weiner (New York: Methuen, 1980),
Lennon taped the lines from a BBC radio production and
did not even know what play it was until years later.

Findings: Right and left stereo tracks of the ending were
compared, but there was little difference. There seem to be
four vocal components to the ending of "I Am the Walrus."

1. A chanted "Goo goo goo joob"—which is in the published
   lyrics and is taken from *Finnegans Wake.*
2. Another chant that seems to be "Oom pah, oom pah."
3. A third chant that has been identified as "Everybody's got
   one," beginning approximately when the "Goo goo goo
   joob" chant dies away.
4. The lines from *King Lear.*

Chant no. 3 makes it nearly impossible to understand the *Lear*
dialogue. But it fades away just before the last line from the play.
For a moment at the very, very end of the record, there is only
the *King Lear* recitation. If you turn the volume way up, you can
hear (on both tracks) "Sit you down, father; rest you." This is a
line from Act IV, Scene iv. Once you turn to the right place in
the play, it isn't too hard to hear the other lines spoken as you
read along. "I Am the Walrus" contains eleven lines from *Lear,*
the three characters speaking in distinct—not the Beatles'—
voices:

OSWALD	Slave, thou hast slain me. Villain take my purse:
	If ever thou wilt thrive, bury my body,
	And give the letters which thou find'st about me
	To Edmund, Earl of Gloucester; seek him out
	Upon the English party. Oh, untimely death!
	Death!
EDGAR	I know thee well. A serviceable villain,
	As duteous to the vice of thy mistress
	As badness would desire.
GLOUCESTER	What, is he dead?
EDGAR	Sit you down, father; rest you.

18. **"Sheep"**
Pink Floyd, *Animals*
Rumor: A Moog-modified voice recites a parody of the Twenty-third Psalm.
Findings: The part in question begins six minutes, thirty-five seconds into the cut, in an otherwise instrumental passage. In stereo you can barely hear a muffled, electronically modified voice begin, "The Lord is my shepherd/I shall not want ..." The voice continues but is drowned out by the music and the bleating of sheep.

The two stereo tracks were split. The voice is relatively clear on the left track, all but absent from the right. Only the first two lines are directly from the Twenty-third Psalm. The rest (thirteen lines) is a passably clever parody of man/ God and man/sheep relationships: "He converteth me to lamb cutlets." Pink Floyd's publisher refused permission to print the lyrics here.

19. **"Revolution 9"**
The Beatles, *The Beatles,* **a.k.a. "The White Album"**
Rumor: Various reversed and/or one-track speech. The reversal of "Number nine" to "Turn me on, dead man" has pretty much been discounted as coincidence (although it is mentioned on Congressman Dornan's list).
Findings: Distinction between lyrics and any hidden message blurs on "Revolution 9." The eight-minute cut is a montage of sounds collected by John Lennon and Yoko Ono (and not by credited co-writer Paul McCartney, per *White Album* usage). It includes discordant music, radio broadcasts, sirens, applause, gunfights, sports cheers, the crackling of a fire, screams, a baby gurgling, a choir singing, and much that cannot be identified. For this investigation, "Revolution 9" was transcribed four times, twice on each stereo channel. One copy of each of the tracks was reversed. The four resulting versions were compared against each other and against the original two-channel version.

"Revolution 9" contains a lot of talking. Played in stereo, forward, the longest stretch of understandable speech is probably an announcer saying, "... every one of them knew that as time went by they'd get a little bit older and a little bit slower ..."

One believable instance of reversed speech occurs: someone saying "Let me out! Let me out!" (once held to represent McCartney in his totaled Aston-Martin). Two iffy reversals occur on the backward recording of the right stereo
track: "She used to be assistant" and "There were two
men . . ." Neither is clear enough or long enough to be
convincing. Some of the music, including the recurring
theme, sounds more natural in reverse.

"Turn me on, dead man" is a typical phonetic reversal.
The forward "number nine" (repeated throughout the cut)
is clear; the reversal is slurred—something like "turn me on
dedmun." It has been claimed that "number nine" must be
pronounced with a British accent or with some careful in-
flection in order to reverse to "Turn me on, dead man."
This seems not to be so. As an experiment, three American-
accent renderings of "number nine" were reversed. All
sounded about as much like "Turn me on, dead man" as the
record did. Like the other phonetic reversals, "Turn me on,
dead man" must be considered a coincidence.

Much of "Revolution 9" is on one stereo track only. Near
the end a voice says "A fine natural imbalance . . . the Wa-
tusi . . . the twist . . . Eldorado . . . Eldorado." "A fine natural
imbalance" is on the right track only, though the words that
follow are in stereo. One of the longer bits of speech—
"Who could tell what he was saying? His voice was low and
his [unintelligible] was high and his eyes were low"—is clear
on the left track, a bare whisper on the right.

There is a stereophonically concealed "secret message" on
"Revolution 9." The words are on the right track. They begin about four minutes, fifty-eight seconds into the cut and
run for about twenty-two seconds. They are not likely to be
noticed in stereo because of the much louder left track. The
sound of applause begins on the left track at about five minutes, one second into the cut. Deafening noises—the clap-
ping, sirens, music—continue on the left track until five
minutes, forty seconds. It may or may not have been
Lennon's and Ono's intention to conceal the spoken passage. Given the haphazard quality of "Revolution 9," the
concealment may have been accidental. To recover the passage, the left track must be switched off. The right track can

then be heard to contain a sound like a stopwatch ticking, behind these words:

So the wife called, and we better go to see a surgeon ... [*a scream muffles a line that sounds like* Well, what with the prices, the prices have snowballed, no wonder it's closed] ... So any and all, we went to see the dentist instead, who gave him a pair of teeth, which wasn't any good at all. So instead of that he joined the bloody navy and went to sea.

20. "A Day in the Life"
The Beatles, *Sgt. Pepper's Lonely Hearts Club Band*

Rumor: The seemingly blank grooves at the end of the record contain a note so high that only dogs can hear it, intended for Paul McCartney's dog, Martha.

Findings: Anyone who examines the record carefully will notice fifteen widely spaced grooves at the end of "A Day in the Life." They seem to contain no music. The record label lists the length of "A Day in the Life" as five minutes, three seconds. Yet, if you time it, the music seems to be over in about four and a half minutes. Certainly the "full" five minutes, three seconds are not played on the radio.

"A Day in the Life" was recorded with a forty-two-piece orchestra from the London Philharmonic. The loud climaxes were created by playing in different keys simultaneously. A synthesizer was also used.

Could a record contain a note too high-pitched for humans to hear? The sound engineer *Big Secrets* consulted didn't think so. Recording hardware is tuned to the human range of hearing and has a very poor response outside that range. The same is true for the equipment that plays back the sound. Even if the Beatles had somehow managed to record such a note, no commercial tweeter would respond to it—not if it was much more than twenty thousand cycles per second, anyway. So much for the idea of Fru-Fru being hypnotized by "A Day in the Life."

Those fifteen grooves aren't really empty, though. The end of "A Day in the Life"—starting with the final loud "daaa" and going all the way into the center of the record—was transferred to master tape and the stereo levels monitored. Initially, the final note is split evenly between stereo

tracks. As it tails off, most of the note is on the right channel. The level never hits zero until the end of the record. By
turning the volume up repeatedly, the final note can be
heard all the way to the end.

Dogs can hear fainter sounds, as well as higher sounds,
than humans. So at a given volume setting, a dog should be
able to hear the final note longer than a human. Whether
the dog hears the entire recorded note depends on the volume level and the dog.[1]

"Secret Messages on Records" from *Big Secrets* by William Poundstone. Text: Copyright © 1983 by William Poundstone. Illustrations: Copyright © 1983 by Permission
of William Morrow & Company, Inc.

[1]English pressings of *Sgt. Pepper's* do contain a high-pitched sound after the final
chord fades out, as does the American rerelease on CD. [Ed.]

18 Scenes of Violence from Bret Easton Ellis's Almost-Banned Novel *American Psycho*

As I was reading through *American Psycho* for this feature, an odd thought occurred to me. For some reason, I was not convinced that the horrific acts the story's central character Patrick Bateman commits against varied and sundry characters in the novel actually take place.

I have not spoken to Ellis about this but during my reading I had the irresistible intuition that all the acts of random and perverted violence Bateman wallows in throughout the book all take place *in his mind.* Even after finishing the book, I do not know this to be true. Ellis never tells us, but I thought you might be interested in my initial reaction. If you've read the book, you'll know what I mean. If you haven't, the following list of acts of violence from the book might shock you, and I'm sure that there will be many of you who will use these scenes as justification for Ellis's original publisher Simon & Schuster's refusal to publish the book. (It was eventually published in 1991 by Random House as a Vintage Original.)

If I am right, though, the joke is on all of those mortally offended and appalled critics and readers who ostensibly defend free speech in one breath but turn around and say that they can almost understand why those who called for a ban of *American Psycho* might have had a point. Indeed, if I am right, *American Psycho* belongs on the shelf with other great contemporary literary chronicles of insanity, including Sylvia Plath's painful *The Bell Jar,* and even Stephen King's *The Shining,* for that matter.

Interestingly, Random House might very well have had the same interpretation of Patrick Bateman as I did. The cover blurb for the novel reads, "In this, his third novel, Bret Easton Ellis has explored incomprehensible depths of *madness,* and captured the *insanity* of violence in our time or any other." [Emphasis added.]

In the end, each reader must be the judge.

Kudos to Random House for having the balls to publish *American Psycho,* and bravo to Bret Easton Ellis for having the balls to seriously attempt to capture *genuine* madness—no matter how sickening and disturbing—on paper, with nothing more than mere, astoundingly powerful *words.*

American Psycho is the story of Patrick Bateman, yuppie extraordinaire. Bateman lives in Manhattan, makes loads of money, and apparently spends much of his free time committing the most horrendous acts of sadistic violence imaginable. Or does he?

The following feature details some of the incredibly nasty things Bateman does and/or remembers doing to men, women, pets, and household pests. (Page numbers are provided for those who would like to go to the novel and read the actual scene for themselves. Page references are to the 1991 Random House Vintage Original trade paperback edition.)

WARNING!

This feature is NOT for the squeamish.

It is gruesome, graphic, and EXTREMELY violent.

If explicit descriptions of grisly torture

and bizarre sex disturb you,

DO NOT READ THIS FEATURE!

1. Patrick Bateman deliberately steps on the leg stump of a blind homeless amputee sitting in a doorway (82).
2. Bateman remembers once raping a waitress with a can of hairspray (94).
3. Bateman stabs Al the homeless guy in the right eye with a knife with a serrated edge, pushing the blade in a full half inch, and popping the retina. Bateman pulls Al's pants down and stabs him repeatedly in the belly, just below the pubic hair. Bateman slices Al's left eye open with a knife. Bateman slices Al's nose into two pieces. Bateman slices open Al's cheek when he cleans off his knife by rubbing it on Al's face. Bateman steps on and breaks the two front legs of Al's dog, Gizmo (131).
4. Bateman disembowels a gay man's sharpei dog (165).
5. Bateman repeatedly stabs a gay man in the face and head,

THE ODD INDEX / 329

slits his throat, and then shoots him twice in the head with a gun equipped with a silencer (166).

6. Bateman sadistically tortures two nude hookers with a sharpened coat hanger, a rusty butter knife, matches from the Gotham Bar and Grill, a half-smoked cigar, and a carton of Italian seasoning salt from Dean & Deluca (176).

7. Bateman binds with wire a naked girl named Alison who is drunk and high on coke. After gagging her with duct tape, he slathers his gloved arm with Vaseline and toothpaste and then tries to push his entire arm up her vagina (207).

8. Bateman slaughters his friend Owen with several ax blows to the face and skull and then covers Owen's body with lime and places his corpse in a bathtub (217).

9. Bateman knocks Bethany unconscious with four blows to the head with a nail gun, after which he nails three fingers of each of her hands to a board with the gun. He sprays Mace in her eyes, mouth, and nostrils, and then shoots more nails into both her hands until they're covered with nails, and then he Maces her again. He cuts off one of her nipples with a scissors, after which he cuts out her tongue. He fucks her in the mouth, ejaculates, and then Maces her at least two more times (245).

10. Bateman slices Elizabeth's jugular with a knife, punches her in the stomach, stabs her five or six times, and then rubs his penis all over her dead face. He then chops off her right arm and left hand and rips out chunks of her right leg with his hands. He then decapitates her, scoops out her eyes, and places her severed head on his kitchen table (289).

11. Bateman ties Christie naked to a futon, stuffs pages from *Vanity Fair* in her mouth, and hooks up jumper cables connected to a car battery to her breasts. Her breasts eventually burst open, electrocuting her. Bateman drops lit matches from Le Relais on her naked belly, chews off one of her nipples and swallows it, and then mashes and rips open her burnt breasts with a pair of pliers (290).

12. Bateman stabs a five-year-old boy in the neck and the child bleeds to death before his mother finds him (298).

13. Bateman rips apart Tiffany's vagina with his mouth. He then nails either Tiffany or Torri's head to the apartment wall, amputates their fingers and arranges the severed digits in a circle around a compact disk player. He bites savagely into

their dead bodies at random and defecates on one of them (305).

14. Bateman poisons a small dog and videotapes its death convulsions (307).

15. After smearing it with Grey Poupon mustard, Bateman eats the brains of one of his victims' corpses (328).

16. Bateman drills a girl's teeth with a power drill (328).

17. Bateman nails a girl's arms to wooden posts, spreads her legs, and smears cheese all over and up into her vagina. He then pours acid on her vagina to eat away enough flesh so that a plastic Habitrail hamster tube will fit inside the girl. He then forces a large rat to run up the tube into the girl's vagina, after which he traps the rodent inside the girl's body. He then slices the girl in two with a chainsaw while she's still alive, sticks a knife up her nose to her forehead, and hacks off her chin. He fucks her mouth three times and then gouges out her eyes with his fingers. He stomps the rat to death when it emerges sated and fed from the girl's vagina, and later bakes the girl's femur and left jawbone in the oven (328).

18. Bateman dismembers and disembowels a girl and tries to make a meat loaf out of her flesh. It doesn't work, so he makes sausage instead.

Postmortem

It is a cliché to say that violence is everywhere today, and that we as a culture have become jaded and inured to its horrors.

There are many misguided pundits who look to art as the *cause* of the endemic violence, and they will often cite such works as *American Psycho, Silence of the Lambs,* Ice-T's song "Cop Killer," and the genre of horror in toto as the primary reasons things are the way they are.

Art is a mirror. It *reflects* what is going on in society. It is a voice that can scream or whisper. Ideologically, art cannot be required to have a purpose; it must simply be allowed to speak—and no matter what it says or how offensive or repellent its message, we are all, in the end, better off for its existence.

10 Common Elements of Near-Death Experiences

A *near-death experience* (NDE) is an ostensibly preternatural event that a person experiences at the point of clinical death. The reason we're even aware of NDEs is that the people who have had them were brought back to life to tell about it.

There are several possible explanations for the experience:

- Some scientists and doctors look to *hypoxia* as a cause for an NDE. Hypoxia is a decrease of oxygen to the brain, and, the theory goes, when the brain is oxygen-deprived, hallucinatory sensory experiences occur.
- More spiritually oriented people such as psychics and clergy choose to believe that a near-death experience is an actual look at—an actual *experience* of—the next world and the afterlife. They believe that we all experience exactly what NDEers do, except that most of us don't come back to life, so the experience remains within the eternal soul of the deceased.
- Carl Sagan, in his book *Broca's Brain,* may have the best explanation of all. His theory is that a near-death experience is a re-experience of our own birth. This would explain why NDEs are especially common (and similarly remembered and recounted) in 3- to 9-year-olds who "die" and are brought back to life. Their latent birth memories are far more recent than those of, say, a 75-year-old. Sagan put it this way:

[E]very human being, without exception, has already shared an experience like that of those travelers who return from the land of death; the sensation of flight; the emergence from darkness into light; an experience in which, at least perceived, bathed in radiance and glory. There is only one common experience that matches this description. It is called birth.

A 1991 Gallup Poll reported that 12 million Americans have had NDEs. Here are ten of the most commonly reported elements of the near-death experience:

1. **Being in Another World or Realm** This is one of the most commonly reported experiences. People feel that they have somehow crossed over into another plane or level of existence.

2. **An Overwhelming Feeling of Peace** The sense of peace, serenity, and contentment is so palpable to NDEers that many have actually chastised the doctor for pulling them away from the afterlife and bringing them back to life.

3. **A Review of the Person's Life** This is the archetypal experience of having your life flash before your eyes. This experience has also been reported by people who believed they were dying but who remained conscious throughout. People falling off buildings or drowning have often reported a life review.

4. **An Out-of-Body Experience** Most NDEs begin with the person's astral body floating up and out of their physical body. Many report then feeling as if they could fly at will.

5. **Accurate Visual Perception** NDEers can often relate details about things they could not have seen while clinically dead, including scenes and events that took place outside the emergency room or site. Perhaps an NDE allows us to tap into some sort of dormant sensory ability that we're not capable of accessing in the material world.

6. **Encountering Other People** Many NDEers claim to have met and had conversations with deceased relatives and friends on the other side. To some, this is the most bittersweet aspect of a near-death experience.

7. **Audible Voices and Sounds** NDEers can also often relate details about things they could not have heard while clinically dead.

8. **The Light** A wondrous and, to some, holy light often bathes and beckons people who have a near-death experience. Most feel that the light is the source of all things or is actually the physical manifestation of God.

9. **The Tunnel** This is often spoken of as one of the most common elements of a near-death experience, yet in fact only 9

percent of people who were interviewed by Raymond Moody reported walking or floating down a tunnel.

10. **Precognition** Precognition, or being able to predict the future, was the least-reported NDE element. Cynics look to this as proof that there is nothing even remotely supernatural going on here, and thus, the paucity of genuinely provable phenomena. But 6 percent of all of Raymond Moody's NDEers reported being able to know at least something of future events after their experience.

The 7 Stages of the Soul's Ascent to God

According to ancient mystic wisdom, the soul must travel through seven stages in order to ultimately know and experience true Divinity. Upon attainment of the seventh stage, God enters the person's soul and the traveler becomes one with God. These seven stages are also known as the Castle of the Interior Man, which is an expressively poetic and metaphorical way of describing this inner journey.

1. **The State of Prayer:** During this stage, the traveler concentrates on God, using meditation and prayer as tools.
2. **The State of Mental Prayer:** Here, one attempts a deeper understanding of all things, with emphasis on the mystical and spiritual significance of existence and of the self as it relates to all things.
3. **The Obscure Night:** This stage is said to be especially difficult to achieve because it demands the total and complete surrender of the Self.
4. **The Prayer of Quietism:** Once the Obscure Night is achieved and the Self is renounced, the fourth stage requires that the traveler willingly give himself over to the will of God, whatever it might be.
5. **The State of Union:** The will of God becomes evident and the traveler begins to understand how that will relates to the will of his own soul.
6. **The State of Ecstatic Prayer:** This is a transcendent state in which awareness of a higher state of consciousness is present and the soul is flooded with joy and love.
7. **The State of Ravishment:** A mystical marriage between God and man is attained and God and the state of eternal bliss called Heaven enter into the soul.

The 26 Stages of Deterioration a Corpse Goes Through from the Moment of Death On

And so, from hour to hour, we ripe and ripe,
And then from hour to hour, we rot and rot:
And thereby hangs a tale."
—William Shakespeare, *As You Like It,* II, vii

Most of us go through life believing that all dead bodies wear a lot of makeup, dress nicely, and have a stoic expression on their faces. Such is the wonder of modern mortuary skills.

But morticians understand the "need for speed" in their chosen profession and this feature will illustrate why. Here is what happens to us physically when we shuffle off this mortal coil.

The Moment of Death

1. The heart stops.
2. The skin gets tight and ashen in color.
3. All the muscles relax.
4. The bladder and bowels empty.
5. The body temperature begins to drop 1½° Fahrenheit per hour.

After 30 minutes

6. The skin gets purple and waxy.
7. The lips, fingernails, and toenails fade to a pale color.
8. Blood pools at the bottom of the body.
9. The hands and feet turn blue.
10. The eyes sink into the skull.

After 4 hours

11. Rigor mortis has set in.
12. The purpling of the skin and the pooling of the blood continue.
13. Rigor continues to tighten muscles for another 24 hours or so.

After 12 hours

14. The body is in full rigor mortis.

After 24 hours

15. The body is now the temperature of the surrounding environment.
16. In males, the semen dies.
17. The head and neck are now a greenish-blue color.
18. The greenish-blue color spreads to the rest of the body.
19. There is a pervasive smell of rotting meat.
20. The face of the person is essentially no longer recognizable.

After 3 days

21. The gas in the body tissues forms large blisters on the skin.
22. The whole body begins to bloat and swell grotesquely.
23. Fluids leak from the mouth, nose, vagina, and rectum.

After 3 weeks

24. The skin, hair, and nails are so loose they can easily be pulled off the corpse.
25. The skin bursts open in many places on the body.
26. Decomposition will continue until the body is nothing but skeletal remains, a process that can take a month or so in hot climates, and two months or more in cold climates.

27 States That Will Execute a Person Under the Age of 18 and the States' Official Method(s) of Execution

This feature looks at those states that will execute an adolescent.

State	Minimum Age	Method of Execution
1. Alabama	No minimum age	Electrocution
2. Arizona	No minimum age	Lethal gas
3. Arkansas	15	Lethal injection
4. Delaware	No minimum age	Lethal injection
5. Florida	No minimum age	Electrocution
6. Georgia	17	Electrocution
7. Idaho	No minimum age	Lethal injection or firing squad
8. Indiana	16	Electrocution
9. Kentucky	16	Electrocution
10. Louisiana	15	Electrocution
11. Mississippi	13	Lethal injection or lethal gas
12. Missouri	14	Lethal injection or lethal gas
13. Montana	No minimum age	Lethal injection or hanging
14. Nevada	16	Lethal injection
15. New Hampshire	17	Lethal injection
16. New Mexico	No minimum age	Lethal injection
17. North Carolina	No minimum age	Lethal injection or lethal gas
18. Oklahoma	No minimum age	Lethal injection

19. Pennsylvania	No minimum age	Electrocution
20. South Carolina	No minimum age	Electrocution
21. South Dakota	No minimum age	Lethal injection
22. Texas	17	Lethal injection
23. Utah	14	Lethal injection or firing squad
24. Vermont	No minimum age	Electrocution
25. Virginia	15	Electrocution
26. Washington	No minimum age	Lethal injection or hanging
27. Wyoming	No minimum age	Lethal injection

The 15 Steps of Field Dressing a Dead Member of Our Wildlife

I have been a vegetarian for almost twenty years. That is the extent of my introduction to this list.

1. Make sure the animal is dead.
2. Lay the animal on its back with its head facing uphill.
3. Cut off its genitals.
4. Slice the underside of the animal open from the groin to the sternum. Twice.
5. Split the pelvis open with your knife.
6. Straddle the animal and split the chest open with your knife.
7. Expose the windpipe with your knife.
8. Cut the windpipe and pull it out of the animal's neck.
9. Cut a horizontal hole in the windpipe.
10. Stick your finger in the hole.
11. Using the windpipe, pull the intestines out.
12. When you reach the bottom of the split animal with your pull, cut off the anus at the end of the intestines.
13. Leave the intestines on the ground.
14. Lift the animal by its front legs and drain the blood from the body cavity.
15. Take your spoils home.

The 11 Steps of Embalming a Body and Preparing It for Open-Casket Viewing

I look where he lies white-faced and still in the coffin—I
draw near,
Bend down and touch lightly with my lips the white face
in the coffin.

—Walt Whitman, "Reconciliation"

The shepherding of the dead to their final resting place is a scary and awe-inspiring duty. Morticians or undertakers (who now prefer to be called funeral directors) are responsible for the last vision a family will ever have of their loved one. It is their job to make the dead person look good, comfort the family in their time of bewildering grief, and handle all of the bureaucratic requirements needed to write a beloved citizen off the books.

Here's what happens from the moment the body arrives at the funeral home and the embalming begins. (Sometimes bodies are stored in refrigerators until the mortician is ready to begin the embalming.) Many of these procedures overlap one another and many morticians have their own ways (and order) of working, but this is the general routine necessary to prepare a dead body for viewing.

1. The body is completely undressed.
2. The limbs are gently stretched and massaged to lessen the effects of the relentless rigor mortis.
3. The body is washed.
4. An artery and vein in either the neck, armpit, or groin are cut open and all the corpse's blood is drained out. This is

usually done on a table with gutters that drain to a receptacle of some sort.

5. The veins are filled with embalming fluid. This is a formaldehyde-based liquid that, ironically, looks like blood. (This is coincidental, not aesthetically intentional.)

6. A large syringe is inserted into the navel and the contents of the stomach and abdomen are pumped out.

7. The abdomen is filled with between 8 and 10 pints of embalming fluid.

8. Cups or pads are placed over the eyeballs to prevent a sunken look and the eyelids are sewn shut. The mouth and cheeks are stuffed with cotton to prevent a hollow look, and the lips are sewn shut. Any necessary reconstructive work is performed.

9. The body is attended to cosmetically: The hair is washed and set on women; the beard is shaved on men. Makeup is applied to both the face and neck *and* the hands. (I once knew a hairdresser who insisted on doing his mother's hair after her death. He insisted that he was the only one who knew exactly how she'd want it to look. He was allowed to do it.)

10. The body is dressed. Usually the family provides something for the deceased to wear but, if necessary, the funeral home has a wide selection of inexpensive, paper-like clothing.

11. The body is placed in the coffin and arranged for viewing. The hands are manipulated so as to have a natural fall, and religious items are sometimes placed in the hands. (In some ethnic communities, it has become the practice to place items of significance in the coffin with the deceased for viewing. I attended one wake where the cover of the coffin held at least six framed photos of the deceased woman's grandchildren, two dancing school diplomas, and notes from the children. The poor thing looked like she was about to be crowded out of her own casket.)

The 21 Steps of a Medical-Legal Autopsy

Sing, my tongue, of the mysteries of the glorious Body.
—St. Thomas Aquinas

In *Cause of Death,* Dr. Keith Wilson defines the circumstances when what's known as a "medical-legal autopsy" is required to be performed.

A [medical-legal autopsy is a] specialized type of autopsy authorized or ordered by the proper legal authorities (usually the medical examiner) in cases of suspicious deaths, including suicide, homicide and unattended or unexpected deaths in order to ensure justice for the purpose of determining the cause of death.

If a person dies without having been attended by a doctor in the past fourteen days, or under suspicious circumstances, or during a surgical operation, the coroner may rule that an autopsy is required. A medical-legal autopsy is required in all homicide cases. [pg. 70]

Here is what happens, step-by-step, during a medical-legal autopsy.

1. **Hello, It's Me:** The dead body arrives at the morgue.
2. **Sign In, Stranger:** The body's identity is confirmed, assigned an identification number, and given a toe-tag, which is a cardboard ticket with all of the corpse's pertinent information written on it. This tag is tied to a big toe.
3. **Smile!** The body is photographed from head to toe, front and back, in the clothing it was wearing when it arrived at the morgue.

4. **Smile! (take 2):** The body is photographed from head to toe, front and back, completely naked.

4. **Statistically Speaking:** The body is weighed on a scale, and the weight is recorded. The body is also measured for length, and completely X-rayed.

5. **Digitally Speaking:** The fingerprints of the corpse are taken. In instances in which hands and/or fingers are missing, prints are taken of what remains of the remains, and missing parts are duly noted.

6. **Exteriors, part 1:** The clothing the deceased was wearing upon arrival at the morgue is carefully and methodically examined. Fiber samples from the garments are taken for later study, and stains on the clothing are noted and examined.

7. **Exteriors, part 2:** Any and all moles, wounds, tattoos, scars (including surgical scars), and other physical body anomalies are noted and examined.

8. **Exteriors, part 3:** The corpse's fingernails, toenails, skin, and hair are examined. The skin of the arms and legs is carefully checked for syringe marks.

9. **Ladies Only:** During a medical-legal autopsy of a female, a rigorous examination of the external genitalia (labia, pubic hair, and so on) is performed to determine whether or not there was a rape or sexual assault committed against the woman prior to (and/or after) her death.

10. **Tapped Out:** Bodily fluids (blood, urine, and so on) are withdrawn from the body and subjected to comprehensive toxicology tests.

11. **Open Wide!** The coroner makes a huge, full-body-length "Y" incision that opens up the entire front of the body. The incision starts at each shoulder, proceeds on an angle down to the mid-chest, and then joins into a straight line that extends all the way to the pubis. This is the most dramatic element of a medical-legal autopsy, and most people who have never seen one performed are stunned by the dramatic way the body is spread wide by this incision. Many people have, at one time or another, seen some sort of surgical procedure performed. The incisions, even for major abdominal surgery, are thin, neat, and relatively "clean." An autopsy incision need not be neat, nor concerned with excessive bleeding. Thus, the corpse is split wide open by a deep cut

that is a very effective reminder that the person being autopsied is, in fact, quite dead.

12. **Let's Do Take-out!** First, the organs of the upper abdominal cavity—the lungs, heart, esophagus and trachea—are removed. The coroner then takes out the lower abdominal organs, which include the liver, spleen, kidneys, adrenals, stomach, and intestines. Slices of each organ are taken and tested.

13. **Open Wide! (take 2):** The internal genitals of both males and females are examined. In the case of females, the uterus and vagina are carefully studied for signs of pregnancy, rape, or some form of sexual assault.

14. **More Take-out:** The organs of the pelvic region, including the bladder, the uterus, and the ovaries, are removed. Samples of each organ are taken and analyzed.

15. **Gut Reaction:** When the cause of death is either drowning or a suspected poisoning or drug overdose, the contents of the stomach are removed, examined, and carefully analyzed. All findings are recorded.

16. **Let's Do Shots!** Any and all bullet wounds are recorded. The number of wounds is noted, as well as the perceived direction(s) of the bullet(s). An estimate, based on the configuration of the bullet entrance wounds, is made as to what distance the gun was from the victim when it was fired. All bullets are removed from the body and placed in plastic bags. The bullets are then examined by a ballistics lab and findings are recorded as evidence.

17. **Mind Games:** First, a deep incision is made in the skin of the scalp. The cut, which is called intermastoid, begins behind one ear, travels over the top of the head, and ends behind the opposite ear. The scalp is then grasped firmly and pulled forward over the face, baring the bony skull. Using an electric saw, a wedge-shaped portion of the skull is cut out and removed, exposing the brain. The brain is then removed in its entirety, weighed, and examined.

18. **Back in the Saddle Again:** Since he or she is now through with them, the coroner returns all of the removed internal organs to the body cavities.

19. **Fatal Findings:** The autopsy findings, complete with a final opinion as to cause of death, as well as all reports and photographs, are turned over to legal authorities. This "pack-

age" becomes a part of the *corpus delecti,* and is used as evidence in a court of law when necessary. The folder containing all of this detailed information is known as the case file.

20. **Signed, Sealed, Delivered:** A final determination is made as to the cause of death, and the death certificate is filled out.

21. **Taps:** The body is turned over to the funeral director the family has selected. The body is then prepared for burial, cremation, or donation. (See "The 11 Steps of Embalming a Body and Preparing It for Open-Casket Viewing" in this volume.)

13 Stigmatics

My marks and scars I carry with me, to be a witness for me, that I have fought his battles, who will now be my rewarder.—John Bunyan, *Pilgrim's Progress*

The miracle of the Church seems to me to rest not so much upon faces or voices or healing power coming suddenly near to us from afar off, but upon our perceptions being made finer, so that for a moment our eyes can see and our ears can hear what is there about us always.
　　—Willa Cather, *Death Comes for the Archbishop* (1927)

One miracle is just as easy to believe as another.
　　—William Jennings Bryan, Scopes trial, July 21, 1925

The *Encyclopedia of the Unexplained* had this to say about the strange physical phenomenon known as stigmata:

[Stigmata are] wounds or marks on the body corresponding to the wounds suffered by Christ on the cross, in the hands, feet, and side; stigmatics may also bear the bruise on the shoulder caused by carrying the cross, rope-marks on the wrists and ankles, the marks of scourging and those of the crown of thorns on the forehead. [p. 240]

Since the first century A.D there have been over three hundred reported cases of stigmatisation. The Catholic Church has been *extremely* cautious about attributing a divine cause for the appearance of stigmata on one of their rank and file faithful. This is in line with their official, usually neutral, position on almost all seemingly supernatural religious phenomena, such as miraculous healings attributed to particular saints and sightings of the Virgin Mary.

Today, skeptics believe that auto-suggestion and religious hysteria are the root causes for stigmatisation, but this still leaves us with some apparently unanswerable questions, such as why do stigmatics only secrete blood and water—never pus—no matter how long the stigmatic wounds are open? And why don't the dead bodies of many stigmatics often never decay—even after hundreds of years—and continue to emit a sweet odor even after death and burial? Also, there are reported cases of the stigmatic's blood acting in a weird fashion, such as in the case of Marie-Dominique Lazzari. She bled from her hands and feet, and when lying prone in bed, the blood from her feet would flow *up* her toes, in an apparent defiance of gravity.

Dermography, or skin writing, is another facet of the stigmata phenomenon. Words and/or symbols appear spontaneously as raised welts or red marks on the believer's skin. The most recent popular depiction of this type of religious physical manifestation was in the 1973 horror film *The Exorcist.* In that chiller, the words *Help me* appeared as raised welts on Regan's abdomen. Regan was possessed by a demon at the time and it seems that the plea for help came from her own subconscious, rather than from a spiritual entity. This feature looks at twenty documented stigmatics and provides some details as to the circumstances and nature of their holy wounds.

1. **St. Paul (died c. 67)** The Apostle Paul was the first recorded case of religious stigmatisation. Paul revealed the appearance of his wounds in his Epistle to the Galatians: "From henceforth let no man trouble me: for I bear in my body the marks of the Lord Jesus" (6:17). According to legend, Paul was also capable of performing miracles and died on the same day as Saint Peter. Nero beheaded Paul in 67 during his vicious persecution of Christians. The former Pharisee was likely between fifty-two and sixty-two years of age at the time of his death.

2. **Lutgardis (1182–June 16, 1246)** Lutgardis was a Benedictine nun whose body dripped blood when she experienced Christ's Passion during religious ecstasies. Her stigmata and visions spanned the twelve years from 1202 through 1214. She is considered one of the leading mystics of the thir-

teenth century and is also reputed to have performed miracles and made prophecies.

3. **St. Francis of Assisi (c. 1181–October 3, 1226)** St. Francis first experienced the stigmata on September 14, 1224, while praying in his cell on Mount Alverna. His stigmata consisted of torn and bleeding flesh at the five sites: hands, feet, and side. The wounds on his hands and feet looked like punctures made by spikes. He suffered severe pain and much bleeding from his stigmata and it is believed that his wounds hastened his death at the early age of forty-five.

4. **Catherine of Siena (1347–1380)** Catherine first received the stigmata in 1375 at the age of twenty-eight. (Twenty-eight, as you will notice, appears quite often as the age for the first manifestation of stigmata.) What was especially odd about her stigmatisation was that her wounds remained invisible throughout her lifetime, but appeared on her body after her death. It must be assumed that she suffered from the pain and bleeding in silence throughout the five years of her stigmatisation. Her death at the young age of thirty-three (the accepted age of Christ at the time of his crucifixion) revealed her wounds.

5. **Rita of Cascia (1381–1457)** Rita's stigmata did not appear until late in her life. In 1441, at the age of sixty, Rita heard a sermon about Christ's crown of thorns. Later, a bleeding "thorn" wound appeared on her forehead. Several miracles were attributed to her intervention after her death and she was canonized a saint in 1900.

6. **La Bienheureuse Lucie De Narni (1476–1544)** Lucie manifested the stigmata for seven years beginning at the age of twenty. She died at the age of sixty-eight, almost forty years after the last appearance of her wounds. In 1548, four years after her death, her body was exhumed and it was found to be free from decay and putrefaction. Her corpse exuded a sweet odor and blood still flowed from the wound in her side. In 1710, 162 years later, her body was yet again exhumed and was found to still be in a perfect state with no decay.

7. **Johanna Della Croce (b. 1524)** Johanna's stigmata appeared every Friday regularly throughout her life and vanished two days later on Sunday. In Catholic theology, Friday is the day Christ died and Sunday the day he rose from the dead.

8. **St. Veronique Giuliani (1660–July 9, 1727)** In 1693, at the age of thirty-three, Veronique's stigmata first manifested itself as a crown of thorns. Bleeding wounds appeared on her forehead in the places where Christ wore his crown of thorns. In 1697, at the age of thirty-seven, Veronique manifested the other five common stigmatic wounds: She bled from her side, her two hands, and her two feet. It is also reported that Veronique could levitate at will. She was acknowledged as one of the most astounding mystics of the eighteenth century and was canonized a saint in 1839.

9. **Jeanne de Marie-Jesus (18th cent.)** Jeanne's stigmata manifested itself in several uncommon ways. Her skin became dark and blue. Blood pooled beneath her fingernails and toenails. Dark bruises appeared on her arms and legs. Jeanne's most alarming stigmatic sign was the sweating of blood from her forehead and elsewhere on her body. Not much other biographical information exists about Jeanne de Marie-Jesus.

10. **Catherine Emmerich (1774–1824)** Catherine was a nun at the Dolmen convent. Her crown of thorns wounds opened regularly every Friday. Throughout her life she manifested eight wounds on her hands and feet (front and back on both hands and feet), which flowed blood continuously with no apparent severe ill effects.

11. **Gemma Galani (1878–April 11, 1903)** It is not known when Gemma first received the stigmata. In addition to the wounds, she also experienced mystical visions of Christ and demonic assaults. She died of tuberculosis of the spine at the young age of twenty-five and was canonized a saint in 1940.

12. **Padre Pio (1887–1968)** Padre Pio da Pietralcini (whose real name was Francesco Forgione) is one of the most well known of the modern stigmatics. He first manifested the stigmata in 1915, at the age of twenty-eight. He was a Capuchin monk who lived in the convent of San Giovanni Rotondo in Italy. In 1918, the wounds on his hands and feet began flowing blood and water at the rate of a glass a day. His other reputed paranormal/supernatural gifts included clairvoyance (seeing or sensing things not visible with ordinary sight such as apparitions and spirits) and precognition (being able to predict the future). The religious faithful

turned to Padre Pio for spiritual guidance, healings, and other help but the Catholic Church maintained a "hands off/no comment" attitude about the much-loved friar.

13. **Teresa Neumann (1898–1962)** Teresa Neumann, who was born at Konnersreuth, Germany, is another modern stigmatic around whom a devotive cult has developed. Like Padre Pio, Teresa's stigmata appeared at the age of twenty-eight, during Lent in the year 1926. She would go into a trance and have visions of Christ's Passion, during which she would bleed from her hands, feet, and forehead, and also cry tears of blood. She rarely ate. As with Padre Pio, Catholics turned to her for all manner of spiritual guidance and intervention, but, again, the Church remained neutral as to whether or not her manifestations had a divine source.

7 More Stigmatics (Including 4 Named Marie) About Whom Not Much Else Is Known

1. **Victoire Courtier** (1811–1888)
2. **Marie-Julie Jahenny**
3. **Louise Lateau** (1858–1883)
4. **Marie-Dominique Lazzari**
5. **Marie de Moerl** (1812–1868)
6. **Crescenzia Nierklutsch**
7. **Marie-Agnes Steiner**

4 of the Stupidest Initiation Rites Known

You have to wonder sometimes, you know?

This feature looks at ridiculous things people will do in order to get accepted by a group of other people who were willing to do ridiculous things to get accepted by other people who were willing to do . . . well, you get the point.

Some of these initiations are just plain stupid. Others are not only incredibly dumb but unbelievably dangerous. (See no. 1.) There have always been the innocent (relatively speaking) initiations such as dumping a guy wearing no clothes on the outskirts of town and leaving him to fend for himself getting back to the dorm. Whatever floats your boat, I guess. But these four are cruel, malicious, and disgusting, and it boggles the mind that people would actually agree to participate in such ritual stupidity.

But fraternity initiations continue, and we can only hope that actually belonging to the groups in question was worth what the initiates had to go through in order to get accepted as members.

1. **Initiation Ritual:** The AIDS Test.
   Group: Unidentified street gang.
   Place: San Antonio, Texas.
   This is probably the most unbelievable of all the initiations I've come across. In order to be accepted into one of the biggest street gangs in San Antonio, several teenage girls ranging in age from fourteen to fifteen (none were of legal age) had unprotected sex with male gang members who were known to be HIV-positive. The purpose of the test was for the girls to prove that they were "tough enough" to beat AIDS. When their initial blood tests came back negative for the HIV virus,

five of the girls who participated in this suicidal game of sexual Russian Roulette all bragged about being able to fight off
the AIDS virus. This single negative test, of course, means
nothing. The HIV virus can lie dormant for years before
turning into full-blown AIDS, and sometimes the virus itself
doesn't even show up in the blood for several months after
the initial, infected sexual encounter. STUPIDITY SCORE: 10.

2. **Initiation Ritual:** Genital branding.
   Group: A noted national fraternity.
   Place: College campuses.
   Even though fake genital branding is common as a pledge
   rite, certain branches of this fraternal organization actually
   brand their initiates with a coathanger that has been heated
   until it is incandescently hot. Like I said earlier, you really do
   have to wonder. STUPIDITY SCORE: 9.5.

3. **Initiation Ritual:** Eating and drinking until you puke.
   Group: A noted national fraternity.
   Place: College campuses.
   This initiation rite involves eating spaghetti and drinking
   wine until you throw up. Then you eat some more and pre-
   sumably throw up some more. STUPIDITY SCORE: 9.

4. **Initiation Ritual:** Mock execution by deadly gas.
   Group: The Black Watch Cadet Corps.
   Place: Montreal and elsewhere.
   Pledges are taken into a room where pellets are dropped into
   a liquid that begins to fill the room with a gas that has a dis-
   gusting odor. Such fun! STUPIDITY SCORE: 8.

Department of Peculiar Parlance:
84 Euphemisms for Vomiting

Vomiting is nature's way of reminding you that your stomach is not
a stainless steel septic tank. Here's how to say "puke" (no. 38) 83
other charmingly inventive and nauseatingly descriptive ways, including yuke and zuke.

1. Barf
2. Blow Beets
3. Blow Chow
4. Blow Lunch
5. Blow Your Cookies
6. Blow Your Groceries
7. Bow to the Porcelain Altar
8. Buick
9. Call Ruth
10. Chew the Cheese
11. Chuck Up
12. Chum the Fish
13. DeFood
14. Drain the Bilge
15. Drive the Porcelain Bus
16. Earl
17. Feed the Fishes
18. Flash the Hash
19. Fred
20. Go to Europe with Ralph and Earl in a Buick
21. Happy Returns
22. Hug the Porcelain God
23. Hug the Throne
24. Hurl
25. Jerk the Cat
26. Kiss the Porcelain God
27. Laugh at the Carpet
28. Launch Your Lunch
29. A Liquid Laugh
30. Lose a Meal
31. Lose Your Cookies
32. Lose Your Lunch
33. Make a Sale
34. Make Love to the Porcelain Goddess
35. Make Pizza
36. Marry Your Porcelain Mistress
37. Pray to the Porcelain God
38. Puke
39. Pump Ship
40. Purge
41. Ralph
42. Retch
43. Reverse Gears
44. Ride the Buick
45. Ride the Porcelain Bus
46. Ride the Porcelain Honda
47. Rolf
48. Ruth
49. Sell Buicks
50. Sell Out
51. Shit
52. Shoot Your Cookies
53. Shoot Your Cat
54. Shoot the Works
55. Skin a Goat
56. Snap Your Cookies
57. Spew
58. Spill Your Breakfast
59. Spill the Blue Groceries
60. Spit Beef
61. Talk into the Porcelain Telephone
62. Talk on the Great White Telephone
63. Talk to Earl
64. Talk to Ralph on the Big White Phone
65. Throw a Map
66. Throw Your Voice
67. Throw Up
68. Throw Up Your Toenails
69. Toss Your Cookies
70. Toss Your Lunch
71. Toss Your Tacos
72. Unspit
73. Unswallow
74. Upchuck
75. Urp
76. Water Buffalo

77. Wheeze
78. Woof Cookies
79. Worship the Porcelain God
80. Worship the Throne
81. Yak
82. Yank
83. Yuke
84. Zuke

7 Tampered-with Products and the Poisons Used to Tamper with Them

Are you afraid of what you put in your mouth?

Ever since the 1982 Tylenol tragedy, every consumer is safety conscious, some to the point of paranoia. Companies are acknowledging peoples' fears by cloaking everything in more safety seals than Carter's got pills. The typical bottle of pills today bears at least four safety features: The box is usually glued closed, there is a plastic seal around the cap, there is a glued safety seal covering the top of the bottle, and the bottle covers themselves all require either finger gymnastics or some form of cryptographic code-breaking ability to open.

The packaging for Extra-Strength Tylenol Liquid Pain Reliever is probably the most extreme example of corporate concern. Realizing that liquids are likely to be the most easily tampered-with product, and recognizing what another Tylenol tamper scare would do to the company, Johnson & Johnson made absolutely sure that no one was getting into Tylenol Liquid, or if they did, that you'd know about it.

First, the box is glued. The bottle of liquid inside the box is completely shrink-wrapped from top to bottom in tight plastic. The cap of the bottle proper is childproof, and then the liquid itself is protected by a glued foil seal. Any one of these precautions would probably be enough. All four virtually guarantee it.

This feature looks at seven horrifying incidents of product tampering, although to this day, Perrier claims that the benzene that got into Perrier in 1990 was due to an error, not tampering.

1. Extra-Strength Tylenol Capsules (1982)

Cyanide. Seven people in the Chicago area died after swallowing capsules of Extra-Strength Tylenol pain reliever that had been laced with cyanide. This is the tampering case that led to putting safety seals on everything from mouthwash to vitamins. This case also led to the eventual almost complete abandonment of the capsule as a delivery medium for over-the-counter medication, and to the development of the solid-core capsule and the caplet, both of which are virtually impervious to tampering. No one was ever charged with the tampering and Tylenol's manufacturer, Johnson & Johnson, settled with the families of the deceased for an undisclosed amount. Johnson & Johnson's corporate response to this crisis is a textbook example of how a company can experience what appears to be an absolutely devastating catastrophe with one of its products and be able to reduce damages to a minimum with the effective implementation of crisis team action and smart and irreproachably correct public relations.

2. Contac, Dietac, and Teldrin Capsules (1986)

Rat poison. These products were all contaminated by a man who was trying to manipulate the price of the company's stock. He was arrested and convicted of the tampering. No deaths were reported.

3. Gerber Baby Food (1986)

Glass fragments. Glass was found in several varieties of Gerber baby food in various areas of the country. The Food & Drug Administration said that some of these cases were due to bottle breakage during shipping but also attributed some of the glass fragments to tampering. No deaths were reported.

4. Extra-Strength Excedrin Capsules (1986)

Cyanide. Two people in Washington state died after ingesting Extra-Strength Excedrin that was contaminated with cyanide. The wife of one of the dead victims was arrested and convicted in the tampering.

5. Perrier Mineral Water (1990)

Benzene. Bottles of Perrier that had been shipped to the United States, Canada, Denmark, and West Germany were found to contain traces of the chemical benzene, a clear, colorless, flammable liquid that is used to manufacture DDT, detergents, motor fuels, and insecticides. Perrier officials claim that the benzene entered the water because of a dirty pipe filter at the underground spring "Source Perrier" at Vergeze in southern France.

6. Sudafed Capsules (1991)

Cyanide. Two people—again in Washington state—died after taking cyanide-laced Sudafed capsules. A man who poisoned the capsules in an attempt to murder his wife was arrested and convicted of the tampering.

7. Diet Pepsi and Diet Crystal Pepsi (1993)

Syringes. Syringes and needles were reported found in cans of Diet Pepsi and Diet Crystal Pepsi in 23 states. PepsiCo immediately went into crisis management mode and did three things: They went to the press, they went to the government, and they showed the public their manufacturing process. At least one syringe report was immediately confirmed to be a hoax and PepsiCo went to great lengths to assure the public that it was virtually impossible for cans of soda to be tampered with during production. They explained that the empty, cleaned cans were only open and vulnerable for .9 of a second each. PepsiCo produced 20 million cans of soda a day at 150 plants. It was eventually proven that the reports of syringes in Pepsi cans were nothing more than a twisted and sick fabrication.

22 Things Invented by Leonardo da Vinci Hundreds of Years Before They Were "Invented"

Leonardo da Vinci lived from 1452 to 1519, when he died at the age of sixty-seven. During his life, he conceived and designed dozens of "devices" we recognize today as the forerunners of many of our modern necessities, including the airplane, eyeglasses, and the life preserver. This list comprises only twenty-two of his most remarkable "brainstorms," all of which were "thought up" hundreds of years before their modern versions came into being. Actual sketches of these inventions are available in the many published editions of Leo's notebooks.

1. The Revolving Stage
2. The Flying Machine
3. The Parachute
4. The Air Conditioner
5. The Oil Lamp
6. The Alarm Clock
7. The Printing Press
8. The Odometer
9. The Pedometer
10. The Magnetic Compass
11. A Clock with Minute and Hour Hands
12. Eyeglasses
13. The Telescope
14. The Differential Transmission
15. The Water Turbine
16. The Horseless Wagon
17. The Machine Gun

19 Things You're Not Supposed to Do with the U.S. Flag

A very specific and quite detailed code of conduct exists regarding the treatment of Old Glory. No American symbol represents more to the people of this country and, thus, the passionate devotion to it in all of its forms.

This passion manifested itself in the early 1990s when the Supreme Court ruled that flag burning was legal. They said it was an expression of free speech that could not be forbidden or suppressed.

Overnight, bumper stickers appeared threatening that the driver of the car would shoot someone if he or she saw an American flag being burned. Feelings run deep about the Stars and Stripes. This feature looks at 19 rules for proper treatment of the American flag.

1. The flag should never be allowed to touch the ground or the floor.
2. When the flag is used to cover a coffin, it should never be lowered into the grave with the casket.
3. The flag should never be dipped to any person.
4. The flag should never be dipped to any thing.
5. The flag should never be displayed with the stars ("the union") pointing down except as a distress signal.
6. The flag should never be displayed on a car, boat, or float on anything but a pole.
7. The flag should never be used as a covering for a ceiling.
8. The flag should never have anything written or drawn on it.
9. The flag should never be used to carry anything.
10. The flag should never be used to cover a statue, a sculpture, or a monument of any type.
11. The flag should never be used for advertising.

12. The flag should never be embroidered on anything dispos-able, such as cardboard boxes, or anything that is to be used once and then discarded.
13. The flag should never be worn as part of a costume.
14. The flag should never be worn as part of an athletic uni-form.
15. No advertising signs should ever be attached to the flag's staff.
16. The flag should never be used as drapery of any sort.
17. The flag should never be hung in any way that prevents it from falling free and unencumbered.
18. When a flag is hung on a pole from a building, the union should be away from the building.
19. The flag should never be thrown away. Burning is prefer-able.

9 Types of Angels

As Catholics, we all grew up believing that every one of us had a Guardian Angel watching over us. This was comforting, but also a little scary. According to the "rules," our angel was with us from the moment of birth until we breathed our last breath, and then even *after* we died as our angel stuck by us and accompanied us into Heaven.

As you can well imagine, this was pretty heady stuff for impressionable grammar school kids. We were taught that our angel was *always there,* you see. In my class, the thought crossed many a juvenile mind that there were a few minor things in our lives that we might not want even our Guardian Angel to see, if you catch my drift.

This feature lists the nine different types of angels that float around outside our earthly plane. This ranking is based on the writings of St. Paul and other theologians. How they all determined that this was the correct arrangement I haven't the foggiest.

Interestingly, there is an actual rank called Angel, and ironically, it is at the bottom of the "spiritual totem pole," so to speak. There are eight angelic ranks superior to just plain old angels. I don't think it's ever been determined just how these spiritual bodyguards get promoted. It just might be who you know, you know? This listing starts with the highest ranking of angels.

First Choir

1. **Seraphim.** They have six wings and are apparently the only holy beings allowed to stand in the presence of God.
2. **Cherubim.** They have large wings, a human head, and an animal body.

3. **Thrones.** The Bible is vague on what Thrones look like, but they are mentioned in Colossians 1:16, and it is assumed that they serve seraphim and cherubim in some capacity.

Second Choir

4. **Dominions.** The chief angels of the Second Hierarchy. They are also mentioned in Colossians.
5. **Virtues.** Angels that report to Dominions.
6. **Powers.** Angels that report to Virtues and that are also mentioned in Colossians.

Third Choir

7. **Principalities.** An angel with power over Archangels and Angels.
8. **Archangels.** A chief angel, in charge of Angels. Gabriel, Raphael, and Michael are Archangels.
9. **Angels.** Supernatural beings garbed in white robes. They have one set of wings and are superior to humans in powers and intelligence. They are usually assigned the day-to-day work of watching over and helping humans.

11 Weird Psychiatric Disorders

This feature lists eleven of the odder psychological derangements we humans are capable of.

1. **Abasia** A person feels that he or she has lost the ability to walk.
2. **Achiria** A person feels that one or both of his or her hands is missing.
3. **Astasia** A person feels that he or she has lost the ability to stand.
4. **Cataphasia** A person frequently repeats the same word or phrase over and over.
5. **Chionophobia** A person has a phobic fear of snow.
6. **Coprophilia** A person has an abnormal interest in feces.
7. **Echolalia** A person compulsively repeats the last thing he or she heard.
8. **Erythrophobia** A person has a phobic fear of blushing.
9. **Heberphrenia** This is a form of schizophrenia distinguished by primitive, regressive behavior and a permanent silly grin.
10. **Logorrhea** This is distinguished by nonstop irrational babbling.
11. **Theomania** A person has the delusion that he or she (usually he) is Jesus Christ.

Department of Peculiar Parlance:
228 Euphemisms for Sexual Intercourse

I am sometimes amazed at the creativity and inventiveness that goes into the concoction of euphemisms. Remember: A slang or euphemistic expression is often intended to be used as a substitute for a cruder or more embarrassing term, and yet some of the following terms for sexual intercourse are far more descriptive and explicit than the blunt, yet accurate, "have sex with."

Here's an illustration: Which of the following two remarks do you think would be more acceptable in conversation among friends?

A. "I had sex last night."

B. "Last night I had a pair of balls against my butt."

Obviously A would be the comment least likely to raise eyebrows, and yet the B statement (no. 49), clearly the more vulgar way of describing the act, was originally coined to *replace* something like the A statement.

And not all euphemisms are understandable. How in the world did "have a Northwest Cocktail" (no. 105) come to serve as a substitute for "have sex"?

Whatever the circumstances of their genesis, the following 228 terms are all inventive and colorful ways of describing the dance of the ages. (Is *your* favorite here?)

1. Adam and Eve It
2. Be in a Woman's Beef
3. Be up to One's Balls
4. Beat Someone with an Ugly Stick
5. Boink Someone
6. Bone Someone
7. Bop Someone
8. Bump Bellies
9. Bunny Fuck
10. Bury the Weenie
11. Buzz the Brillo
12. Cream Someone
13. Dance the Buttock Jig
14. Dance the Matrimonial Polka
15. Dance the Mattress Jig
16. Dip Your Wick
17. Do a Bit of Front Door Work
18. Do a Dicky Dunk
19. Do a Dive in the Dark
20. Do a Four-Legged Frolic
21. Do a Grumble and Grunt
22. Do a Lewd Infusion
23. Do Boom-Boom

24. Do Dirty Work at the Crossroads
25. Do Horizontal Exercises
26. Do Some Ladies' Tailoring
27. Do Some Nose Painting
28. Do Some Rump Work
29. Do Some Twat Raking
30. Do Target Practice
31. Do the Act of Darkness
32. Do the Bone Dance
33. Do the Chores
34. Do the Featherbed Jig
35. Do the Horizontal Hula
36. Do the Naughty
37. Do the Ugly
38. Drive Home
39. Eat Cauliflower
40. Eat Hymeneal Sweets
41. Enjoy a Flesh Session
42. Exchange Spit
43. Fan Someone
44. Feed the Dummy
45. Fit End to End
46. Fix Her Plumbing
47. Flop in the Hay
48. Get a Belly Full of Marrow Pudding
49. Get a Pair of Balls Against Your Butt
50. Get a Shove in Your Blind Eye
51. Get into Someone's Pants
52. Get Jack in the Orchard
53. Get Oats from Someone
54. Get Your Ashes Hauled
55. Get Your Chimney Swept Out
56. Get Your End Wet
57. Get Your Hair Cut
58. Get Your Leather Stretched
59. Get Your Nuts Cracked
60. Get Your Oil Changed
61. Give a Hole to Hide In
62. Give a Woman a Shot
63. Give Hard for Soft
64. Give Her a Hosing
65. Give Her a Past
66. Give Her the Business
67. Give Juice for Jelly
68. Give Pussy a Taste of Cream
69. Give Someone a Stab
70. Give Someone the Works
71. Give the Dog a Bone
72. Go Bed-Pressing
73. Go Belly-to-Belly
74. Go Fishing
75. Go Like a Belt-Fed Motor
76. Go Like a Rat up a Drainpipe
77. Go Like a Rat up a Rhododendron
78. Go on Bush Patrol
79. Go Rump-Splitting
80. Go Star-Gazing on Your Back
81. Go to Town
82. Go to Work with Someone
83. Goose Someone
84. Grease the Wheel
85. Grind Your Tool
86. Hammer Someone
87. Haul Your Ashes
88. Have a Bit of Curly Greens
89. Have a Bit of Fish
90. Have a Bit of Fun
91. Have a Bit of Giblet Pie
92. Have a Bit of Pork
93. Have a Bit of Skirt
94. Have a Bit of Split Mutton
95. Have a Bit of Sugar Stick

168. Poke Someone
169. Pop It In
170. Pork Someone
171. Post a Letter
172. Pound Someone
173. Pray with the Knees Upward
174. Pump Someone
175. Put Four Quarters on the Spit
176. Put the Bee in the Hive
177. Put the Boots to Someone
178. Put the Devil into Hell
179. Ram Someone
180. Ride Someone
181. Ride the Hobby Horse
182. Roller Skate
183. Rub Bacons
184. Sacrifice to Venus
185. Saw Off a Chunk
186. Screw Someone
187. Shake a Skin Coat
188. Shake the Sheets
189. Shoot Between Wind and Water
190. Shoot Your Wad
191. Shtupp Someone
192. Sink It In
193. Sink the Soldier
194. Slam Someone
195. Slip Someone the Hot Beef Injection
196. Smoke Someone
197. Spear the Bearded Clam
198. Split Someone
199. Stab a Woman in the Thigh
200. Stain Someone
201. Stretch Leather
202. Suck the Sugar-Stick
203. Take a Belly Ride
204. Take a Trip up the Rhine
205. Take a Turn in the Stubble
206. Take a Turn on Shooter's Hill
207. Take Nebuchadnezzar Out to Grass
208. Take the Starch Out of Someone
209. Taste Someone
210. Tear Off a Piece
211. Tell a Bedtime Story
212. Thread the Needle
213. Throw a Leg Over
214. Tie the True Lover's Knot
215. Trade a Bit of Hard for a Bit of Soft
216. Trim the Buff
217. Trot Out Your Pussy
218. Varnish Your Cane
219. Wank Someone
220. Wet Your Bottom
221. Wet Your Wick
222. Whitewash Someone
223. Wind Up the Clock
224. Work Out
225. Work the Hairy Oracle
226. Wriggle Navels
227. Yield Your Favors
228. Zig-Zag Someone

67 Ways People Described Themselves in the "Personals" Column in One Issue of *The New York Review of Books*

■■■■ ■ ■■■ ■■■ ■ ■■ ■ ■■■

The New York Review of Books "Personals" column is a veritable Home Shopping Club of romance. Week after week, amour-minded bibliophiles advertise their "wares" for perusal by fellow book-minded "shoppers."

This list is probably the best advertisement for the magazine's readership—if all of the descriptions are for real, that is. If all of the people who advertise in the personals are what they say they are, *The New York Review of Books* has the most sophisticated, intelligent, creative, and gorgeous readers on the planet.

Are there truth-in-advertising laws for personals ads? I guess a "reader beware" caveat is the best we can hope for. This feature lists some of the more interesting personal descriptions found in one issue of the magazine.

1. Above-average brains
2. Academic
3. Accessible
4. Adept
5. Almost shy
6. Artistic
7. Attentive
8. Attorney
9. Baby-boomer
10. Brimming with mischief, humor, and libido
11. Capable of love with great passion and commitment
12. Curvaceous
13. Divorced [several times]
14. Doctorate
15. Earthy
16. Eclectic
17. Elated by the prospect of discovering a first edition of Gide
18. Exhilarated by white-water rafting
19. Feminist with strong family values
20. Francophile

21. Gay [more than once]
22. Geographically exploratory
23. Grace Kelly good looks
24. Humanist values
25. Humanistic career [several times]
26. Iconoclast
27. Interested in duplicate bridge and/or jazz
28. Interested in film, art, and theater
29. Ivy-educated
30. Ivy-league graduate degree
31. Jewish Mensch
32. Jewish-flavored
33. Joi de vivre
34. Leggy
35. Live and work in Westchester
36. Lousy hours
37. Love my companion animal
38. Lover of social conscience
39. Loves blues
40. Loves Egyptian art
41. Loves folk
42. Loves Impressionists
43. Loves Italian food
44. Loves music (Chopin to Gladys Knight to Gospel)
45. Loves old houses
46. Loves sea kayaks
47. Miss NYC
48. Moderately but not completely sane
49. Multilingual schmoozer with unusual background
50. Not bad-looking
51. Not-uncomely
52. Now working in the area of multicultural relations
53. Political
54. Quite selective
55. Researcher
56. Riding wave of exuberance
57. Seasoned
58. Sings (blues/popular)
59. Singularly appealing
60. Suzanne Pleshette type
61. Thinking man's blonde
62. Transplanted New Englander
63. Uncertain age
64. Wine buff
65. Winsome
66. Woman of exceptional qualities
67. Writer escaped from gruesome glamour career

9 of the Ways TV Gets It Wrong

Television? The word is half Latin and half Greek. No good can come of it.—attributed to C. P. Scott (1846–1932)

In July of 1993, *USA Today* published a report that compared the way American life is depicted on television, and what American life was *really* like.

Their research involved watching all of the prime time shows airing on ABC, CBS, NBC, and the Fox network the week of April 24–30, 1993. (I hope the *USA Today* staff is paid well.) *USA Today* explained their methodology:

> We profiled all characters with two or more speaking lines and counted how often various activities occurred on screen. Advertisements were not included.
>
> Violent incidents include those depicted on screen and those visually implied. Counted are such acts as pushing and slapping, assaults, rape, and killings—most of which could be either criminal or noncriminal. Accidental acts or purely verbal references to violent acts were not counted.

USA Today's sources for "real life" information came from the U.S. Census Bureau, the Bureau of Justice Statistics, Gallup, Clairol, the Boy Scouts of America, the Girl Scouts of America, Mediamark Research, the President's Committee on Employment of People with Disabilities, and the National Association to Advance Fat Acceptance. Barbara Hansen of *USA Today* did the analysis and the result was a revealing, impeccably researched study of just how "off" American television was when looked at as a mirror of American life. These statistics speak volumes about American TV's warped and distorted representation of America. Here are 9 of the ways American TV gets it wrong.

1. In TV Land, **63 percent** of the characters are male. In real life, men make up only **49 percent** of the U.S. population. On TV, **37 percent** of the characters are female. In real life, women make up **51 percent** of the U.S. population.

2. In TV Land, **60 percent** of the employed characters fall into the Professional/Executive category. In real life, the figure is only **26 percent.**

3. On TV, only **21 percent** of the employed characters work in the labor/service/clerical fields. In real life, a whopping **72 percent** of the American workforce labor in those fields.

4. In TV Land, **19 percent** of the employed characters work in law enforcement. In real life, the figure is only **2 percent.**

5. In TV Land, only **1 percent** of the characters are handicapped. In the real world, **17 percent** of the population has some form of disability.

6. On TV, only **10 percent** of the characters are overweight. In the real world, a whopping **68 percent** of the population are heavier than they should be.

7. On TV, the violent crime rate is **59** victims per 1,000 people. In real life, that figure is only **32** victims per 1,000.

8. In TV Land, only **5 percent** of the characters practice religion in any way at all. In real life, **42 percent** of the population say that religion plays some role in their lives.

9. On TV, **27 percent** of the female characters are blondes. In real life, only **20 percent** of America's women are towheads.

15 Weird Movies That Contain Bizarre Sex, Unusual Practices, or That Are Just Plain *Strange*

The duty of the chronicler is not to sweeten the truth but to report it objectively.—Opening narration, *Mondo Cane*

This is an abitrary look at some genuinely strange movies. This feature does not profess to be comprehensive or definitive. It is instead just a look at some randomly selected films I thought had a high enough bizarre quality to qualify.

What I did was to visit my friendly video rental store (Tommy K's in Branford, Connecticut—they will one day give Blockbuster Video a run for their money, mark my words) and ask my friend Linda to steer me toward the weird stuff. She led me by the hand to the Cult section and the Adult room. The Cult section was a goldmine of the weird and wondrous, and the Adult room had several X-rated videos that had the word *freak* or *bizarre* in the title.

I picked and chose among Tommy K's inventory and this list is the result. So go get your Frequent Renter's card out and check out some of these cinematic curiosities.

1. *Akira* (1990)

Akira is an animated Japanese film that you ain't *never* gonna confuse with the Jetsons, that's for sure.

This is an "adult" film, and by that I mean that it is thematically complex, very violent, and incredibly detailed. Each frame of this film could exist as an individual piece of gorgeous comic art.

This science fiction tale, directed by Katsuhiro Otomo and based on the Japanese comic book of the same name, takes place in the post-nuclear holocaust twenty-first century, thirty-one years after

World War III has devastated Neo-Tokyo. A member of a motorcycle gang is empowered with telekinesis after the government experiments on him (shades of *Firestarter!*), and when he runs amuck,
his fellow gang members try to stop him.

Akira has a very high-tech, *Blade Runner* look. It is so well drawn
there are times when the action actually looks live. The film has superb point-of-view camera angles and a smooth fluidity of motion
that rivals some live-action features. If you're into sophisticated animation and "cyberpunkish" science fiction, rent *Akira*.

2. *Baby Snakes* (1979)

This film by the late Frank Zappa is an electronic video collage. It
is part documentary, part concert film, and part drug hallucination.
The cast includes Joey Psychotic, Donna U., Wanha, Frenchy the
Poodle, Ms. Pinky's Larger Sister, Angel, Janet the Planet, and Diva.

Baby Snakes tells the story of the making of a claymation feature,
which itself is incredibly bizarre. We get to see Zappa directing the
soundtrack of the film. He uses an exotic aural conglomeration of
electronic noises, shrieks, claps, and laughs.

We also see Zappa in concert with the Mothers of Invention.
One of his best jokes is the one about the three mistakes God
made after creating light: man, woman, and the poodle.

Baby Snakes has a cult following due to its unabashed strange-
ness. When it was originally released theatrically in 1979, it ran 166
minutes long. It was reissued in 1984 at 91 minutes. I'm not sure
if both versions are available on video. (The version I screened was
the longer one.) The film can be boring at times but if you approach it as the cinematic oddity that it is, you'll probably enjoy
the experience.

3. *Beyond the Valley of the Dolls* (1970)

This one has to be seen to be believed. Notwithstanding its title,
this is *not* a sequel to the 1967 Patty Duke no-brainer *Valley of the
Dolls*. *Beyond the Valley of the Dolls* is the cinematic result of the unlikely teaming of Roger Ebert (yes, the post-ampersand part of the
film critical duo Siskel & Ebert) and large breast devotee (addict,
actually) Russ Meyer. Supposedly, *Beyond* was intended to be a sat-
ire of both the Hollywood scene and those ludicrously moralistic
Innocent-Young-Artist-Actress-Musician-Whatever-Moves-to-

Tinseltown-and-Gets-Corrupted movies. I don't know. I can see where Ebert and Meyer intended it to be satirical, but it's all done with such a straight face that in the end *Beyond* just comes off as a bad, bad movie. The film includes such nauseants as

- A transvestite rock star named Z-rock who only speaks in Shakespearean dialect (one of the most ridiculous and irritating elements of the flick)
- An all-girls band that is originally called The Kelly Affair but later changes its name to The Carrie Nations(!)
- Cringe-inducing seventies hippie lingo ("It's a stone gas, man!" and "Don't bogart that joint!")
- Hairdos that look as though the guys in the Brady Bunch (*especially* Greg) all dropped acid and decided to get experimental perms
- The decapitation (with a sword) of a guy in leopard-skin bikini underwear
- A Nazi named Otto
- The spontaneous curing (by love) of a wheelchair-bound, suicidal, rafters-diving band manager
- Edy Williams as a porn star
- The Strawberry Alarm Clock performing in gargantuan bell-bottoms and mustaches at a party
- An oh-so-serious (and thus, even more laughable) closing narration that sums up the disastrous moral choices made by each character
  and (of course)
- Naked women everywhere, all of whom possess *enormous* breasts (except for the flat-chested transvestite rock star)

Like I said, it has to be seen to be believed.

Beyond the Valley of the Dolls and the original unrelated *Valley of the Dolls* were both released on video for $19.98 each in May of 1993. I can unequivocally assure you that either is worth at least one rental.

4. *The Big Shave* (1967)

The Big Shave is a short film—all of six minutes—by Martin Scorsese. *The Big Shave* has *no* dialogue, and in it a young white man shaves.

We see the unnamed guy stumble into the bathroom, remove his shirt, wash and lather his face, and then shave, using one of the twist-open double-sided safety razors our dads used before the industry came up with disposables. Many of us learned to shave with those types of razors, and many of us cut our faces to ribbons in the process. They might have been *called* "safety razors," but the term was dubious.

After the young man rinses the razor one last time and wipes the shaving cream residue off his face, something goes wrong. He stares at himself in the mirror, and then bewilders us by once again spreading shaving cream all over his face. Is he going to shave again? Yes, he is, we realize. And he does. Only *this* time, he intentionally slices his face with each sweep of his razor.

Ignoring the blood, he continues to cut his face with the razor: He slices himself under his nose, on his cheeks, on his chin. The blood begins to flow and drip down his face onto his neck and into the sink. The bathroom and fixtures are stark white (Scorsese acknowledges Herman Melville in the credits for "whiteness"); the blood is vividly red.

The young man continues to shave until his face and neck are a red mask. Then he carefully and deliberately slits open his throat—one swipe from each side—unleashing a flood of blood down his neck, down his chest, into the sink, and all over the floor.

And that is how *The Big Shave* ends.

But what is this film about?

In it a man "cleanses" himself by shaving off his facial hair. He then confronts his newly shaven face in the mirror and comes to the conclusion that the shaving was not enough. He must now draw blood. He must pay for his sins with his blood. To atone for *what*, we are never told.

The religious symbolism is fulfilled and thoroughly explicated at the conclusion of the film immediately after the man cuts his throat. We see the blood slide down his chest and the resemblance to similar ubiquitous images of Christ are unmistakable.

This is an odd piece of work, as are all artistic creations that operate solely on a metaphorical level, and yet it is striking and gripping in its use of the red and white imagery throughout its brief and bizarre six minutes.

5. *Bizarre*

Just the title of this video alone mandated that it be included. The sleeve of the film didn't offer any clues as to what it might contain so I was ready for anything as I popped it into my VCR.

Bizarre is a German film (date unknown, but it looks fairly modern) with no soundtrack other than music. The video consists of 55 minutes of two naked women fighting and then 5 minutes of lesbian oral sex.

The two slender, thirtysomething women are completely naked except for high heels, and throughout most of the film the two frauleins kick, slap, scratch, and beat each other with sticks and branches. (The entire film takes place outdoors.) They pull and slap each other's breasts, twist each other's nipples, and at one point one of the women actually urinates on her opponent. The movie ends with one woman hosing the other down, erotically playing the stream of water over her breasts and genitals, and then the two of them engage in oral sex on a lawn chair.

This film was obviously designed for that segment of the X-rated audience that gets off on watching two women fight. I do not happen to find that scenario particularly erotic and throughout the film I sat there awestruck at the deliberate, unrelenting effort these two cat fighters put into their "performance." They did not let up for a minute, from rolling around on the grass to chasing and kicking each other. After the novelty wears off, though, it was all actually quite boring.

6. *Boobs, Butts, and Bloopers, Part 2* (1992)

This is a compilation of outtakes from X-rated movies. It is hosted by porn star Ron Jeremy, who is "famous" for being able to fellate himself (he's done it on film) and time his own orgasms to the second.

This film is included here because it provides a behind-the-scenes look at the weird and unique world of the X-rated movie industry. This film humanizes what many consider to be an exploitative fringe industry. The X-rated film business is most definitely not a "fringe" business, as this film shows, and as far as exploitation goes, what we see in this collection is an industry peopled by young, attractive, intelligent actors and actresses who are in this strictly as a job.

These people bring no moral baggage to their work site, and there is genuine affection among the cast members in these films. Watching this blooper reel, we realize that X-rated films are masterpieces of human plumbing, and it is not difficult to understand why so many of these actors say it's not the most erotic thing in the world to have sex under hot lights, with people watching, and with the camera—and the clock—running. The people in the sex film industry are experts at creating the "hot and sweaty sex" illusion on screen and it is quite illuminating to see them turn "passion" (and, of course, sexual prowess and expertise) on and off at will. They literally switch in and out of the "sex animal" persona on command.

There is humor here, too. We see the actresses get their clothing caught in their earrings and their hair as they are doffing their tops. We see guys who can't get it up, and guys who can't get off. There are a lot of "inside" jokes on the set, many of them sexual, but many of them not. Ron Jeremy's blossoming weight gets its fair share of gags, and one director even gets a "hot foot" as he sleeps by the side of a pool during a break from shooting.

Boobs, Butts, and Bloopers, Part 2 is worth renting if you've ever rented an X-rated film and want to see how they're made. (And since X-rated films now constitute close to 40 percent of the video rental business, you very well might have.) Because this film does contain hardcore sex scenes, though, you will find it in the Adult section of the video store.

7. *Eraserhead* (1978)

You thought *Wild Palms* and *Twin Peaks* were weird? A suggestion: Reserve judgment until you see *Eraserhead*. *Eraserhead*, David Lynch's first full-length feature film, is a filmed nightmare. It is a bizarre, black-and-white journey into some kind of weird alternate reality where cooked chicken carcasses bleed on their dishes, and people give birth to fetus-like heads that survive without bodies.

Beyond those cursory images, *Eraserhead* is almost beyond description and has to be experienced to be believed. (Notice I didn't use the word *seen*.)

Is it about the creation of the universe? Is that guy shown at the beginning of the film sitting at a darkened window supposed to be God? What's actually going on beneath the radiator? And to paraphrase a question David Letterman once asked Don King, "Hey, Eraserhead, what's the deal with the hair?"

Eraserhead is hallucinatory, surrealistic, and just plain *weird*. In fact, it's *mega-weird*.

Rent it.

And then strap yourself into your Barcalounger.

You will be given your rational mind back when the movie's over.

8. *European Sex Freaks* (1980s)

This is a grainy half-hour video that is narrated in German with English subtitles. The film is notable for the presence of Long Dong Silver, the black porno star whose name recognizability went through the roof after the Clarence Thomas/Anita Hill Supreme Court Senate confirmation hearings. (Hill accused Thomas of unwelcomely discussing Long Dong and his movies with Hill. It wasn't revealed if this was the film alleged to have been discussed, but it might have been.) For those of you who are not familiar with Mr. Silver (or is it Mr. Dong?), his claim to fame is a purportedly genuine 19-inch penis.

In *European Sex Freaks*, Long Dong is first seen dancing naked on a stage next to a similarly naked dancing woman. He has this silly grin on his face as he swings his pendulous penis back and forth. It does look like the real thing. We then see a picture of Long Dong with his penis tied in a knot.

The next scene shows Long Dong in bed with an X-rated film starlet named Fiona Flaps, whose anatomical peculiarity is having *enormous* labia majora. (A woman I know once described Fiona's labia as "looking like a pair of chicken cutlets." I thought that metaphor was hilarious—and incredibly accurate, too.)

Fiona caresses Long Dong's penis as he runs his hands over her naked body and then masturbates her. He never achieves an erection throughout their encounter.

The next segment features a woman with enormous breasts, who first masturbates herself and then ties her labia in a knot. (Tying body parts into knots is apparently a big thing with "sex freaks," eh? Would anyone actually be turned on by seeing that? I know I wasn't.) A guy then performs cunnilingus on her while she's "tied up."

The film then moves on to a woman, wearing an open bra and a garter belt, posing for pictures. She spreads open her legs and a guy snaps pictures. It isn't really clear just what qualifies her for inclusion here as a "freak," but I think she possessed a huge clitoris. The tape was so grainy it was kind of difficult to tell, though. She holds open her vagina for a while and then a *white* guy with a long penis (it looked to be about 15 inches or so flaccid) enters the picture. The woman giggles at his *"Schwanz"* and they then pose for photos with the woman holding his penis as though she were milking a cow.

As in the case of Long Dong, this chap never gets erect either. For one series of photos, he hangs his penis over her shoulder while she feigns lust.

The next segment features a pretty blond girl who first poses topless and then pulls down her dress to expose her pubic hair. She eventually removes the dress entirely and is sprayed down with water by a woman assistant. She then spreads her legs and we see that she (he?) has an uncircumcised penis *and* a vagina. Pictures are taken during which the penis never becomes erect, and then he/she gets on his/her knees and masturbates his/her vagina, but not his/her penis. (There should be an appropriate pronoun for hermaphrodites, don't you think?)

The next segment begins with a person dressed in a parka and hood entering a photographer's studio. The person has a mustache and long hair, but when the parka is removed we realize it's actually a woman who happens to be literally *covered* with hair from head to foot. She has thick dark hair all over her breasts, her stomach, her legs, and her back. The photographer snaps pictures as the woman poses on a bed and holds open her vagina with her fingers. The photographer then removes his shirt and embraces the woman.

The next segment features a Marilyn Monroe lookalike who might be the hermaphrodite from earlier. Long Dong shows up and pictures are taken of him alone and then with "Marilyn." There is no actual sex and once again Long Dong does not become erect. There is posed, feigned sex, though, for the pictures. In one shot, the actress holds her mouth close to his penis, and then they pose with his organ between her breasts.

There is then a short segment on a woman named Chesty Morgan, famous for having gargantuan breasts, and the film concludes with another hermaphrodite playing with itself on a bed.

This film was supposed to show the behind-the-scenes making of sex films and sex photographs involving people with physical sexual peculiarities, but it was so obviously staged that it lost any educational or "scandalous" power it might have had if it had been a genuine sexual documentary.

9. *Head* (1968)

The ingredients in the *Head* recipe include the Monkees ("a manufactured image"); the psychedelic era; a script by Jack Nicholson and Bob Rafelson (both still two years away from *Five Easy Pieces*) that had absolutely no coherent plot; clips from old movies; Terri Garr and Frank Zappa; and acid-inspired animation and imagery.

The result is High Weirdness that includes Nehru shirts, Jack Nicholson in a walk-on, the Monkees as living dandruff flakes, and a pro-drug subtext that had to be deliberately oblique so as not to jeopardize the Monkees' enormous teen following.

One interesting bit of staging you might want to watch for is the scene in which Davy Jones plays the violin on the steps of a brownstone while a woman sits in the window and listens. You look at this scene and tell me if it doesn't remind you—*a lot*—of the scene in Spike Lee's brilliant *Do the Right Thing* in which Mother Sister sits in the window of a brownstone and watches the world go by on the sidewalk beneath her. Maybe Spike was a Monkees fan growing up?

Head is worth checking out if you're interested in late-sixties psychedelia and culture. Just don't expect a storyline.

10. *Koyaanisqatsi* (1983)

Koyaanisqatsi is a film that has no cast, no dialogue, and no script. What it does have is an incredible Philip Glass soundtrack over scenes of hectic city life contrasted with beautiful nature vistas.

Koyaanisqatsi is a Hopi Indian word that means "life in turmoil, life disintegrating, life out of balance, a state of life that calls for another way of living."

The photography in this film (which is technically a documentary but is really much more than that) is spectacular and the editing and direction are inspired. Time-lapse photography is used brilliantly to show entire days in an eye-blink. The images are so powerful that this "silent" movie ends up speaking volumes about man and his relationship with nature.

In *Koyaanisqatsi*, director Godfrey Reggio truly shows us a world that most of us do not know, and many of us will never understand. In 1988, Reggio followed *Koyaanisqatsi* with *Powaqqatsi*, which was subtitled *Life in Transformation* (also worth your time). I can assure you that you have never seen anything quite like *Koyaanisqatsi* and *Powaqqatsi*.

11. *Meet the Hollowheads* (1988)

This overlooked 1988 sci-fi comedy is notable for the presence of Juliette Lewis and for its absolute, unequivocal devotion to its main premise. The story revolves around a family that lives in some sort of bizarre parallel world where everything is based on properties of fluid transfer and delivery—a liquid-based habitat and lifestyle.

The movie doesn't always work, and one critic noted that a brief explanatory introduction at the beginning of the film might have saved the audience a half hour or so of confusion, but what does go on in the film is so weird that it is definitely worth a look.

Daddy works at United Umbilical as a meter reader. UU pumps fluids into people's homes for all manner of uses. The family has a pet eye on a tentacle in a tank, as well as a human-faced dog. Doors are called orifices, and food and drink are blue. Grandpa is kept chained up in the basement and is fed with a huge syringe, and someone who is drunk is described as "liquefied."

The meticulous attention to detail in creating and showing the Hollowheads' world is admirable. After a period of total bewilderment, we get the joke and begin to enjoy the genuinely offbeat humor. *Meet the Hollowheads* might be a little difficult to find, but it's definitely worth a rental for those interested in the gleefully bizarre.

12. *Mondo Cane* (1963)

This Italian documentary begins with the following disclaimer (heard over scenes of caged, barking dogs):

All of the scenes you will see in this film are true and are taken only from life. If often they are shocking, it is because there are many shocking things in this world. Besides, the duty of the chronicler is not to sweeten the truth but to report it objectively.

Mondo Cane was the first of the "Mondo" films and I suppose it must have been rather shocking back in 1963. But now, after the more extreme and genuinely startling later "Mondo" films, in retrospect, *Mondo Cane* seems quite tame.

Food and death seem to be the main focus of *Mondo Cane* in that the "shocking things" we see all seem to revolve around eating and dying. Some of the more intriguing segments include the following:

- A Pasadena dog cemetery
- A restaurant on the Island of Formosa where dogs are served as the main course
- Geese being force-fed in Strasburg with huge funnels with crank handles so that their prized livers will grow to grotesque proportions
- A New York restaurant that specializes in insect dishes. Specialities of the house include lava rats, fried ants, stuffed beetles, butterfly eggs, worms au gratin, and rattlesnake and muskrat dishes. In 1963, it cost about $20 for a light lunch.
- Mutated fish and animals on the Bikini Atoll. (Radiation from the nuclear explosions that took place on the island caused the mutations.)
- Chinese fishermen who so hate sharks that they stuff poisonous sea urchins down their throats so that the sharks will suffer for a week before dying
- A Japanese parlor filled with weird medical and exercise devices
- A U.S. auto graveyard
- French models who cover their nude bodies with paint and then roll around on canvases to create physical erotic art
- The running of the bulls in Portugal, complete with the inevitable gorings

13. *Mondo Magic* (1975)

This is one of those sensationalistic, pseudo-documentary "Mondo" series of films [*Mondo New York*, *Mondo Cane*, and *Mondo Topless* (a Russ Meyer spoof of the "Mondo" concept) and others].

Mondo Magic is notable because of the narration written by famed Italian novelist Alberto Moravio, as well as for its attempt to seriously document some of the more bizarre goings-on on our planet. In that endeavor, it more than succeeds.

This film contains some of the strangest things you will ever see: scenes that are disgusting, cruel, and yet at the same time genuinely enlightening.

The New York *Daily News*'s Phantom of the Movies described *Mondo Magic* as a "semi-sleazoid, semi-serious" film and recommended it for the "I-can't-believe-what-I'm-seeing" value and the aforementioned Moravio narration. Here is a look at some of what is included in *Mondo Magic*:

- Male and female members of the Mundari tribe running around stark naked
- A man picking lice out of a woman's pubic hair
- Mundari tribespeople bathing in cow urine (they put their heads right under the cow) and then covering themselves with powdered cow dung. (It keeps the insects away.)
- A tribesman puffing into a cow's vagina to restore the animal's fertility. Immediately after he pulls his face away, the cow has a bowel movement. The tribesman waits until the cow is through and then puts his face right back into the animal's vagina.
- A tribal witch sucking on an old woman's body as a curative
- The Mundari consider cow manure to be "precious." They are shown using it for pillows and bedding and rolling around in it.
- The tribesmen hunting, killing, and eviscerating a buffalo, a giraffe, and an elephant
- Vultures coming to feast on the remains of the slaughtered animals but will not touch the body of a dead witch doctor. (Corpses are left unburied to "melt" into the ground.)
- Tribesmen cutting open the jugulars of cows and drinking their blood. This is painless for the cow, we are told, and they heal quickly. The Mundari children live on a diet of milk and blood.
- The Yonowama tribe—food-gathering nomads that live in the rain forest between Brazil and Argentina—engaging in sexual foreplay out in the open. The sex act itself is done in the relative privacy of the forest
- The tribesmen tying their penises to their belts
- Tribeswomen breast-feeding puppies at the same time as their children
- The tribe eating live lice and cooking and eating spiders and caterpillars

- The tribe has three rules: never have fear; never forgive; always hit back.
- The Yonowama punishment for adultery, consisting of allowing the offended husband to hit the adulterer in the head with a stick with all his might
- A favored pastime of the Yonowamas, snorting a hallucinogenic drug called epina
- Rituals of the Filipinos including naked body painting, consuming the crushed bones of their ancestors, and watching decapitated chickens run around as a form of divination
- Filipinos removing the eyes of slaughtered elephants so that the animal's spirits cannot witness the evisceration of its body
- Healing ceremonies involve urinating on the ill person
- Mutilation, considered a preventative measure against illness
- The cure for weight loss, slitting the skin near the kidney and inserting a mineral
- The cure for genital disorders, requiring the man to stand naked and hold his penis over a fire
- Young boys who must be punished (for any of a number of offenses) having their penis yanked by a rope tied around the organ at its base
- Witch doctors performing exorcisms on people suspected of being possessed. A woman is seen being exorcised. She is completely naked and lying on a bed. The witch doctor first smells her vagina. He then puts a funnel-like horn into her vagina and inserts magical herbs. Then he inserts a tube into her rectum and literally blows smoke up her ass.
- The witch doctor's cure for a migraine headache is to brutally amputate the end of the patient's little finger with a knife. (I guess you're in so much pain from the amputation that you forget about the headache.)
- We see brutal floggings and self-flagellation, which are considered therapeutic.
- In Sri Lanka, yogis lying on beds of nails for forgiveness
- A Sri Lankan having fish hooks put through the skin on his back
- Another man having a needle pierced through his cheeks, horizontally across his mouth
- A man being lifted by hooks that pierce his back, and his body being swung on a rope

- A man wearing shoes of nails, while others burn the soles of their feet and dance on fire and hot coals
- Sri Lankans sipping water that has been used to wash off words from the Koran that were written in charcoal on a slate
- As an infertility treatment, the Marabu (a woman witch doctor) watching two people have sex and caressing their bodies with paper on which words from the Koran are written
- The Marabu's job is also to confirm a bride's virginity before a marriage. She does this by opening the girl's vagina, inserting her fingers, and feeling for the hymen, all of which is shown.
- Native women stretching the lips of their vulva so that their vaginal secretions are kept away from their bodies
- Nuns who are not allowed contact with real live men performing daily ritual masturbation on a giant wooden phallus

14. *Multiple Maniacs* (1970)

Director John Waters has of late been trying to reinvent himself and move into mainstream filmmaking (e.g., *Hairspray* and *Cry-Baby*), but there was a time in the seventies when he was as over-the-edge as you can possibly get. *Multiple Maniacs* is unquestionably one of those guaranteed-to-offend films. This black-and-white film was Waters and company's tribute to Herschel *(Blood Feast)* Gordon Lewis's 1964 camp gorefest classic *2,000 Maniacs,* itself a quintessential drive-in experience and the granddaddy of today's naked-dead-teenager-woods-summer-camp-slay flicks.

Multiple Maniacs has something to piss off literally *everyone.* The movie begins with an onscreen warning that it contains "explicit material," which is somewhat of an understatement.

The story, such as it is, is about a traveling carnival-like show called Lady Divine's Cavalcade of Perversions, which promises "Fags, Sluts, Dykes, and Pimps." (Divine, played by obese transvestite comic actor Harris Milstead, was once described by film scholar Danny Peary as a "perverted Miss Piggy." I find that apt.)

This unrelentingly stupid film boasts primitive production values and horrible acting. Some of its "treats" include the following:

- A woman kissing a bicycle seat
- A guy kissing a bra
- Divine being raped by a giant lobster
- A topless girl having her armpits smelled

- A guy having a cigarette snuffed out on his back
- A human pyramid made up entirely of topless women
- A nude woman having her vagina photographed
- Two homosexual men French kissing
- A junkie going through cold turkey withdrawal
- A man eating vomit
- Divine being raped by a bearded guy who is wearing a dress
- Jesus making cans of tuna fish and sandwich buns miraculously appear
- The Infant of Prague appearing to Divine
- People in long robes stuffing tuna fish in their mouths
- A woman anally raping Divine with a crucifix in a church

Plus, references to the Charles Manson/Sharon Tate murders (Divine and the Cavalcade Barker supposedly had something to do with the murders); and numerous other outrageous religious and sexual enactments and references.

Would I recommend a rental of *Multiple Maniacs?* Yes, if you're curious *and* you have a high tolerance for disgusting religious and sexual imagery. Overall, though, there's no doubt about it: *Multiple Maniacs* is one weird sumbitch of a movie and thus simply viewing it must, I suppose, be counted as an experience.

15. *Surf Nazis Must Die* (1987)

This is one of those weird Troma offerings that one critic called "vile, stupid, and pointless." He was right and I've listed it here only to make you aware of Troma's stuff, which is supposed to be so bad it's good. If vile, stupid, and/or pointless floats your boat, *Surf Nazis* might be worth a rental. I found it unwatchable.

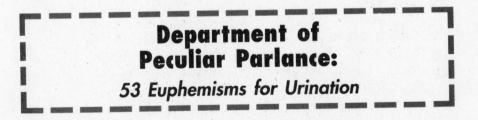

Department of Peculiar Parlance:
53 Euphemisms for Urination

Bill Murray's character, Bob, in the 1991 film *What About Bob?*, complained to his psychiatrist (played masterfully by Richard

Dreyfuss) that one of his biggest worries in life was that someday
he would have to urinate, he wouldn't be able to find a bathroom,
and his bladder would explode. (A bladder would only rupture if
it was filled with many times its capacity and not allowed to void.
This was a common torture in ancient Rome. They would pour gallons of wine down a slave's throat and then sew up his urethra so
that he couldn't urinate.) This feature lists 52 other ways to say
"take a leak" (which happens to be no. 42).

1. Answer Nature's Call
2. Burn the Grass
3. Check the Ski Rack
4. Do Pee-Pee
5. Drain the Crankcase
6. Drain the Dragon
7. Drain the Lizard
8. Drain the Main Vein
9. Drain the Suds
10. Drain Your Radiator
11. Drain Your Snake
12. Give the Chinaman a Music Lesson
13. Go and See If the Horse Has Kicked Off His Blanket
14. Go to Egypt
15. Kill a Tree
16. Look Upon a Hedge
17. Make a Piss Stop
18. Make a Pit Stop
19. Number One
20. Pay a Visit
21. Pee
22. Pick a Daisy
23. Piddle
24. Piss
25. Pluck a Rose
26. Point Percy at the Porcelain
27. Post a Letter
28. Powder Your Nose
29. Pump Ship
30. See a Man About a Horse
31. See Johnny
32. See Mrs. Murphy
33. Shake Hands with an Old Friend
34. Shake Hands with the Guy You Enlisted With
35. Shake Hands with Your Wife's Best Friend
36. Shake the Dew Off the Lily
37. Shoot a Lion
38. Spring a Leak
39. Squeeze the Lemon
40. Squirt
41. Syphon the Python
42. Take a Leak
43. Take Your Snake for a Gallop
44. Tap a Kidney
45. Tinkle
46. Train Terrence on the Terra Cotta
47. Visit the Sandbox
48. Wash Your Hands
49. Water the Dragon
50. Water the Horses
51. Water Your Pony
52. Wring the Rattlesnake
53. Wring Your Sock Out

109 Weird, Bizarre, Strange, Insulting, or Just Plain Disgusting Names of Rock Bands

My favorites of this motley crew (sorry) are *Bad Livers, The Dead Kennedys, The Fat Chick in Wilson Philips, Sandy Duncan's Eye, The Shitbirds,* and *Vulgar Boatmen.*

Here, for your listening pleasure, is a breakdown of some notable rock band names, grouped into a few descriptive, self-explanatory categories.

It's only rock and roll, but I like it.

- **Completely Incomprehensible:** Birdsongs of the Mesozoic, Bite the Wax Tadpole, Black Tape for a Blue Girl, Digital Poodle, The Disposable Heroes of Hiphoprisy, The Importance of Being Chuck, The Makers of the Dead Travel Fast, Myself a Living Torch, Pop Will Eat Itself, Smack Dab Queen Crab, That Petrol Emotion.
- **Culturally, Historically, or Literarily Referential:** Agent Orange, Catherine Wheel, Chia Pet, Babes in Toyland, The Dead Kennedys, Exploding White Mice, Jonestown, The Loud Family, Mojo Nixon, Sisters of Mercy, Skinnerbox, Thinking Fellers Union Local 282, Vulgar Boatmen, Women of the SS.
- **Gleefully Macabre, Sexual, Tasteless, or Gross:** Body Count, Butthole Surfers, Cadaver, Cannibal Corpse, Carcass, Come, Coroner, Dead German Tourist, Deceased, Defecation, Foetus, The Fried Abortions, Fudge Tunnel, Gorefest, Grave, Obituary, Spread Eagle, Sucking, Suffocation, Swallow, Trenchmouth, Undead, Vomit.
- **Mercilessly Self-Deprecating:** Bad Brains, Bad Livers, Cosmic Psychos, Cultivated Bimbo, Dickless, Dirt, Dog Faced Her-

mans, Fat, Perfect Disaster, Pungent Stench, Rancid Hell Spawn, Revolting Cocks, Righteous Pigs, Shitbirds, The Subhumans, Swinging Swine, Toiling Midgets, Unsane, White Trash, Zero Boys.

- **Possessing a Charming and Self-Confident Sexual Bravado:** Bang Tango, Bedhead, Bitch Magnet, Carter the Unstoppable Sex Machine, Date Bait, Godflesh, Miranda Sex Garden, Revolting Cocks, Righteous Pigs, The Stiffs, Supersuckers, These Immortal Souls, Throbbing Gristle, Young Fresh Fellows.
- **Possessing a Clever Sense of Humor:** Circle Jerks, Club Foot Orchestra, Crash Test Dummies, Every Mother's Nightmare, The Fat Chick in Wilson Philips, Happy Fingers Institute, House of Large Sizes, Meat Beat Manifesto, Mourning Sickness, Overwhelming Colorfast, Porno for Pyros, Sandy Duncan's Eye, Thirteenth Floor Elevators, United Dairies.
- **Violent as Hell:** Boiled in Lead, Cop Shoot Cop, Deicide, Dismember, Lynch Mob, Napalm Death, Nurse with Wound, Splatter Trio, Thrill Kill Kult, Uzi.
- **Admirably In-Your-Face Honest:** Drugs 'N' Booze, Lords of Acid, Lush.

Works Consulted

Andrews, William. *Old Time Punishments* (1890 edition). New York: Dorset Press, 1991.

Augarde, Tony. *The Oxford Dictionary of Modern Quotations*. New York: Oxford University Press, 1991.

Bernard, André, ed. *Rotten Rejections: A Literary Companion*. Wainscott, NY: Pushcart Press, 1990.

Bernard, Jami. *First Films: Illustrious, Obscure and Embarrassing Movie Debuts*. New York: Citadel Press, 1993.

Berra, Tim M. *Evolution and the Myth of Creationism: A Basic Guide to the Facts in the Evolution Debate*. Stanford, CA: Stanford University Press, 1990.

Bord, Janet, and Colin Bord. *Unexplained Mysteries of the 20th Century*. Chicago, IL: Contemporary Books, 1989.

Brooks, Tim, and Earl Marsh. *The Complete Directory to Prime Time Network TV Shows 1946–Present*. New York: Ballantine Books, 1988.

Campbell, Colin, and Allan Murphy. *Things We Said Today: The Complete Lyrics and a Concordance to The Beatles' Songs, 1962–1970*. Ann Arbor, MI: Pierian Press, 1980.

Cavendish, Richard, ed. *Encyclopedia of the Unexplained: Magic, Occultism and Parapsychology*. New York: Penguin/Arkana, 1989.

Cheetham, Erika, translator and ed. *The Prophecies of Nostradamus*. New York: Berkley Books, 1981.

Chilnick, Lawrence D., ed. *The Pill Book*. New York: Bantam Books, 1992.

Cooper, Margaret. *The Inventions of Leonardo Da Vinci*. New York: Macmillan, 1965.

Corliss, William R. *Ancient Man: A Handbook of Puzzling Artifacts*. Glen Arm, MD: The Sourcebook Project, 1980.

_____. *Incredible Life: A Handbook of Biological Mysteries*. Glen Arm, MD: The Sourcebook Project, 1981.

————. *Mysterious Universe: A Handbook of Astronomical Anomalies.* Glen Arm, MD: The Sourcebook Project, 1979.

————. *Unknown Earth: A Handbook of Geological Enigmas.* Glen Arm, MD: The Sourcebook Project, 1980.

De Thuin, Richard. *The Official Identification and Price Guide to Movie Memorabilia.* New York: House of Collectibles, 1990.

Delacoste, Frédérique, and Priscilla Alexander, eds. *Sex Work: Writings by Women in the Sex Industry.* Pittsburgh, PA: Cleis Press, 1987.

Delaney, John J. *Pocket Dictionary of Saints.* New York: Doubleday, 1983.

Drimmer, Frederick. *Until You Are Dead: The Book of Executions in America.* New York: Pinnacle Books, 1992.

Ebert, Roger. *Roger Ebert's Movie Home Companion, 1993 Edition.* Kansas City, MO: Andrews and McMeel, 1993.

Ellis, Bret Easton. *American Psycho.* New York: Vintage Books, 1991.

Ellis, James Anthony. *Preparing for the Best: A Guide to Earth Changes for 1993 and Beyond.* San Diego, CA: JAE Publishing, 1993.

Fargis, Paul, and Sheree Bykofsky, editorial directors. *The New York Public Library Desk Reference.* New York: Stonesong Press, 1989.

Fedler, Fred. *Media Hoaxes.* Ames, IA: Iowa State University Press, 1989.

Ferm, Vergilius. *Lightning Never Strikes Twice (If You Own a Feather Bed) and 1,904 Other American Superstitions from the Ordinary to the Eccentric.* New York: Gramercy Publishing Company, 1989.

Fletcher, Barbara. *Don't Blame the Stork!: The Cyclopedia of Unusual Names.* Seattle, WA: Rainbow Publications, 1981.

Fletcher, Lynne Yamaguchi, and Adrien Saks. *Lavender Lists: New Lists About Lesbian and Gay Culture, History, and Personalities.* Boston, MA: Alyson Publications, 1990.

Flexner, Stuart, with Doris Flexner. *The Pessimist's Guide to History.* New York: Avon Books, 1992.

Fodor, Nandor. *Encyclopedia of Psychic Science.* New Hyde Park, NY: University Books, 1966.

Fricke, John, Jay Scarfone, and William Stillman. *The Wizard of Oz: The Official 50th Anniversary Pictorial History.* New York: Warner Books, 1989.

Gatten, Jeffrey N., compiler. *The Rolling Stone Index: Twenty-Five Years of Popular Culture, 1967–1991.* Ann Arbor, MI: Popular Culture, Ink., 1993.

Gipe, George. *The Last Time When.* New York: World Almanac Publications, 1981.

Gittleson, Bernard, and Laura Torbett. *Intangible Evidence.* New York: Simon & Schuster, 1987.

Givens, Bill. *Film Flubs, the Sequel: Even More Memorable Movie Mistakes.* New York: Citadel Press, 1992.

_____. *Film Flubs: Memorable Movie Mistakes.* New York: Citadel Press, 1990.

_____. *Son of Film Flubs: More Memorable Movie Mistakes.* New York: Citadel Press, 1991.

Gold, Gari. *Crystal Energy: Put the Power in the Palm of Your Hand.* Chicago, IL: Contemporary Books, 1987.

Gomez, Dr. Joan. *A Dictionary of Symptoms.* New York: Bantam Books, 1967.

Graves, Kersey. *The World's Sixteen Crucified Saviors.* New York: The Truth Seeker Company, 1875.

Hale, Mark. *Headbangers: The Worldwide MegaBook of Heavy Metal Bands.* Ann Arbor, MI: Popular Culture, Ink., 1993.

Hammond, Allen, ed. *The 1993 Information Please Environmental Almanac.* New York: Houghton Mifflin Company, 1993.

Harmetz, Aljean. *The Making of The Wizard of Oz.* New York: Dell Publishing/Delta, 1977.

Hockinson, Michael J. *Nothing Is Beatleproof: Advanced Beatles Trivia for Fab Four Fanciers.* Ann Arbor, MI: Popular Culture, Ink., 1990.

Hoffman, Mark S. *The World Almanac and Book of Facts 1993.* New York: Pharos Books, 1993.

Hosoda, Craig. *The Bare Facts Video Guide.* Santa Clara, CA: The Bare Facts, 1992.

Jacobs, Dick. *Who Wrote That Song?* New York: Betterway Publications, 1988.

Jones, Judy, and William Wilson. *An Incomplete Education.* New York: Ballantine Books, 1987.

Key, Wilson Bryan. *Media Sexpolitation.* New York: New American Library/Signet, 1976.

Klimo, Jon. *Channeling: Investigations on Receiving Information from Paranormal Sources.* Los Angeles, CA: Jeremy P. Tarcher, 1987.

Krantz, Les. *The Best and Worst of Everything.* New York: Prentice Hall, 1991.

Lavigne, Yves. *Hell's Angels: Taking Care of Business.* New York: Ballantine Books, 1989.

Lenburg, Jeff, Joan Howard Maurer, and Greg Lenburg. *The Three Stooges Scrapbook.* New York: Citadel Press, 1982.

Lewisohn, Mark. *The Beatles Recording Sessions.* New York: Harmony Books, 1988.

Love, Brenda. *The Encyclopedia of Unusual Sex Practices.* Fort Lee, NJ: Barricade Books, 1992.

Lucaire, Ed. *The Celebrity Almanac.* New York: Prentice Hall, 1991.

MacEachern, Sally, ed. *Illustrator's Reference Manual: Nudes.* Secaucus, NJ: Chartwell Books, 1989.

Madonna. *Sex.* New York: Warner Books, 1992.

Maltin, Leonard, ed. *Leonard Maltin's Movie and Video Guide 1993 Edition.* New York: New American Library/Signet, 1993.

Mannix, Daniel P. *Freaks: We Who Are Not As Others.* San Francisco, CA: Re/Search Publications, 1990.

Margulies, Edward, and Stephen Rebello. *Bad Movies We Love.* New York: Plume, 1993.

Martin, Elizabeth A., ed. *The Bantam Medical Dictionary.* New York: Bantam Books, 1982.

Martin, Mick, and Marsha Porter. *Video Movie Guide 1993.* New York: Ballantine Books, 1993.

Matthews, Peter, ed. *The Guinness Book of Records 1993.* New York: Bantam Books, 1993.

McArdle, Phil and Karen. *Fatal Fascination: Where Fact Meets Fiction in Police Work.* Boston, MA: Houghton Mifflin, 1988.

McNeil, Alex. *Total Television: A Comprehensive Guide to Programming from 1948 to 1980.* New York: Penguin Books, 1980.

Mitchell, Margaret. *Gone with the Wind.* New York: Macmillan, 1936.

Monestier, Martin. *Human Oddities: A Book of Nature's Anomalies.* New York: Citadel Press, 1987.

Morse, L. A. *Video Trash & Treasures.* Toronto: HarperCollins, 1989.

———. *Video Trash & Treasures II.* Toronto: HarperCollins, 1990.

Nash, Bruce, and Allan Zullo. *The Misfortune 500.* New York: Pocket Books, 1988.

Neiss, Charles P., ed. *The Beatles Reader: A Selection of Contemporary Views, News & Reviews of The Beatles in Their Heyday.* Ann Arbor, MI: Pierian Press, 1984.

Oglesby, Carl. *The JFK Assassination: The Facts and the Theories.* New York: New American Library/Signet, 1992.

The Oxford Dictionary of Quotations, Third Edition. New York: Oxford University Press, 1979.

Paglia, Camille. *Sexual Personae: Art and Decadence from Nefertitti to Emily Dickinson.* New York: Vintage Books, 1990.

Panati, Charles. *Panati's Extraordinary Endings of Practically Everything and Everybody.* New York: Harper & Row, 1989.

Parker, Tom. *Rules of Thumb 2.* Boston, MA: Houghton Mifflin Company, 1987.

Peary, Danny. *Cult Movie Stars.* New York: Simon & Schuster/ Fireside, 1991.

Pelosi, Michael. *A Date to Remember.* New York: deLuxx Editions, 1982.

Pelton, Robert Wayne. *Loony Sex Laws That You Never Knew You Were Breaking.* New York: Walker and Company, 1992.

The Phantom of the Movies. *The Phantom's Ultimate Video Guide.* New York: Dell Publishing, 1989.

Pinckney, Cathy, and Edward R. Pinckney. *The Patient's Guide to Medical Tests.* New York: Facts on File, 1982.

Poundstone, William. *Big Secrets: The Uncensored Truth About All Sorts of Stuff You Are Never Supposed to Know.* New York: William Morrow and Company, 1983.

_____. *Bigger Secrets: More Than 125 Things They Prayed You'd Never Find Out.* Boston, MA: Houghton Mifflin Company, 1986.

Puckett, Newbell Niles, compiler. *Black Names in America: Origins and Usage.* Boston, MA: G. K. Hall & Co., 1975.

Purvis, Kenneth, M.D., Ph.D. *The Male Sexual Machine: An Owner's Manual.* New York: St. Martin's Press, 1992.

Rosenfeld, Isadore, M.D. *Symptoms.* New York: Bantam Books, 1989.

Rovin, Jeff. *The Encyclopedia of Superheroes.* New York: Facts on File Publications, 1985.

_____. *Laws of Order: A Book of Hierarchies, Rankings, Infrastructures, Measurements, and Sizes.* New York: Ballantine Books, 1992.

Schaffner, Nicholas. *The Beatles Forever.* New York: McGraw-Hill, 1977.

Schultheiss, Tom. *The Beatles: A Day in the Life, The Day-by-Day Diary 1960–1970.* Ann Arbor, MI: Pierian Press, 1981.

Schwabe, Calvin W. *Unmentionable Cuisine.* Charlottesville, VA: University Press of Virginia, 1979.

Schwartz, J. R. *The Official Guide to the Best Cat Houses in Nevada.* Boise, ID: J. R. Schwartz, 1993.

Shepherd, Chuck, John J. Kohut, and Roland Sweet. *News of the Weird.* New York: Plume, 1989.

Spears, Richard A. *Slang and Euphemism: A Dictionary of Oaths, Curses, Insults, Sexual Slang and Metaphor, Racial Slurs, Drug Talk,*

Homosexual Lingo, and Related Matters. New York: New American Library/Signet, 1991.

Spence, Lewis. *An Encyclopaedia of Occultism: A Compendium of Information on the Occult Sciences, Occult Personalities, Psychic Science, Magic, Demonology, Spiritism, Mysticism and Metaphysics.* New Hyde Park, NY: University Books, 1960.

Spignesi, Stephen J. *The Complete Stephen King Encyclopedia.* Chicago, IL: Contemporary Books, 1992.

_____. *Mayberry, My Hometown: The Ultimate Guidebook to America's Favorite TV Small Town.* Ann Arbor, MI: Popular Culture, Ink., 1987.

_____. *The Official "Gone with the Wind" Companion.* New York: Plume, 1993.

_____. *The Woody Allen Companion.* Kansas City, MO: Andrews and McMeel, 1992.

Stannard, Neville. *The Beatles' The Long & Winding Road: A History of the Beatles on Record.* New York: Avon Books, 1982.

Stern, Jack I., M.D., and David L. Carroll. *The Home Medical Handbook.* New York: William Morrow and Company, 1987.

Stern, Jane and Michael. *The Encyclopedia of Bad Taste.* New York: HarperCollins, 1990.

_____. *Jane and Michael Stern's Encyclopedia of Pop Culture: An A to Z Guide of Who's Who and What's What, from Aerobics and Bubble Gum to Valley of the Dolls and Moon Unit Zappa.* New York: HarperPerennial, 1992.

Stevens, Serita Deborah, with Anne Klarner. *Deadly Doses: A Writer's Guide to Poisons.* Cincinnati, OH: Writer's Digest Books, 1990.

Trager, James, ed. *The People's Chronology: A Year-by-Year Record of Human Events from Prehistory to the Present.* New York: Holt, Rinehart and Winston, 1992.

Treffert, Darold A. *Extraordinary People: Understanding "Idiot Savants."* New York: Harper & Row, 1989.

Walters, Mark Jerome. *Courtship in the Animal Kingdom.* New York: Doubleday, 1988.

White, John. *A Practical Guide to Death and Dying.* Wheaton, IL: The Theosophical Publishing House, 1980.

_____. *Pole Shift: Scientific Predictions and Prophecies of the Ultimate Natural Disaster.* Virginia Beach, VA: A.R.E. Press, 1980.

Wiener, Tom. *The Book of Video Lists.* Kansas City, MO: Andrews and McMeel, 1992.

Wilkins, Mike, Ken Smith, and Doug Kirby. *The New Roadside America*. New York: Simon & Schuster, 1992.

Wilson, Keith D. *Cause of Death: A Writer's Guide to Death, Murder and Forensic Medicine*. Cincinnati, OH: Writer's Digest Books, 1992.

Woodward, Kenneth L. *Making Saints: How the Catholic Church Determines Who Becomes a Saint, Who Doesn't, and Why*. New York: Simon & Schuster, 1990.

Wurman, Richard Saul. *Medical Access*. Los Angeles, CA: Access-Press, 1985.

Zimdars-Swartz, Sandra L. *Encountering Mary: Visions of Mary from La Salette to Medjugorje*. New York: Avon Books, 1992.

Zuramski, Paul, ed. *The New Age Catalogue*. New York: Doubleday, 1988.

Magazines Consulted

The Atlantic Monthly
Celebrity Sleuth
Circus
Cosmopolitan
Crime Beat
Details
Discover
Entertainment Weekly
Esquire
Far Out
Field & Stream
Film Threat
Gauntlet
Glamour
Harper's
Hustler
Inner Light
Leg Show
Life
MacUser
Macworld
Movieline
Musician
The National Lampoon

New Woman
New York
The New York Review of Books
The New York Times Book Review
The New Yorker
Newsweek
Omni
Option
Penthouse
People Weekly
Playboy
Premiere
Prevue
Publishers Weekly
Pulse!
Rolling Stone
Science Digest
Soldier of Fortune
Spy
Time
True News
TV Guide
U.S. News & World Report
UFO Review
US
The Utne Reader
Whole Earth Review
Yankee

Newspapers Consulted

The Advocate
The Boston Globe
The Boston Herald
The Boston Phoenix
The Connecticut Post
The Hartford Courant
The National Enquirer
The Los Angeles Times
The New Haven Advocate

The New Haven Register
The New York Daily News
The New York Post
The New York Times
The Star
The Washington Post
The Weekly World News
USA Today
The Village Voice

About the Author

Stephen Spignesi is a writer and popular culture expert who lives in New Haven, Connecticut, with his wife, Pam, and their remarkable cat, Ben.

In addition to *The Odd Index*, Spignesi is also the author of the "Andy Griffith Show" encyclopedia, *Mayberry, My Hometown* (Popular Culture, Ink.); *The Complete Stephen King Encyclopedia* (Contemporary Books); *The Stephen King Quiz Book* (New American Libarary); *The Second Stephen King Quiz Book* (New American Library); *The Woody Allen Companion* (Andrews and McMeel); *The Official "Gone with the Wind" Companion* (Plume); and *The V. C. Andrews Trivia and Quiz Book* (New American Library).

Spignesi was described as "The world's leading expert on Stephen King" by *Entertainment Weekly* magazine, and his work has appeared in *Harper's, Cinefantastique, Saturday Review, Midnight Graffiti*, and *Gauntlet* magazines, and *The New York Times*.

He is currently working on a number of nonfiction projects involving film, music, and popular culture, including a novel, *Sunspots*.